REMAINS

Historical and Literary

CONNECTED WITH THE PALATINE COUNTIES OF

Lancaster and Chester

VOLUME XXVI—THIRD SERIES

MANCHESTER:

Printed for the Chetham Society

1979

The publication of this book has been
assisted by a generous award
from the Twenty-Seven Foundation

METHODIST SECESSIONS

The origins of Free Methodism
in three Lancashire towns:
Manchester, Rochdale, Liverpool

by
D. A. GOWLAND, B.A., Ph.D.

MANCHESTER:
Printed for the Chetham Society
1979

© The Chetham Society 1979

Published for the Society by
Manchester University Press
Oxford Road, Manchester M13 9PL

British Library cataloguing-in-publication data

Gowland, D A
  Methodist secessions.— (Remains historical
  and literary connected with the Palatine
  counties of Lancaster and Chester : 3rd
  series; vol.26).
  1. United Methodist Free Churches in
  Manchester, Eng.
  2. United Methodist Free Churches in
  Rochdale, Eng.
  3. United Methodist Free Churches in
  Liverpool, Eng.
  1. Title   11. Series
  287.97   BX8278M

  ISBN 0 7190 1335 6

Printed in Great Britain by
W & G Baird Ltd at the Greystone Press,
Caulside Drive, Antrim.

CONTENTS

For my parents
Margaret and William Gowland

PREFACE

This book deals with one chapter in the division of nineteenth-century Wesleyan Methodism. During the second quarter of the century internal opposition to Wesleyan polity crystallised in three major crises which gave rise to Protestant Methodism, the Wesleyan Methodist Association and the Wesleyan Reform movement. These bodies eventually combined to form the United Methodist Free Churches in 1857, the third largest Methodist denomination after the Wesleyans and the Primitive Methodists; it should be noted that the generic term 'Free Methodist', loosely applicable to all Methodist bodies which protested against the Wesleyan constitution, is here employed to refer only to the constituent elements of the UMFC.

The subject matter of this book concerns the origins and early development of the Association and, to a lesser extent, of the Reform movement within the context of three Lancashire towns —Liverpool, Manchester and Rochdale—each of which played a prominent role in the evolution of Free Methodism. The study has two main objects in that it attempts to analyse the peculiar features and varied fortunes of the seceders in each town, and it seeks to explain secessions in terms of the interaction of specifically denominational practices and general social patterns.

I should like to express my gratitude to Professor W. R. Ward of the University of Durham for help and advice at various stages of writing. Needless to say, the errors and misunderstandings which may be found in the book are all my own work.

D. A. Gowland
University of Dundee

Beelzebub's Message to his friend Jabez

I send this, friend Jabez, to tell thee that I,
On a visit for business, will call bye and bye,
Meanwhile, do not fail, I beseech thee to send
Such a mandate to Rochdale as I recommend.

Bid each of thy servants who values his place,
In the eyes of the Master would wish to find grace,
To be and bestir him, and do what he can
To send Tory Royds as a Parliament man.

If any poor Brother or Friend be so weak,
As a cause for the change in his conscience to seek,
Press him hard, nor give him time to recover his strength,
But beat out his conscience to Conference length.

Our principal friends I've no doubt will be true,
Their praises in Churches again we'll renew,
Should others less Orthodox, dare to refuse,
Vote with or leave us, now take which you choose.

Do this now friend Jabez, t'will oblige even me,
And strengthen the powers I've given to thee,
May'st thou like the Pope hold the conscience of men,
And wear lawn in full length e're I write thee again.

Rochdale parliamentary election squib, 1837.

CHAPTER 1

THE POST-WESLEY CONNEXION

For two generations after the death of John Wesley in 1791 Wesleyan Methodism underwent remarkable growth and considerable fragmentation. In the period 1800–1830 the membership almost trebled from 90,619 to 248,592, thus increasing from 0·85 to 1·53 per cent of the population. By 1860, however, when the membership stood at 310,311 or 1·38 per cent of the population, it was evident that the earlier rate of growth had not been maintained and that the age of unbridled expansion had given way to a chequered period of less spectacular gains and more dramatic losses. In the intervening period the Wesleyans increasingly encountered some of the intractable problems of a social and religious order which rarely allowed one party to grow at the expense of another. The monopoly of an extraordinary mission was challenged by evangelical Anglicanism and revived Dissent, while the sharp rise in population and the spread of urbanisation made heavy demands on all denominations. Moreover external restraints on further rapid growth were joined by internal conflicts which culminated in the loss of one-third of the membership during the mid-century Reform controversy.

With the important exception of doctrines concerning the church and the ministry, Wesleyan divisions were rarely attributable to theological disagreement. The teachings of Wesley were upheld in all quarters and the spiritual pilgrimage from conviction of sin to entire sanctification possessed the same meaning for each group. Divisions usually took one of two forms, in that spontaneous revivals were largely responsible for the emergence of the Primitive Methodists, of the Bible Christians and of the Independent Methodists, while the character of connexional government assumed primary importance in the formation of the Methodist New Connexion and in the subsequent rise of Free Methodism. Each of the three Free Methodist secessions originated in protests against allegedly constitutional irregularities especially in relation to the role of central administration, the function of the ministry, the authority of local courts and the rights of the laity. The main arguments were first advanced by extensive references to the constitutional settlement of the 1790s.

Landmarks in the construction of the Wesleyan system of

government were closely associated with exceptional circumstances and emergencies. This feature was as evident in 1795, 1797, 1835 and 1853 as when Wesley himself had acted in response to the needs of a growing movement. The connexional framework, the itinerant system and the form of discipline were necessary expressions of an unusual mission rather than the products of established guidelines and preconceived ideas. On Wesley's death his legal successor by the Deed of Declaration (1784), the Conference of one hundred preachers, faced competing claims concerning the status and identity of the connexion. The conflict of interests between the defenders of the societary character of the movement and the advocates of a separate denomination was raised in an acute form by the question of the administration of the sacraments which ranged the bulk of the trustees against a large majority of the preachers and people. The attendance of Methodists at Church services and communion was still customary, yet there was growing pressure to open the chapels during the hours of Church services and to arrange for the administration of the sacraments by the preachers. The trustees resisted this programme on the grounds that it amounted to separation from the Church, that it put at risk their considerable investment in buildings, and that it involved association with a dissenting community which was sliding into all kinds of political and theological errors. While Conference vacillated on the sacraments issue and first left the initiative to individual preachers (1791), subsequently prohibited the practice (1792) and finally allowed the societies to vote on the matter (1793), it soon became clear that a general settlement was required to avoid a widespread division. In 1795 a working compromise was devised which effectively constituted a defeat for the pro-Church trustees; the administration of the sacraments was allowed to continue where already established practice but its introduction elsewhere was made conditional on the consent of a majority of the trustees, of the stewards and leaders, and of the Conference.

This arrangement formed part of the Plan of Pacification which had wider significance as the first major statement on administration and discipline in the post-Wesley period. Conference hereby reaffirmed its exclusive right to appoint preachers and also denied the trustees any authority to expel preachers from the chapels. But some mechanism was required to ensure that the preachers discharged their duties in a proper manner. Since 1791 the preachers had sought a substitute for Wesley's personal and unbroken oversight over the connexion. Wesley had no heir apparent and most preachers were unwilling to elevate one of their number to such a position, nor were they prepared to support a separate order of preachers without normal circuit responsibilities. Hostile reactions to the proposed introduction of bishops, the Lichfield plan of 1794, indicated the popular bias against the designs of some of the senior preachers and reinforced support for a system of District Meetings which had been introduced in 1792 and which was now clearly defined as the instrument responsible for the oversight of the preachers in the intervals between Conference. In its presentation of this Plan Conference pleaded for a more settled state of affairs but was soon confronted by a campaign which was headed by Alexander Kilham, the first of a succession of rebel preachers associated with lay demands.

Kilham held the view that the substance of the Plan fell far short of a desirable mode of government. In the belief that oversight of the preachers by the preachers offered insufficient protection to the laity, he pressed the case for lay representation in all official bodies including Conference. Leading preachers were immediately fearful of a radical agitation led by a man of pronounced dissenting sympathies, for besides the unwelcome prospect of a mixed Conference there was a real danger that the public authorities might view widespread unrest as further evidence of patently disruptive social forces within Methodism. What alarmed leading preachers, however, scarcely restrained Kilham who combined a general protest against the failure to consult the people with charges of financial malpractices, the recurring themes of reform movements a generation later. Conference eventually met this challenge in two ways Kilham was expelled in 1796 and a fundamental review of connexional law was undertaken in the following year.

Only some judicious concessions could limit losses to the Kilhamite organisation, the Methodist New Connexion, and satisfy widespread grievances forcefully expressed by some two hundred lay delegates who besieged the Leeds Conference of 1797. Conference decided to revise the entire body of connexional law, hitherto contained in the *Large Minutes* and Wesley's *Nature, Design and General Rules of the Methodist Societies* (1743), and the result of this exercise was *The Form of Discipline*. Moreover it was agreed to introduce certain new rules, commonly known as the Leeds Regulations and later included in *The Form of Discipline*.

The significance of these measures was twofold. First, the Plan of Pacification and *The Form of Discipline* amounted to a basic constitution which was unchanged in form until 1835 but subjected to conflicting interpretations in the intervening period. Conference maintained its legislative authority and rejected lay representation as incompatible with the necessary conditions for the preservation of the connexional system. This ruling also applied to the District Meeting whose Chairman, a Conference appointment, and members, all preachers in the area, were held responsible for the execution of the laws, on the basis of which this body became an increasingly important and eventually highly controversial instrument for the maintenance of peace and order. Secondly, the Leeds Regulations involved considerable concessions to the lay-dominated circuit and society courts. At the circuit level the Quarterly Meeting was granted more extensive powers to supervise both the financial support of the preachers and the process of circuit reorganisation, in addition to which it was given a one-year delaying veto on the introduction of any new law. It was officially declared that the Quarterly Meetings thus became 'the sources from whence all temporal regulations, during the intervals of Conference, must now originally spring'. There was an equally emphatic but more debatable characterisation of the measures concerning the admission and expulsion of officers and members. Prior to 1797 the right of the preachers to appoint leaders and stewards as well as to admit or to expel members was qualified only by provision for an ill-defined form of consultation with the leaders and stewards. The Leeds Conference reached three important decisions in that it allowed the Leaders' Meeting to declare against any applicant for membership and bound the senior itinerant preacher in the circuit, the superintendent, to accept such a decision; it conceded that no person could be expelled for immorality until the charge had been proved at a Leaders' Meeting; and it declared that the appointment or removal of a leader or steward had to take place in conjunction with the Leaders' Meeting and that while the superintendent retained the right of nomination the leaders had to approve of any nominee. In the opinion of Conference these arrangements meant that 'we have given up to you far the greatest part of the Superintendent's authority . . .'.[1] By any standards, however, this declaration contained an element of exaggeration if only because the superintendent still possessed exclusive authority to preside over all official meetings and to nominate officers. It was in the disputed difference between the substance and the shadow of these measures that conflicts arose in later years, but in the immediate circumstances a decidedly pragmatic approach successfully limited the Kilhamite secession to 5,000 members, approximately five per cent of the Wesleyan membership.

In terms of effective government at the turn of the century, however, Wesleyanism was still a loosely-controlled community of proliferating societies vulnerable to a host of centrifugal forces and capable of constitutional development in various directions. During the next thirty years the connexion became a highly organised unit with a much more expansive central administration designed to provide close supervision of the societies. The principal architect of this transformation, Jabez Bunting, entered the ministry in 1799 at a time when none of the leading preachers commanded either the personal authority or the administrative ability to dominate Conference. Supporters and opponents alike never doubted that Bunting occupied such a position, for he was variously regarded as the indispensable ecclesiastical statesman, the Methodist Pope, the Conference 'buttoned up in a single pair of breeches', and 'the power-drunk minister of Christ'. The son of a radical Manchester tailor, Bunting was educated by Unitarians and preached his trial sermon in a revivalist hothouse. Although his pulpit talents first suggested high office, his keen regard for order and discipline proved his greatest asset. At the unusually early age of thirty-five he was appointed Secretary of Conference in 1814 and held the post until 1820 when he entered upon the first of four spells of office as President of Conference. After service as connexional editor in the period 1821-4 and further circuit duties he was permanently stationed in London as Secretary for foreign missions in 1833 and a year later he secured his most controversial appointment as President of the Theological Institution.

During the first half of a ministry that ended in 1851 Bunting laid the foundations of a form of systematic government that came under attack in the three major crises of the second half of his career. His insistence on efficient and extensive administration was as evident in his first minor commission to sort out some of the muddled connexional accounts as in his provision of a sound basis for the Methodist Missionary Society and his formulation of Sunday school policy. At an early stage he was convinced that the ministerial office originated in and guaranteed sound doctrine and discipline. While Wesley had never regarded his preachers as ministers, Bunting was confident of his own standing as a minister and he sought to instil the same assurance into his colleagues. The pro-Church trustees of the 1790s had rejected this view of the preacher, but Bunting won over their successors and forged an alliance between the ministry and the wealthy laity which was based on overlapping interests in the maintenance of public order and disciplined societies. This arrangement first materialised in the second decade of the century when Wesleyanism was fast acquiring a range of substantial chapels and when some of the large connexional business committees, formerly the preserve of the preachers, were thrown open to laymen whose high social status and liberal contributions to the funds won the fulsome praise of the preachers and frequently suggested superior wisdom, piety and experience. While this system attracted the support of the lay notables, it did not guarantee the unquestioning loyalty of a far larger number of class leaders and local preachers whose social standing and financial resources were invariably less impressive, whose functions and outlook were essentially local, and whose distaste for central controls could be as strong as their opposition to any elevated view of the ministry. By the 1820s signs of unrest within this body of activists became increasingly apparent especially in the large urban societies of the North where the differentiation of social interests had reached an advanced stage and where a series of disputes, as in Leeds, eventually led to a major conflict.

The Leeds controversy marked a significant stage in the development of Wesleyan polity and resulted in the first Free Methodist secession. Throughout the 1820s Leeds Wesleyanism was divided by issues currently in evidence in Liverpool and Manchester, only here a crisis was precipitated by the celebrated Brunswick organ. Opened in 1825 the Brunswick chapel attracted a predominantly middle class congregation. When a majority of the chapel trustees applied for the installation of an organ, a large number of local preachers and leaders opposed the project. Notwithstanding this opposition and the rejection of their application by the District Meeting, the Trustees appealed to Conference and secured their objective. Some fifty local preachers immediately withheld their services and supported their principal spokesman, Matthew Johnson, when he was suspended from further duties by Edmund Grindrod, superintendent of the Leeds East Circuit. Grindrod summoned a Special District Meeting to deal with a deteriorating situation and it was this body which threw into sharp relief two contrasting views of Wesleyan government.

The Special District Meeting was convened on the basis of certain 'Sundry Miscellaneous Regulations' which had been drawn up by the Conference of 1797. These Regulations explicitly stated that the District Meeting had responsibility for the execution of the laws, but since they did not appear in the Conference 'Letter to the Societies', which listed the other new rules, the dissentients argued that they were not part of the 1797 agreement. According to the 'Sundry Miscellaneous Regulations' there was no doubt that the President of Conference had a right to preside on such occasions, but the presence of Bunting as the President's special adviser had no precedent while the absence of three of the nearest Superintendents, none of whom seemed fit for the task in Grindrod's view, was contrary to the Regulations of 1797. The proceedings of this commission, however, had more important consequences, because the main decision to sanction the expulsion of members without a trial before a Leaders' Meeting became the centrepiece of every Free Methodist litany thereafter.

Formally designating themselves Protestant Methodists in August 1828, the Leeds dissentients devised a constitution based on lay and local powers. Only two features, in fact, distinguished this constitution from Independency; the Yearly Meeting drew representatives from all circuits and was empowered to alter the rules, while the full-time missionary could be appointed to any circuit where he performed a preaching function but possessed neither the power nor the status of the Wesleyan minister.

Immediately prior to the launching of the Protestant Methodist connexion Conference delivered its verdict on the controversy. The result of the debate was scarcely a foregone conclusion; only two loyal circuit addresses surfaced from a pile of memorials and a number of preachers expressed grave doubts. In one of the most powerful speeches of his career, however, Bunting argued that firm action had been required to deal with nothing less than an insurrection against the Pastoral Office or, as he noted elsewhere, an outbreak of 'Methodistical Luddism'. The preachers were thereby persuaded to support the crucial resolution 'That it is the judgment of the Conference, that the Special District Meeting, held in Leeds, was both indispensibly necessary, and, in the most extraordinary emergency, constitutional also . . .'[2]

This judgment, however, required some explanation in terms of a comprehensive definition of the Pastoral Office. Since 1791 there had been a conspicuous absence of any serious study of the doctrine of the ministry, and apart from occasional intimations there was no formal statement which pointed the way to the authoritarian concept of the ministry now developed in the wake of these events. Two publications immediately offered a systematic exposition of the high Wesleyan view of the ministry. By virtue of his considerable reputation as a theologian in Methodist circles Richard Watson provided the most authoritative assessment of the duties and responsibility of the Wesleyan minister while a more detailed elaboration of this theme was produced by one of the younger preachers, John Beecham, who faithfully reflected Bunting's point of view.[3] Beecham argued that Methodism recognised the legitimate and scriptural authority of the Pastoral Office as committed to the regular ministry. In support of this claim and to nail the idea that the government of the church was vested in the whole church as the Kilhamites and Leeds dissentients variously supposed, he sought to demonstrate that the Pastoral Office, first filled by Christ and entrusted to the ministers in the church, involved the nurturing and governing of the people and that the only possible conclusion to be drawn from scripture was that ministers of the gospel alone acted as pastors. Within this framework Beecham maintained that the preachers in Conference constituted a collective pastorate that could not be shared with or surrendered to laymen. For one of the distinctive features of the pastor involved separation from secular employment and as such both local preachers and class leaders, whose respective preaching and counselling activities might have suggested otherwise, were barred from the office of pastor. In relation to Wesleyan polity this analysis meant that the constitutional provisions of the 1790s had offered safeguards for the people but had not dispossessed the preachers of their power. Beecham summarised his argument thus:

We have seen that. in 1795 and 1797, the power of the Pastor was not taken away from him, and given to others, or even shared with them; —that all the privileges then conceded by the Conference were only so many fences and guards thrown around the Pastor, to prevent him from using his power injuriously . . . that the final decision of extraordinary questions is not with the people, but rests with the collective pastorate.[4]

The Leeds Special District Meeting was hereby vindicated on account of its 'extraordinary power' that guaranteed the maintenance of Wesley's personal superintendence of the connexion.

Two recent studies arrive at different conclusions on this question. Dr J. C. Bowmer argues that the Wesleyan doctrine of the Pastoral Office was implicit in Wesley's system and was formulated as circumstances demanded, and he continues 'This is not to say that there was anything artificial about the doctrine, or that it was devised to defend an otherwise intolerable situation. Had it not been challenged, it would have continued as an accepted but more or less undefined tradition; but, being challenged, some sort of formulation became necessary'. Professor W. R. Ward, however, holds the view that 'what took place was not so much the definition of a deposit from John Wesley as of the new pastoral functions which the preachers were performing as they moved from an old-style itinerancy to the sham church-based itinerancy they have maintained ever since', and he detects a particular change of emphasis in the Peterloo period when, against a background of social, financial and disciplinary problems, the feeding and guiding tasks of the preachers were overshadowed by teaching and ruling functions which accorded with Bunting's long-held view of the ministerial office.[5]

In their opposition to the nature and constitutional implications of the Wesleyan doctrine of the ministry, the Free Methodists insisted that they were reacting against a situation which was not of their own making. Two general features characterised their arguments. First, their understanding of Wesleyan polity was governed by what they regarded as a binding and comprehensive contract which had been made between preachers and people in 1795 and 1797. By the terms of this arrangement and especially with reference to the Regulations of 1797 it was held that Conference had transferred important powers to the local courts and in particular that a system had been established whereby the superintendent and the Leaders' Meeting shared pastoral authority. Secondly, it was claimed that during and after the Leeds conflict preachers had taken the initiative in advancing a form of ministerial authority which was based on false premises and which destroyed the scriptural and constitutional rights of the people. Whether in references to 'the fiction of the Pastorate' or in protests against 'an authority which neither the Gospel, nor the Methodists' compact justifies . . .', the Free Methodist leaders rejected the Wesleyan doctrine of the Pastoral Office on the ground that it was neither a datum of scripture nor the underlying principle of the constitution.[6] The preachers had in effect invented an artifice to enhance their own powers and status and to overwhelm allegedly undesirable elements.

One of the most reasoned expositions of the Free Methodist case was produced by Robert Eckett, the Association leader, who sought to prove two propositions based upon the Regulations of 1797, the first of which concerned the disciplinary function of the Leaders' Meeting and the other related to the right of local meetings to memorialise Conference. The first issue was of major importance, for while the Wesleyans believed that the right to expel members was vested in the Pastoral Office Eckett contended that no member could be expelled without the consent of a majority of the Leaders' Meeting. The controversy turned on the meaning and significance of one of the Leeds Regulations which stated that 'no person shall be expelled from the Society for immorality till such immorality be proved at a Leaders' Meeting'.[7] In support of the view that this rule transferred the power of expulsion to the Leaders' Meeting, Eckett first maintained that any other interpretation necessarily implied inconsistency and deception on the part of the Conference of 1797. For since the Conference had claimed to have given up 'far the greatest part of the Superintendent's

authority' and since the superintendent still retained considerable powers, it was reasonable to suppose that the main concessions had concerned the administration of discipline and that
the Conference had indeed 'intended to give the leaders' meetings the same authority as to the exclusion of members, which
it allowed them to have in respect to the admission of members . . .'.[8] Eckett proceeded to demonstrate that this inference
was substantiated by evidence from two sources.

First, he cited a collection of rules compiled by the connexional Book Steward, published by the Book Room in 1798,
and entitled *The Nature, Design and General Rules of the
Methodist Societies established by the Rev. John Wesley*. Besides
its composition of the *Form of Discipline* the Conference of
1797 had agreed to publish a smaller collection of rules comprising all the rules relating to local officers and meetings
together with the Rules of the Society. Eckett claimed that the
above publication answered the description of this collection of
rules, one sentence of which was particularly important, 'Neither
can any member of the Society be excluded, but by a majority
at a leaders' meeting'. On the basis of this rule Eckett concluded
that the Leaders' Meeting was empowered not only to try the
question of guilt in the manner of a jury but to assess the
amount of punishment in the role of a judge. He showed moreover that this rule was confirmed by usage until the Leeds controversy, after which it became increasingly common for the
preachers to uphold the view that the leaders constituted a jury
while only the superintendent, as judge, awarded the punishment. During the course of the Association controversy of 1835,
when the law of expulsion sharply divided some societies,
Wesleyan apologists argued that the dissentient case was based
on mistaken conclusions drawn from an inadmissible source.
They maintained in effect that the Book Room publication of
1798 was an unauthorised and inaccurate paraphrase of the
Form of Discipline and that the smaller collection of rules,
promised by Conference, did not appear until 1804 when the
superintendent's power of expulsion was confirmed by the
following statement, 'No person must be expelled from the
Society for any breach of our rules, or even for manifest immorality, till such fact or crime has been proved at a Leaders'
Meeting'. Eckett pointed out, however, that this view failed to
explain why Conference had neither withdrawn nor repudiated
the 1798 paraphrase, besides which the 1804 edition of the rules
gave no indication as to whether the superintendent or the
Leaders' Meeting had the right to determine the sentence in a
disciplinary case.

In a detailed examination of this issue Dr Bowmer distinguishes between the official view which was based on the letter of the law and the dissentient case which rested on current usage, and he comes to the conclusion that 'while the *Form of Discipline* did in theory leave the power of expulsion with the superintendent, in actual practice he always acted in consultation with his Leaders' Meeting'.[9] Two pieces of precise evidence support this interpretation. The *Form of Discipline* did state that the superintendent was 'to take in or put out of the Society', as had been the case during and immediately after Wesley's lifetime. In view of the local importance of this ruling, however, there is at least an element of doubt as to why neither the 1798 paraphrase nor the 1804 edition of the rules made any reference to the subject and as to why Conference failed to correct the omission in reprints of the 1804 publication. Defenders of the official view have also cited the testimony of individual preachers, and particular emphasis has been given to the fact that James Wood, who had travelled with Wesley and was elected President on two occasions, declared in 1835 that he had always understood the law of expulsion to mean that 'the fact was with the Leaders' Meeting, but the sentence was with the superintendents'.[10] But the recorded impressions of the preachers of 1797 also formed the second source of evidence in support of the dissentient argument. Eckett himself indicated that Wood's opinion, delivered almost forty years after the event and at a time when there was every reason to uphold the official view, had to be compared with other assessments made by preachers shortly after the Conference of 1797. During the course of this Conference Henry Moore, a senior preacher and one of Wesley's literary executors, firmly believed that the preachers 'have conceded by one act, all their authority, thereby violating Mr Wesley's wish and intentions in reference to the work'. A less hasty but similar judgment was made by James McDonald, one of the leading Irish preachers in the English Conference, who reviewed the proceedings in 1804 and came to the conclusion that Conference had parted with so much authority that the preachers had 'put it out of their own power to dismiss a leader from his office, without the sanction of a leaders' meeting. . . . The leaders and stewards being constituted judges of themselves and people'. Then there was the weighty opinion of Jonathan Crowther expressed in 1810, 'For fear of a larger division, the conference agreed to make considerable sacrifices, the preachers resigning considerable portions of power, respecting temporal matters, divisions of circuits, receiving and excluding members, the appointment and removal of leaders, stewards and local preachers'. A few years later Crowther, who

was a President of Conference like Moore, confirmed this view
in his biography of Thomas Coke, the President of Conference
in 1797 whose own distaste for the Leeds Regulations was held
responsible for the failure to insert the Regulations in the Conference Journal.[11]

It was in the aftermath of the Leeds crisis that conflicting
attitudes towards this type of issue and evidence became increasingly apparent. In 1829 Beecham concluded his essay on an
optimistic note, 'The more carefully the Constitution of
Methodism is studied, the more clearly will its excellence be
perceived'. Yet the recent controversy had scarcely subsided before renewed agitation was occasioned by the opposition of one
of the Manchester preachers, Dr Samuel Warren, to the introduction of a Theological Institution in 1834. The first signs of
widespread protests appeared in South Lancashire where a
number of Manchester and Liverpool laymen assembled in
Manchester on 6 November 1834 to form the Grand Central
Association. Denominated the Wesleyan Methodist Association
in 1835, this body was larger than the Protestant Methodists
whose membership, 4,000 in 1830, mainly consisted of the Leeds
concentration and small societies elsewhere in Yorkshire and
Lancashire. The Association founded branches as far apart as
Camelford and Dundee, and there were some particularly
flourishing causes in the West Country and the Midlands. The
northern counties, however, yielded the largest number of
recruits, and Liverpool, Manchester and Rochdale together
accounted for 6,208 of the 21,275 members by 1837.

Between the unveiling of its original programme and the
adoption of a constitution the Association was supervised by a
Central Committee consisting of officers and twenty-four members, all of whom were drawn from Liverpool and Manchester.
In its opening declaration the Association publicised three main
complaints and proposed remedies. The principal grievance
concerned the Leeds case while specific protests were entered
against the failure of Conference to handle memorials in a
satisfactory manner and to consult local meetings on legislative
matters. The memorials issue had been a source of grievance
since 1828 when Conference had set aside criticism of the Leeds
action on the ground that a circuit had no business to submit
memorials which involved a judicial review of proceedings in
another circuit. Critics of this policy insisted that there was no
rule to this effect and that the Conference of 1796, which had
provided the most explicit advice on the subject, had indicated
its willingness to receive information from the societies 'on
whatever concerns themselves or their people'. The accompanying criticism of the Institution on constitutional grounds was

based on the Leeds Regulations by which a Quarterly Meeting could delay the adoption of a new rule for one year. Conference refused to concede that the Institution came within that category, since the project neither affected the 'Societies at large' nor involved an appeal for funds; the source of general financial support for the preachers and the question of recurrent expenditure had no bearing on the issue. On the basis of these grievances the Association resolved to obtain from Conference a disavowal of the powers exercised by the Leeds Special District Meeting, a revision of the Leeds Regulations so as to eliminate any ambiguity, and a commitment to the admission of laymen to Conference as spectators.

It was a measure of the often conflicting purposes of the original leadership that this programme could be developed in several directions, for it could be viewed as a conservative charter wholly devised to nullify the effects of the Leeds case, as the first instalment of a Kilhamite plan for an omnicompetent but mixed Conference, and as the beginnings of a concerted effort to demolish central administration and to assert local rights. Each possibility presented a threat to Bunting's view of the ministry. The Association was pronounced an 'illegal' organisation and superintendents of troubled circuits expelled the ringleaders, often in the face of hostile Leaders' meetings. The Central Committee organised two delegates' meetings in 1835, the first of which was held in Manchester, 20-3 April, and the second took place in Sheffield, 31 July-6 August, and composed an Address to Conference.

The Sheffield Address contained a set of proposals that laid claim to 'the right of interference on the part of the members of the church, in the regulation of all its affairs'.[12] Most of these proposals were eventually incorporated in the Association's constitution which was provisionally settled in 1836 and confirmed a year later after a prolonged struggle between the supporters of a Kilhamite scheme and the advocates of circuit independence and free representation. The essential feature of the new system was the right of each circuit to govern itself through the Quarterly Meeting and without the interference of an external authority. The connexional principle survived in the emasculated form of the Annual Assembly and the itinerant system. The Assembly was largely a stationing committee responsible for the admission, appointment and expulsion of preachers, besides which it managed all connexional funds and submitted plans for the approval of the circuits. The circuits annually elected the Assembly on the basis of free representation, and the Assembly in turn appointed a Connexional Committee to transact its general business during the course of the year.

Under these arrangements the preacher was no more than a 'hired servant' or a 'speaking brother' in that he was denied the pastoral authority of the Wesleyan preacher, he had no special right to representation in the Assembly and he could be suspended from his duties by a Quarterly Meeting. This constitution remained in being until 1857 when it was inherited by the United Methodist Free Churches without any major amendment.

For its own part the Conference of 1835 dismissed the Sheffield Address in the strongest possible language. At his most active throughout the controversy Bunting virtually dictated the answer to the delegates and singlehandedly drafted a number of new rules which were designed to offer additional safeguards to the people and left the pastoral authority of the preachers intact. First, it was agreed to extend the system whereby mixed committees of preachers and laymen managed the connexional funds; the Contingent and Preachers' Auxiliary funds were now supervised in the same way as the Missionary, General Chapel and School finances. Bunting thus completed one of his major administrative innovations, but his critics frequently observed that lay members of the committees were outnumbered by the preachers, always appointed by Conference, and were drawn from the upper social strata of the societies. Secondly, the new rules concerning discipline clearly stated that once the Leaders' Meeting had given a verdict the case was left in the hands of the superintendent. The rules aimed to avoid a recurrence of the unholy rows that had accompanied the trials of leading agitators. The superintendents were directed to defer judgment until at least one week after the trial and after consultation with colleagues and with experienced leaders. An excluded member retained the right of appeal to the District Meeting and Conference, but provision was now made for a Minor District Meeting comprising two preachers of the District chosen by the appellant, two preachers selected by the superintendent, and the Chairman of the District, all of whom were authorised to review the sentence. This means of redress was also made available to any superintendent who considered that the verdict of a refractory Leaders' Meeting was inconsistent with the facts. These procedures restrained the heavy-handed superintendents who had not hesitated to expel the agitators, and they strengthened the position of those superintendents who had shown little liking for stern disciplinary action and some of whom were already bearing the cost of the intense strain in the form of ill-health or premature retirement. To the opposition, however, these measures merely regularised the unconstitutional proceedings of the post–1827 period, for the Leaders Meeting had been robbed of its power of expulsion and its verdict could be reversed by a body of preachers.

The third major aspect of these new rules concerned memorials to Conference. A Special Circuit Meeting was instituted for the purpose of composing memorials, all of which had to be consistent with the established constitution and had to carry the signatures of supporters. The latter requirement facilitated the detection of troublemakers, while the meeting was so composed as to exclude some of the most likely rebel officers, class leaders and local preachers of less than ten years' standing. Moreover the meeting could be summoned only within seven to ten days after the June Quarterly Meeting and at the request of the stewards. Severely restricting the opportunities for continuous disturbances, these conditions attracted strong criticism. There was the familiar complaint that the regular local courts had been deprived of a right to memorialise Conference on all connexional issues. It was also argued that the Special Circuit Meeting was at variance with the Leeds Regulations which had allowed for other formal meetings besides the Quarterly and Leaders' Meetings but which had specified neither the timing nor the composition of such meetings. And it was further maintained that the right of initiative given to the stewards was unduly oppressive; as nominees of the superintendent and as some of the wealthiest individuals in the societies the stewards were least likely to provide a platform for popular protest.

Such criticism was indicative of structural strains and social conflicts which could not be overcome and were in fact accentuated by a vigorous assertion of pastoral authority. In an assessment of the new rules George Smith, the Conference historian, considered that they were 'too limited and too late'.[13] In effect it seemed unlikely that so many protective clauses could guarantee stability or prove workable now that contrasting attitudes towards the authority of the ministry and towards the relationship between connexional and local jurisdiction had clashed so violently. The rules clearly illustrated the alliance between the ministers and the leading laymen, yet they offered little to the class leaders and local preachers, amongst whom there were always spokesmen inclined to view themselves as the main casualties of a new order which had turned the itinerant preacher into a regular minister. It was no accident that the Conference of 1836 agreed to introduce ordination by imposition of hands, for the use of this symbol of ministerial office was the most significant reply to the Sheffield Address.

Both the Leeds and Association crises strengthened the position of Bunting; he was re-elected President in 1828 and 1836. Special responsibility for mission affairs and for the Theological Institution was now but one aspect of his dominance in Conference proceedings and of his preponderant influence in the connexional committees like the Stationing Committee where his patronage was sought by preachers and laymen alike. It was virtually impossible moreover to conduct business without him. In 1829 the Committee of Privileges met behind his back to compose an official and highly popular address against Catholic Emancipation, but his unexpected appearance defeated the purpose. Eight years later one of the Conference sessions was adjourned on the ground that no business could be transacted in his absence. Nor could much be done to restrain him when, as the Conference of 1837 demonstrated, he chose to bully one of his colleagues, Thomas Galland, for publishing a letter against church rates. Liberal elements in Conference bitterly complained of the way in which Bunting not only used the official apparatus to advance his own party political purposes and to deny themselves fair representation but refused to submit to the same interrogation which they endured at his hands.

The policy and character of this administration attracted two types of resistance amongst the preachers. The 'official opposition' in Conference included Thomas Galland, Joseph Beaumont, Jacob Stanley, Samuel Jackson and Joseph Fowler. Occasionally personality clashes but more commonly policy differences accounted for this anti-Bunting league. Usually of liberal and dissenting views, such preachers voted against the platform on issues like Church-State relations, education, temperance and revivalism but largely upheld the official view on the role and power of the ministry. After a barren period of opposition this group was in a position to bid for power by the mid-1840s. In 1844 Bunting was elected President for the fourth and last time, but it was evidently the beginning of the end of his regime; measures were carried against his advice and at one stage he threatened to dissolve Conference before the completion of its business. A fierce battle for the Presidential chair occurred in the next few years. Stanley was elected in 1845 much to the horror of the Buntingites whose candidate in 1846, Thomas Jackson, was heavily defeated by the nonpartisan William Atherton. After the election of Samuel Jackson in 1847 the Buntingites finally rallied, and the ailing Robert Newton, Bunting's inseparable partner and the most popular of pulpit personalities, easily defeated Fowler to become President for the fourth time in 1848. Flushed with this success the Buntingites now aimed to smoke out their other critics, the underground opposition responsible for the *Flysheets*.

Published anonymously between 1844 and 1848 the *Flysheets* savagely criticised Bunting's system of government under the heading of location, centralisation and secularisation. Charged with the basest of motives Bunting and his lieutenants were held responsible for the construction of a London-based bureaucracy that was riddled with exclusiveness, favouritism and selfishness, that was contrary to the pristine qualities of Methodism, and that was removed from and opposed to the provincial character of Methodism. It was commonly assumed at the time that one of the preachers, James Everett, was principally or wholly responsible for these leaflets. Everett spent almost half of his ministry as a supernumerary, although his plea of ill-health for circuit work never interfered with his extensive writing, speaking and business engagements. He did not admit to authorship of these leaflets, yet they were consistent with his preference for secrecy, his muck-raking talents and, most importantly, his long-standing hatred for Bunting whom he described as 'a mere manufacturer of tools . . .' as early as 1823; characteristically the first reference to the leaflets in his diary is preceded by two pasted over sheets entitled 'The Buntings'.[14] The *Flysheets* might have remained simply the sharpest and most comprehensive of a series of criticisms but for the fact that they were used as a means to reinforce support for the administration amongst the preachers. At the Conference of 1848 George Osborn, a leading Buntingite, secured backing for a declaration of loyal behaviour on this basis. Everett ignored this test, and a year later Samuel Dunn, William Griffiths and himself were expelled for their refusal to indicate whether they were associated with the *Flysheets*. Dunn had long since publicised his opposition to the Buntingite oligarchy, while Griffiths had pursued a stormy but hitherto inconsequential' career as a radical politician.

Few preachers were now more appreciative of the dangers of a witch-hunt than Bunting. The Warrenite agitation was a constant reminder of how easily the ministerial rebel could be pressed into the services of dissident laymen. It mattered little that the expelled had neither the talent nor the policy to lead a revolt, for they had only to appeal to the country and to transform the brotherly question into question by penalty to gain the response which Bunting feared and which he had hoped to avoid by means of suspension rather than expulsion. Founded in the wake of these expulsions the Wesleyan Reform movement was basically a more extensive, more prolonged and more devastating re-enactment of the Association controversy; mass meetings and disciplinary proceedings were set in motion as predictably as a lay leadership emerged to overshadow the expelled ministers. At the first delegates' meeting in London, 12–15 March 1850, a General Reform Committee was established to work in conjunction with local committees, and five months later the second delegates' meeting reiterated the immediate objectives: the rescinding of the rules of 1835 and the introduction of lay delegation. It was expected that large-scale disruption would force Conference to introduce reforms, but as the delegates trailed from one Conference town to another in the course of the next few years it became increasingly clear that the movement could only survive as an independent body. The Conference of 1850 virtually turned itself into a council of war and no preacher was left in any doubt that firm discipline was required where members proved unconciliatory. At the following Conference, where only five of the 500 preachers voted for some communication with the delegates and were ordered to identify themselves by standing, a committee was appointed to examine possible constitutional changes. Adopted in 1853 the report of this committee defined the composition of the Quarterly Meeting, provided for the re-trial of an excluded member by a Special Circuit Meeting chosen by the Quarterly Meeting, and permitted the June Quarterly Meeting to deal with memorials.

These measures were small beer to the Reform leaders, many of whom were calling for circuit independency and were increasingly preoccupied by the problems of consolidating their support. By 1854, when the controversy was on the wane, the Reformers had secured a membership of 49,177 and the Wesleyans had suffered a net loss of 94,109 members. There was a leakage to other churches and some members were lost to organised religion altogether, yet as Professor Ward suggests part of the net loss arose from the failure of demoralised societies to recruit at the same rate as in less troubled times. The Reformers scored spectacular successes in parts of the north but some of their most significant gains were in the rural and small town societies of the southern and eastern counties. Previously disaffected areas yielded some disappointing returns; in the period 1849–57 a reduction of ten per cent in the Lancashire membership compared with a reduction of 22.4 per cent in the connexional membership.

The Reformers were increasingly confronted by a problematical future as a few of their supporters drifted back to the parent society, either mollified by the concessions of 1853 or disenchanted by continuous agitation. The question posed in 1853, as in 1835, began to elicit a different kind of answer, 'Shall the Reformers now abandon their principles of no secession, no surrender, by uniting with either the New Connexion or the Association or, by becoming a distinct body, cease to struggle for readmission—on scriptural grounds, into their own church? God forbid!'[15] There was no support for a Reform denomination independent of other Methodist connexions, and in August 1854 the delegates' meeting agreed to negotiate with the Association and the New Connexion with a view to union. A few leaders pressed for an agreement with the New Connexion but they never reached the negotiating table, because a large majority was determined to ensure the independence of the local courts and the New Connexion refused to compromise on the question of connexional authority. A scheme for union with the Association was accepted in 1856 and entered into force in the following year. The last institutional break in Methodism was thus terminated by the first major Methodist union.

Significant stages in the development of this union were closely associated with the three towns examined in this book. The first informal union of Associationists and Reformers occurred in Liverpool in 1853. Two years later Association representatives agreed on union in Manchester, and in 1857 the uniting Assembly took place in Rochdale. Particular developments during the pre-secession generation formed the basis of such strong, local identification with the Free Methodist alternative to Bunting's Wesleyanism.

REFERENCES

1 *Minutes of the Methodist Conference*, i. p. 394.

2 S. Warren, *A Digest of the Laws and Regulations of the Wesleyan Methodists* (2nd ed. London, 1835), p. 151.

3 R. Watson, *An Affectionate Address to the Trustees of the London South Circuit* (London, 1829); J. Beecham, *An essay on the constitution of Wesleyan Methodism* (2nd ed. London, 1850).

4 J. Beecham, *op. cit.*, p. 108.

5 J. C. Bowmer, *Pastor and People: A Study of Church and Ministry in Wesleyan Methodism from the death of John Wesley (1791) to the death of Jabez Bunting (1858)* (London, 1975), p. 202; W. R. Ward, *Religion and Society in England, 1790–1850* (London, 1972), p. 104.

6 J. Hull, *A short and plain answer to the statement in Mr William Read's 'Candid Address', with a few brief remarks on the recent 'Declaration'* (Manchester, 1834), p. 10; *Wesleyan Times* 6 August 1852.

7 *Minutes of the Methodist Conference*, i. p. 391.

8 R. Eckett, *An exposition of the laws of Conference Methodism* (London, 1846), p. 16.

9 J. C. Bowmer, *op. cit.*, p. 130.

10 Quoted in *Remarks in reply to certain caluminous Mis-statements*, p. 2.

11 Quoted in R. Eckett, *op. cit.*, pp. 24–7; J. Crowther, *The Methodist manual* (Halifax, 1810), p. 31.

12 *Propositions and resolutions of a provisional meeting of delegates from various parts of the Kingdom* (London, 1835), p. 11.

13 G. Smith, *History of Wesleyan Methodism* iii (London, 1864), pp. 315–16.

14 MS. J. Everett, Memoranda 1 February 1823.

15 *Wesleyan Methodist Penny Magazine* August 1853 p. 121.

CHAPTER 2
PROBLEMS OF THE EXPANDING SOCIETY

During the first half of the nineteenth century few parts of the Wesleyan connexion commanded the same substantial support and vast resources as the large societies in South Lancashire. Connexional leaders like Bunting and Newton, both of whom spent almost half of their circuit careers in Manchester and Liverpool, always acknowledged the general importance of these societies, while other established preachers willingly accepted or besought the choicest appointments in the area. In the aftermath of the Leeds crisis Bunting commenced his sixth consecutive year in Manchester, evidently convinced that 'it is of much importance to the whole connexion that this immensely populous and influential part of it should be kept in good feeling'.[1] By 1830 Lancashire accounted for 9.2 per cent or 21,928 of the total Wesleyan membership, half of which was concentrated in the Liverpool, Manchester and Rochdale circuits. Several of these circuits contained some of the wealthiest laymen in the connexion, the oft-dubbed lay lords whose financial resources ensured, for example, that almost one-fifth of the Centenary Fund was raised in the area. Besides this numerical and financial strength, however, there existed a set of circumstances that turned South Lancashire into a major centre of Wesleyan conflict. In the course of one dispute a Liverpool superintendent noted in 1825 'I well know of what sort of stuff the Lancashire materials were composed off, when religious politicks were blended with radical feelings';[2] many of the tensions in the evolution of post-Wesley Methodism often emerged at an earlier date in this environment than in other localities.

There was in the first instance a strife-torn period of adjustment to new realities in the 1790s. At the beginning of the decade it was apparent that the single chapel in each town, Pitt Street Liverpool, Oldham Street Manchester and Toad Lane Rochdale which were opened in 1750, 1781 and 1771 respectively, no longer accommodated either the growing membership or the increasing demands for separate communion. The founders of new chapels, Mount Pleasant Liverpool (1790), Gravel Lane Salford (1793) and Union Street Rochdale (1793), invariably favoured the full provision of Methodist services and often swept the preachers themselves towards adoption of this policy. In Liverpool, for example, Thomas Taylor, the superintendent in the period 1791–3, responded to popular pressure and acted on his own dissenting inclinations by accepting the case for services in Church hours; his subsequent agreement to administer the sacrament, after a threat to appoint two laymen for this purpose, angered the pro-Church leaders, ten of whom immediately withheld their services while the remainder harried Taylor's successor, John Pawson, who came to the town as President of Conference. Pawson's initial doubts about separate communion were soon dispelled by the weight of popular opinion and by the unattractive features of the 'cold, frozen, crooked and perverse' pro-Church party mainly associated with Pitt Street. By September 1794 Pawson was claiming that he would 'most willingly die a martyr for the Sacrament',[3] and a year later it was a measure of the Mount Pleasant leaders' success that their chapel was cited in the Plan of Pacification to confirm the practice.

The struggle over separate communion proved less disorderly than the Kilhamite campaign which aroused the fiercest passions in Liverpool as opposing groups battled for control of the pulpits. Under the leadership of Isaac Wolfe, a prosperous brewer and owner of a private chapel, the pro-Kilham party initially attracted a large body of support including a number of trustees who invited Kilham to address a meeting at Mount Pleasant. This move was vigorously opposed by the superintendent, Henry Moore, who immediately seized bundles of Kilhamite pamphlets and buried them in his garden. On his visit to Mount Pleasant Kilham was nailed in to the pulpit to prevent forcible ejection but pandemonium broke loose when Moore's servant arrived with instructions to clear the chapel. Many members were so shocked by these violent proceedings that the tide of opinion began to turn against Wolfe, and while he complained that many of his supporters failed to declare their true allegiance because 'it would raise Mr Moore's rage to a great Height against them, and so incur his displeasure which is terrible indeed . . .'[4] he also recognised that most members were awaiting the outcome of the Conference of 1797. The Leeds Regulations effectively put an end to the possibility of a large division. A New Connexion circuit was founded with a membership of 250 but with little potential for further development. There existed a more substantial body of support for Kilham in Manchester. Although a loyal address issued in October 1796 and signed by fifty officers claimed that there was only a handful of disaffected leaders there was a sizable minority of rank and file support particularly connected with the Gravel Lane chapel, the first dissenting place of worship in Salford. This response made Manchester the

largest of the New Connexion circuits with a membership of
790 by 1801, yet like the Liverpool cause one chapel was still
sufficient to cater for the bulk of the membership fifty years later.

These divisions caused little more than minor fluctuations in
the underlying trend of striking increases in Wesleyan membership. Served by an earnest army of preachers and leaders, preaching rooms and classes proliferated as periodic revivals swept
through the ranks of migrant workers and as the population of
Manchester and Liverpool swelled from 76,788 to 129,350 and
from 82,295 to 138,354 respectively in the period 1801–21. Between 1796 and 1810 the Manchester membership increased from
2,322 to 3,790, Liverpool expanded from 1,000 to 2,900 and even
Rochdale, still largely unaffected by significant population
mobility, advanced from 780 to 1,080. This rapid growth was
accompanied by a sharp division of opinion between the upholders of discipline and the practitioners of wildfire revivalism.
Conflicting attitudes towards the process of assimilation and towards the maintenance of order assumed particular significance
in Manchester where the North Street Band Room controversy
revealed an official policy that immediately led to the emergence
of Independent Methodism and soon accounted for the separate
development of the Primitive Methodists and of the Bible
Christians. Opened in the 1790s as a recognised Wesleyan meeting house, the Band Room owed its existence to John Broadhurst, the founder of the famous textile firm, whose support for
uncontrolled revivalist activities first attracted official opposition
in 1803. The main charge against Broadhurst concerned his refusal to admit only members of Society to the weekly experience
meetings as prescribed by the rules. Broadhurst was unmoved by
such a consideration and he continued to supervise meetings
which largely consisted of a working class audience, usually involved unrestrained public prayer, exhortation and addresses,
and generally horrified 'the most sober minded and respectable
Wesleyans'.[5] In 1806 the Manchester Leaders' Meeting firmly
resolved to impose its authority on the Band Room management;
the promiscuous admission of strangers to the meetings was immediately banned and preachers were appointed to preside at all
functions. These tight controls were necessary because the Band
Room constituted 'an innovation on the practice of the Christian
Church at large, and an innovation on the established regulations of Methodism in particular', according to an uncompromising statement issued on behalf of the preachers and leaders
but drafted by Bunting who had been appointed to the town
in the previous year.[6] As a youth Bunting himself had been
turned away from a society meeting on account of non-member-
ship and now as a preacher he claimed to act on the same prin-

ciple; the advanced course in scriptural holiness required firm discipline to maintain the distinction between the Society and the world and to protect serious religion from the 'animal exertions' and 'agitated passions' of the Band Room company.

This determined stand was closely followed by a division. The Band Room merged with a number of other revivalist offshoots elsewhere in Lancashire and Cheshire to form the Independent Methodist connexion which staged its first conference in Manchester. Broadhurst secured the support of approximately 250 members but he failed to carry a number of the younger activists, some of whom served their apprenticeship in his business. In fact Bunting mounted a particularly successful rescue operation, for several of these apprentices, including Francis Marris, Robert Henson, Luke Gray and Edward Westhead, eventually became substantial manufacturers and principal supporters of his administration.

The Band Room division coincided with another controversy which was also symptomatic of revivalist tendencies but which had an altogether different outcome. In 1803 Joseph Cooke, a preacher of above-average learning, was appointed to Rochdale where he quickly established a personal following by virtue of his preaching ability. Cooke was appalled by what passed for religion amongst some of the members whose wild enthusiasm appeared to consist of a stream of raptures and impressions devoid of theological substance. In answer to such emotional excesses he preached two sermons on, 'Justification by Faith' and 'The Witness of the Spirit', for which he was summoned to the Conference of 1806 and ordered to retract views considered dangerously akin to Unitarianism. Cooke was unrepentant and his immediate expulsion divided the Rochdale Circuit which reported a net loss of 104 members in 1807. Many of the seceders were turning against the raw revivalism of working-class appeal in much the same way as their social peers in Manchester; they were placed 'in respectable circumstances' according to one of their number,[7] sufficiently prosperous to hire Cooke as a full-time preacher and to erect the large Providence chapel which headed a small network of Methodist-Unitarian societies based on a mixture of Methodist organisation and increasingly Unitarian doctrine. Shortly after Cooke's death in 1811 the bulk of his followers joined the local Unitarian chapel and opened their own recognised Unitarian chapel in 1818. This division meant the loss of a sizable proportion of Wesleyan leaders and it paved the way for a new and younger type of leadership that was to cause even greater havoc.

In spite of official opposition to some of its by-products, revivalism continued to boost Wesleyan membership in the second decade of the century, especially in the years of acute social tension immediately preceding the Peterloo upheavals. But although both the Manchester and Liverpool Circuits made substantial gains in 1810–1 and 1815–7, there were fewer examples of a massive influx of new recruits on the scale of the Liverpool revival of 1800–4 when the membership had almost doubled. Moreover some of the more remarkable happenings and most extensive recruitment occurred on the fringes of town circuits in societies far less organised and settled than the increasingly chapel-oriented town societies. Urban Wesleyanism was beginning to reveal its limitations as a vehicle for revivalism amongst the working class, and by the 1820s there were various indications of the waning influence of the extraordinary appeal. The Liverpool membership increased by 550 as a result of spontaneous revivalism in 1820–1, but there was a marked deceleration in the rate of growth during the rest of the decade and by 1830 the membership was the same size as ten years earlier. At the same time the singularly unsuccessful efforts of the Tent Methodists in Manchester indicated that both general circumstances and Wesleyan conditions no longer favoured the revivalist group. Under the leadership of one of their full-time missionaries, John Pyer, the Tent Methodists entered the town in 1821, intending to penetrate working class Ancoats but only capturing the imagination of several Wesleyans opposed to the formalities of chapel life. Peter Arrive, a Salford local preacher, who was expelled for assisting Pyer, concluded that the Wesleyans had chosen respectability in preference to revivalism, 'Alas! Alas! Wesley is no more. Where are the old paths—where is the good way? Remember Benson's fears of Wealth, Power and Influence, and Bramwell's warning'.[8] Pyer secured the financial backing of Samuel Stocks, a cotton manufacturer, who withdrew from the Wesleyans and built the Canal Street chapel for the extension of the work. The chapel proved a disastrous failure; poor attendances at the services and Pyer's preoccupation with the furtherance of his own career soon convinced most of the trustees that the work of revival was not advanced by such means. In 1827 Stocks and a large majority of the leading supporters abandoned the venture.[9]

During the Peterloo period, in fact, revivalism melted away as rapidly as the Wesleyan authorities commanded the rank and file to meet political unrest and economic distress with loyal addresses. Opposition to radical politics had an immediate effect on a membership which had increased annually since 1800 with the exception of the period 1806–7. Between 1818 and 1820 the Liverpool membership remained at 3,250, Rochdale declined from 1,200 to 1,020 and Manchester was reduced from 3,540 to

3,025. The most serious controversy raged in Manchester where the superintendent, John Stephens, a martinet and stiff-necked conservative, emerged from periodic bouts of depression to preach patriotic sermons and to purge the ranks of political disaffection. Like his junior colleague, Thomas Jackson, who patrolled the streets as a Special Constable, Stephens expressed the conventional wisdom of the Wesleyan hierarchy. Disdainful of party politics and inspired only by the politics of the Bible, he insisted that members were duty-bound to support the monarchy, the constitution, and 'the mild and liberal government'. He was no less orthodox in his assessment of the existing social order that encouraged industry, contentment, temperance and gratitude in the poor and offered full scope for the exercise of condescension, humility and compassion by the rich. In its attacks on such views the radical *Manchester Observer* reserved some of its strongest criticisms for the ruthless punishment meted out to members who failed to conform to official standards. Stephens dealt with these offenders in magisterial style always aiming 'To cure those of them who are worth saving' and 'To take the rest one by one, and crush them when they notoriously commit themselves'.[10] This policy had the unqualified support of substantial businessmen like James Wood, an unbending Church and King tory who acted as chief prosecutor in the Leaders' Meeting, and Francis Marris who assured the Home Secretary, after the expulsion of 400 members, that 'the Wesleyan Methodists, even in Manchester, retain their cordial and conscientious attachment to the person, family and government of our venerable King . . .'.[11]

Opposition to this administration was led by working class local preachers and leaders. Non-radical critics objected to sermons that not only made a mockery of the 'No Politics rule' governing the behaviour of the preachers in the pulpit but seemed to betray a peculiar insensitivity to the general situation as when Stephens, a few weeks after the St Peter's Field debacle, declared in one of his most famous sermons 'Believe me, my poor brethren, your governors, your ministers, your masters, are your best, your only *real* friends'.[12] There were also strong protests against class discrimination in the exercise of discipline, particularly when wealthy members neglected their duties without censure while a poor, conscientious local preacher suffered expulsion 'for assuring a company of half-starved weavers at Miles Platting, that the Almighty had promised that bread should be given them . . .'.[13] Radical opponents viewed preachers and magistrates alike as the detestable agents of unreformed administrations. Much of their support was concentrated in the Swan Street chapel where the preachers rarely completed a service without disturbances and where the symbol of opposition, the

white hat, was often in evidence. A series of formal trials effectively depleted this congregation and the ringleaders were usually
expelled on the ground that they had supported radical declarations. By 1821 Stephens was able to report that he had floored
his opponents, that Methodism now 'stands high among the
respectable people', and that as radical agitation subsided so religion would revive; the resurgence occurred, however, in the
expanding suburbs rather than the downtown working class
areas. Other superintendents met the crisis in the same way as
Stephens. Thus, the Rochdale preachers interrogated any member suspected of radical leanings; a class leader, arraigned for
his use of radical literature and his attendance at New Connexion meetings, was reminded of the privileges enjoyed under
the present system of government, but he remained unconvinced
'We enjoy no other privileges under the present system of government, except an empty pantry, an empty pocket, an empty belly,
a bare leg and a bare foot . . .'.[14]

The tensions and divisions of the Peterloo period were indicative of certain general trends in the structure and organisation of the Methodist community. Particular developments
were determined by the size and character of the town. By the
early 1820s the Rochdale Wesleyans served a compact and comparatively underdeveloped industrial town in which the features
of a traditional order still predominated while new social
interests revealed few of the contrasts evident in larger towns.
It was possible in this situation to retain the original infrastruc-
ture of urban Wesleyanism for a considerable period of time;
one circuit, a single chapel, and numerous preaching rooms
covered the town and outlying areas. The Union Street chapel
moreover had a wide social appeal in that it attracted the depressed weaver and the rising manufacturer, both of whom shared
a growing distaste for the power and influence of the parish
church and of the local gentry alike.

Liverpool and Manchester Wesleyanism, however, had reached
a different stage of development in a new, increasingly stratified
society. One of the most obvious consequences of Wesleyan expansion in these towns concerned the emergence of the chapel
as the principal place of worship and organisation, 'the focus of
our life' observed one Manchester member.[15] Unlike the preaching room the chapel provided a settled form of existence, a
systematic management of Society affairs, and an enlarged range
of responsibilities and functions. Furthermore the large chapel
building programme undertaken in the period 1800–30 reflected
the impact of early suburban development and upward social
mobility. In Liverpool three main chapels were built to accommodate the growing membership, Leeds Street (1800), Brunswick

(1811) and Stanhope Street (1827), while the Manchester Wesleyans opened chapels in Great Bridgewater Street (1801), Chancery Lane (1817), Grosvenor Street (1820) and Oldham Road, Great Ancoats Street, Oxford Road and Irwell Street (1826). The rising and declining fortunes of most of these chapels were chiefly influenced by the migration of affluent members. The major development in Manchester occurred to the south of the town centre where Chancery Lane first attracted some of the leading Oldham Street members who soon removed to Grosvenor Street and eventually drifted towards the more prestigious Oxford Road chapel. A comparable if less pronounced movement took place in Salford and usually involved transfers from Gravel Lane through Irwell Street to Higher Broughton. In Liverpool the burgeoning wealth of a mercantile and professional class produced a similar pattern; Mount Pleasant initially attracted a large number of the most prosperous Pitt Street members, some of whom later dispersed via Leeds Street to Brunswick on the eastern fringe of the town, while Stanhope Street subsequently catered for a similar clientele in the southern suburb of Toxteth Park.

This flight of wealth to the suburbs accentuated social divisions and stored up trouble for the future. It had been possible to maintain a high degree of social cohesion when only one or two chapels served a town. Yet once the old, central chapels like Pitt Street and Oldham Street were abandoned by influential laymen and faced an uncertain future in a working class neighbourhood, they fell into the hands of leaders for whom the Church-based practices of the suburban establishments represented an altogether separate and increasingly hostile order. Several external features of the wealthy chapels invariably aroused criticism and prompted endless contrasts between the primitive simplicity of the tabernacle and the hideous adornments of the temple. Some of these chapels embodied a distinct change in Methodist architecture as the plain and entirely functional building gave way to more distinguished premises; Brunswick had an Ionic porch and semi-circular interior of acknowledged elegance while the tastefully decorated Stanhope Street chapel was so constructed that ' a semi-religious light fell through an oval window of stained glass and imparted a sacred shade to the communion table'.[16] Often served by paid choirs, door keepers and pew openers, these prosperous chapels moreover introduced fully liturgical services. Brunswick set the pattern in Liverpool with a clerk in attendance to read the versicles while the Grosvenor Street trustees were assisted by Stephens but opposed by a majority of class leaders when they pioneered the practice in Manchester. The fiercest opposition to the new style of worship, however, was usually directed against the organ installed in each of these chapels at the outset. The Brunswick trustees in fact established a precedent when they pressed the Conference of 1811 to lift the general ban on organs. Although the Quarterly Meeting (including the superintendent) opposed the project, the trustees had a powerful spokesman in Bunting who was then stationed in the town and who made his first major speech in Conference on this issue.

The provision of new chapels for a growing and increasingly dispersed membership eventually forced organisational changes which emphasised the contrasts between and within circuits. By 1824 the Liverpool and Manchester circuits contained 2,468 and 3,288 members apiece. There was a strong administrative case for the division of both circuits on the ground that one Quarterly Meeting in each town no longer provided adequate supervision. Manchester was first divided into the North and South circuits in 1824, each of which was headed by the Oldham Street and Grosvenor Street chapels, Further reorganisation occurred three years later and resulted in the formation of four circuits: First —Oldham Street, Second—Irwell Street (previously the Salford circuit), Third—Grosvenor Street and Fourth—Great Bridgewater Street. Much of the support for these changes came from the wealthy Grosvenor Street leaders who were equally determined to dismantle the unwieldly, often unsympathetic Quarterly Meeting and to secure the exclusive services of outstanding preachers. The disparity between the new and old chapels was evident in the stationing of preachers. Whereas Grosvenor Street successfully lobbied for an unrivalled succession of talented superintendents (Bunting, Watson, Lessey and Newton), Oldham Street attracted less well-known preachers and by the early 1830s its influence was so reduced that it was obliged to accept a superintendent without any consultation. The Grosvenor Street leaders also wielded considerable power and influence in the disputes that commonly attended circuit divisions. For besides exercising strong pressure whenever the Oldham Street authorities failed to hand over £100 p.a. in accordance with a five-year agreement of 1824,[17] they successfully resisted the Great Bridgewater Street leaders who lodged a strong claim to a projected chapel on the circuit boundary line; the Conference of 1831 settled the issue after Bunting quoted scripture against the case of the weaker circuit and insisted that it would be impolitic to oppose the Grosvenor Street leaders.[18]

The introduction of smaller circuits often meant that concerted opposition to official policy was concentrated in a particular locality. By the early 1830s the Oldham Street circuit was the most likely source of trouble and a few of its local preachers figured as possible rebel leaders. Disaffection among the local preachers was scarcely novel, nor was the opposition of the regular ministry towards any exclusive combination of local preachers. In 1819 Stephens had attempted to liquidate a fund raised by local preachers to assist any of their number in distress. Twenty years later Conference refused to make use of the Centenary Fund for disabled local preachers, and in 1849 the formation of the Local Preachers Mutual Aid Association was viewed with considerable suspicion by the connexional leaders. It was consistent with this attitude, therefore, that when some of the Oldham Street local preachers helped to found a Local Preachers' Friendly Society in 1833 they were immediately opposed by the circuit authorities. Under its first President, Thomas Taylor, an Oldham Street cabinetmaker, the declared purpose of the Society was to save its members from the unhallowed company of secular societies, yet one of the Oldham Street leaders voiced the alarm of official Wesleyanism: 'In my opinion it is attempting the formation of what may turn out to be a mighty Empire to be used to the injury of Methodism, in any unpleasant circumstances'.[19] The actions of individual superintendents scarcely diminished this possibility, for Stephens had his imitators like John Burdsall, the Oldham Street superintendent in 1830, who ruled that only the respectable members of the Quarterly Meeting should be allowed to vote on a particular resolution; the decision angered several local preachers, one of whom challenged Burdsall to draw a line between respectable and contemptible members.

The division of the Liverpool circuit was more keenly contested than the Manchester scheme and nearly assumed the significance of the imminent Leeds controversy. Serious disturbances first occurred in Liverpool after the Conference of 1824 requested Thomas Wood, the superintendent, to prepare for a division. Local preachers and class leaders immediately recognised a major threat to the unity and power of local courts in which they themselves enjoyed a governing role. The large, influential Quarterly Meeting, indeed, brooked no interference with or opposition to its management of affairs; it threatened one set of obstinate trustees with legal action in 1809 and ten years later it caused other trustees to take legal advice before challenging one of its decisions.[20] And the single Leaders' Meeting, formed after a merger of three meetings in 1814, was no less aware of its status; on one occasion it flatly refused to admit a deputation from a trustees' meeting and always conducted its business in such a manner that one of the preachers observed

The Leaders meeting sometimes act as a parli[a]ment, make Rules,

have a secretary beside the Stewards, who writes down what they call
their measures and orders. Sometimes as a Court of Justice; and when
they wish to use harsh language towards the Preacher, as a Court of
Inquisition. . . .[21]

In these circumstances Wood confronted so much opposition to
his unenviable task that eventually he lost his temper, and his
summary expulsion of Peter McClintock, one of the most obstructive of the aged leaders, was accompanied by the suspension
of David Rowland, one of the young ringleaders. The circuit
was now so thoroughly agitated that the Conference of 1825,
petitioned by some 100 officers, appointed a Presidential Commission to resolve the dispute. The Commission judged that
Wood was in breach of the rules and accordingly reversed his
disciplinary decisions. Wood himself was removed from the circuit; his health had broken under the strain and his death in
1826, closely followed by that of his successor, demonstrated that
every preacher required a tough constitution to survive the
battles ahead.

The Commission refused to make any concessions on the
question of reorganisation, and the new superintendent, John
Riles, was directed to establish separate Leaders' Meetings at each
of the main chapels and to divide the circuit in accordance with
a plan which separated the least prestigious Pitt Street, Leeds
Street, Pottery and Welsh chapels in a West circuit from the
prosperous Mount Pleasant, Brunswick and projected Stanhope
Street chapels in an East circuit. This was a formidable undertaking, and Riles himself scarcely slept for weeks before he
finally screwed up his courage and announced the break-up of
the Leaders' Meeting. While the opposition leaders were confounded by this move and claimed that their consent was required in such a matter, Riles dismissed any suggestion of consultation and insisted that the leaders had only 'To hear what
I have to say, and do what I bid you, as your Pastor'.[22] Supported
by the local plutocracy Riles hoped to 'kill or cure' his principal
opponents who were associated with the Leeds Street chapel,
and he promptly appointed one of the wealthiest laymen,
William Comer, a cotton broker, to serve as a Leeds Street
steward and to keep a watchful eye on the rebels. Shortly afterwards the original plan for the division of the circuit was modified and implemented in 1826 with a view to forestalling a powerful alliance of dissident elements in one circuit; the Brunswick
and Leeds Street chapels were placed in a new North circuit and
Mount Pleasant, Pitt Street and Stanhope Street formed the
South circuit. A 3:2 division of membership and of income in
favour of the South circuit caused considerable friction par-

ticularly when the South circuit emphasised its seniority yet compelled its neighbour to provide funds for the support of an additional preacher for Stanhope Street.

A more serious difference of opinion was soon revealed in the course of the Leeds controversy. The South circuit contained several disgruntled leaders like John Russell, an aged local preacher and basketmaker, and William Johnson, a brother of the Leeds campaigner, yet they were heavily outnumbered by the loyal officers, for whom the Mount Pleasant preacher, John Beecham, published his *Essay on the Constitution* and from whom the Conference of 1829 received one of only two loyal addresses. The Leeds Street leaders in the North circuit, however, swiftly composed seven resolutions which condemned the Leeds Special District Meeting and declared that 'the local government of every circuit is vested in the Leaders, Local Preachers, and Quarterly Meetings with the Superintendent at their head'. This view of circuit authority was rejected by John Scott, the superintendent, as nothing less than parish vestry government. Scott refused to allow any discussion of the resolutions in the Quarterly Meeting, but he was eventually obliged to convene a special circuit meeting which carried the resolutions and dispatched the memorial to Conference. His opponents hotly disputed his interpretation of the memorials rule of 1796 which he took to mean that the Quarterly Meeting had no business to discuss the affairs of another circuit. Yet it was symptomatic of the current confusion concerning this rule that in a letter to Bunting during this episode Scott enquired as to whether his judgment was correct and, if so, whether excessive restrictions were thus imposed on the freedom of the people.[23] In this same letter Scott portrayed an increasingly familiar picture of a loyal preacher who was determined to uphold the pastoral office, to retain the support of the respectable members and to inflict stunning defeats on the 'paltry faction' of radicals.

Bunting considered the opposition sufficiently large and troublesome to justify his own appointment as Scott's successor in 1830. By this time two of the young radical leaders, David Rowland and James Picton, had launched an anonymous fortnightly publication, the *Circular to Wesleyan Methodists*, which ran from January 1830 to July 1833 and pioneered a popular brand of polemical journalism in Methodist circles. In its spirited attacks on the ministry the *Circular* ranged freely from detailed analysis of financial administration to general criticism of ministerial authority, while favourite topics usually involved the partiality of connexional publications, the misuse of connexional funds by the preachers, the status of class leaders as pastors, and the idea of parity of esteem between itinerant and local preachers.

Moreover the alliance between the preachers and the laymen of
substance attracted a stream of adverse comments. At the outset
it was asserted that 'the spirit of Methodism does not accord well
with the wealthy'.[24] And periodic references to local conditions
were usually designed to show that sharply contrasting facilities,
forms of worship and degrees of pastoral supervision signified a
widening gulf between powerful congregations supported by the
preachers and less influential agencies ignored or despised by the
hierarchy. Bunting made strenuous efforts to suppress this criticism and in the process further antagonised his opponents, most
of whom were increasingly prepared to contemplate an organised
campaign.

By 1830 the Rochdale leadership was also acquiring a notorious
reputation for its remonstrances at a time when the town was
fast becoming one of the boom circuits in the connexion. Between 1827 and 1835 an unprecedented rise in membership from
1,145 to 1,911 coincided with a period of marked expansion in
the development of the town, particularly as the population,
8,542 in 1801, increased from 14,170 to 19,410 in the period
1821–31. In this situation the preachers enjoyed exceptionally
high stipends and the leaders of the Union Street chapel kept
long waiting lists of applicants for private pews. The circuit was
also free from the heavy debts which so burdened many societies
and which radical opinion often held responsible for the failure
of the trustees to uphold the rights of the people instead of the
power of the preachers. The most distinctive feature of circuit
life, however, became apparent during the Leeds crisis when the
lay notables led the protest movement and the Quarterly Meeting
directly addressed the Conference of 1829. This address strongly
criticised the failure of Conference to repudiate the actions of the
Leeds Special District Meeting and also declared that the
preachers were in no position to reflect the views of the rank and
file, 'Our Leaders and Stewards are their proper representatives
and are best qualified to give the sense of the people'.[25] Bunting
was equally forthright in his response; he commended the wayward leaders to the prayers of their preachers and instructed Conference to send a curt reply concerning the proper purposes of
a memorial. Undeterred by this rebuke the leaders returned to
the subject in June 1830 when thy requested James Townley,
President of Conference, to offer a satisfactory answer to their
objections. Townley's conciliatory but evasive reply prompted
a second address to Conference and yet another was drafted but
eventually withdrawn in June 1831. The second address was
composed by an increasingly militant leadership which was
battling with the preachers for popular support. The preachers
of the circuit were attacked for their successful efforts to subdue

some of the members, while a majority of the leaders, claiming that 'had not our minds been grieved beyond measure, we too had sat down in silence',[26] showed a capacity for real trouble-making when they requested advice concerning trustees who had signed the first address and who had been invited to serve on the new Union Street trust. Any controversy was now likely to engage this leadership and by the early months of 1834 only the threatened resignation of the superintendent forestalled an attempt to secure the support of the Quarterly Meeting for a set of resolutions against official policy and in favour of financial sanctions.

This last incident occurred as a result of the Stephens' case which immediately preceded and was soon overshadowed by the Warrenite controversy. In his declining years the Peterloo veteran, John Stephens, was constantly embarrassed by the rebel activities of two talented members of his family. His eldest son, John, was the editor of the first unofficial Methodist newspaper, the *Christian Advocate,* which appeared in 1830 and was soon given to unrestrained criticism of the Bunting administration. Stephens was so shocked by such apostasy that he publicly expressed his opposition to his son's principles, while Bunting effectively exploited the scurrilous attacks to discomfit some of his ministerial opponents; the liberal Jacob Stanley was almost certainly denied the presidential Chair because of the false suggestion that his purchase of the newspaper indicated support for its views. There was evidently a highly sympathetic readership amongst the restive ranks of South Lancashire laymen; the Manchester bookshop of James Everett served as a main distribution centre, the Liverpool *Circular* merged with the paper in 1833, and one of the preachers complained that 'The abominable "Christian Reprobate" is read in nearly all our influential families in Rochdale'.[27] Sales of the newspaper moreover were boosted by extensive coverage of a controversy surrounding Stephens' second son, Joseph Rayner, who had entered the ministry in 1825. Shortly after his appointment to the Ashton-under-Lyne circuit in 1832 Joseph plunged into disestablishment politics with an evident determination to recruit and to register Wesleyan support for the local Church Separation Society. An undisclosed but no doubt influential number of laymen reported Stephens to the Chairman of the District, Robert Newton, on the grounds that his campaign was not only contrary to the views of a large majority of members and the interests of peaceful societies but foreign to the work of a preacher. Stephens was thus summoned before the Manchester District Meeting on 29 April 1834 to answer specific charges concerning his public identification of Wesleyanism with the disestablishment cause.

The outcome of this District Meeting was largely determined by a difference of opinion over the issue at stake. Stephens freely admitted the charges yet insisted that his actions were beyond reproach in the absence of a Conference ruling on the disestablishment issue. The Chairman, however, rejected this argument on the ground that the meeting had not been convened to pronounce on the abstract question but to judge Stephens' public acts as a preacher. It was on this basis that he was found guilty of disruptive activities and suspended from ministerial duties after his refusal to abstain from further agitation. Apart from the fact that the resolutions of the meeting had been drafted beforehand, Stephens might have had little cause for further complaint if the meeting had not also gone beyond its declared purpose and judged his opinions 'inconsistent with those sentiments of respect and affection towards the Church of England which our Connexion has, from the beginning, openly professed and honourably maintained'.[28] The liberal opposition in Conference protested that this resolution made nonsense of any notion of neutrality and embodied a high and unreciprocated regard for the Church. None of the preachers, however, defended Stephens when he refused to abandon his public campaigning. Bunting rightly sensed that he had opted for an independent course, and unlike most ministerial rebels who underwent formal expulsion Stephens promptly resigned from the ministry and proceeded to organise his supporters who were already withdrawing from some of the societies in North-East Cheshire and South Lancashire. This division was mainly confined to the Ashton, Oldham and Bolton circuits which incurred net membership losses of 650, 195 and 170 respectively. The seceders established seven preaching places, only two of which remained under the pastoral charge of Stephens when he embarked upon his hell-raising career in the anti-poor law campaign and the factory reform movement.

The Conference of 1834 consisted of two major debates, the first of which on the Stephens' case produced several frosty exchanges between Bunting and Warren including a disdainful comment by Bunting that 'When a revolution takes place we will consult Dr Warren about a new house'.[29] There were surprises in store for both men during the next twelve months, because the second debate on the Theological Institution formed the prelude to an organised campaign against Bunting's view of Methodism. The establishment of an Institution in 1834 was the culmination of various plans for the training of the preachers. Wesley himself had contemplated the use of Kingswood School for this purpose, and by 1808 the connexional magazine made the claim that 'no Institution among us would be better supported than an Institution for the Improvement of serious and promising young men for the Methodist Ministry'.[30] Yet preachers continued to serve their apprenticeship in the circuits and only after 1815 were their studies subjected to the close supervision of the Chairmen. During the 'twenties Bunting and Watson in particular pressed the case for more systematic instruction in order to equip candidates for overseas missions, to cater for the interests of a more highly educated membership, and to ensure the effective and uniform administration of discipline. In 1830 Conference discussed a proposal for a seminary, and a year later it appointed a committee under Bunting to report on the training of young candidates; the committee recommended a course of study designed to provide a thorough understanding of Methodist doctrine and discipline as well as some appreciation of classical knowledge. Only shortage of funds now delayed a major initiative, and when the Irish Conference proposed to use a legacy of £1,000 for the training of preachers the Conference of 1833 formed a committee to prepare a plan. This committee met in October 1833 when it unanimously agreed to recommend the establishment of a Theological Institution and also proceeded to nominate three of its members to the staff. In July 1834, a week before Conference, an enlarged committee completed preparations and proposed the purchase of a disused academy in Hoxton. Conference accepted the plan and confirmed the nominations; Bunting was appointed Visitor (soon exchanged for the title of President), Joseph Entwisle was made House Superintendent and John Hannah secured the post of Theological Tutor.

Thirty-one preachers voted against the plan in Conference. Of this number a few primarily opposed the principle of full-time training; James Wood, one of the fathers of Conference, warned against the proverbial evils of college life, John Burdsall pleaded for the 'simplicity of our ministry', and James Bromley, whose arguments and motives were more mixed, complained of the prolongation of the enforced celibacy of probationers. While the virtues of untutored evangelical passion still had an appeal, more mundane professional considerations undoubtedly convinced some of the opponents that college-trained preachers would snap up the choice appointments. Several liberal spokesmen like Galland, Beaumont and Atherton, however, had no need to fear such a possibility. They supported the principle but opposed the management of the Institution, largely because they believed the establishment would be used to ensure that young preachers learnt the advantages of loyalty to Bunting's administration. At the Conference of 1833 Bunting had reflected on the possibility that 'younger brethren who have not known me in my better days may hereafter treat me harshly',[31] yet through such means as the Institution he had a remarkable hold over this body and significantly the ministerial rebels of 1849–50 all belonged to a pre-college generation. The third and largest element in the anti-Institution party opposed both the principle and management of the project. The most skilful and comprehensive attack appeared in an anonymous work by James Everett, *The Disputants* (1835), but more controversial criticism was immediately voiced by Samuel Warren who moved the opposition amendment in Conference and afterwards published his speech under the title *Remarks on the Wesleyan Theological Institution* (1834).

The substance of Warren's argument was that the Institution overthrew a system of proven efficiency and success, lacked popular support, and failed to take account of a general improvement in educational standards which automatically guaranteed a supply of intelligent young candidates. His principal objection, however, was that the whole enterprise concentrated power in the hands of a few individuals and, as such, endangered the liberty of the preachers and the unity of the connexion. The possibilities were frightening in the extreme, as he observed in his conclusion

Does not every one see that we have only to suppose the President of the Institution to be possessed of *Episcopal propensities*, and it follows, as a matter of course, that the Institution will soon become, neither more nor less, neither better nor worse—if indeed worse can come of it—than a *Dominant Episcopal Faction*. From hence the Connexion must prepare itself to receive a liturgical Service, a splendid Ritual, an illegitimate Episcopal Ordination, a cassocked race of Ecclesiastics, and whatever else may render this new—this improved edition of Methodism, imposing and magnificent in the eyes of the world.[32]

This general argument amounted to a *volte face* by Warren. As a member of the October committee he had favoured the plan, recommended the adoption of a college title, supported the decision to nominate the staff and approved of the nomination of Bunting. His main reservations had concerned the appointments to the posts of Theological Tutor and Classical Tutor (the latter post was left vacant until 1835), for which he nominated two of his friends, John Burdsall and John Crowther, neither of whom belonged to the committee. At the July committee, however, he rejected the entire scheme, refused to offer an explanation until Conference, and caused Bunting to complain of the most unprincipled opposition.

What induced this change of mind is a matter of some conjecture. His own explanation was that he began to detect 'the sinister intentions of the parties' on the rejection of his nominees and once it became clear that Bunting intended to continue as Secretary for foreign missions while undertaking both supervisory and teaching functions at the Institution. In brief Warren suddenly recognised the shape of a horrifying bureaucracy dominated by a man whose unlimited ambition fed on an accumulation of offices, whose power was uncontrolled, and whose influence was so great that one of his acolytes seriously proposed that he should appoint the staff to the Institution. Warren's opponents, however, soon attributed his opposition to other reasons. It was rumoured that he had hoped to fill the vacancy created by Bunting's possible resignation from the secretaryship for foreign missions, yet clearly he had neither the ability nor the inclination to serve as a full-time administrator. The common and perhaps most plausible of the uncharitable explanations was first formally advanced by Robert Newton who claimed that Warren himself aspired to one of the offices in the Institution. Warren strongly denied any such ambition and insisted that his own age and mode of life proved that the charge was absurd. Yet at the age of fifty-three in 1834 he was in fact fourteen years younger than Entwisle and two years younger than Bunting. More importantly he might have expected to secure the appointment of Classical Tutor and almost certainly his support for Burdsall and Crowther, both of whom were to oppose the Institution, was a gambit to draw attention to his virtually unrivalled qualification amongst the preachers. His classical studies had commenced in the strange surroundings of a French academy during the revolutionary wars when he and his father, a sea captain, had spent two years as prisoners of war. Later, as a young preacher, he had been so tutored that he was 'furnished with every inducement to persevere with ardour in the acquisition of classical learning',[33] and on his appointment to the Glasgow circuit in 1815 he continued his classical studies through a university course for which he was awarded an M.A. and eventually a doctorate. By the early 1830s moreover Warren had cause to conclude that his services had received insufficient recognition. His recent handbook of Wesleyan law was not entirely to the liking of some connexional leaders who discountenanced such publications. Worse still the possibility of a first choice appointment now seemed almost as remote as the prospect of election to the Presidential Chair. After thirty years in the ministry, mainly confined to peripheral circuits, he was unable to persuade the modest Bury circuit to accept his services in 1832. A year later he was equally unsuccessful in his strenuous efforts to secure a London appointment; ironically he was sent as superintendent to the Manchester (Oldham Street) circuit on the recommendation of Bunting and against the wishes of the local leaders.

In view of his hitherto scholarly and largely uneventful ministry Warren was one of the most unexpected and least experienced of ministerial rebels. Before 1834 he was not a recognised member of the anti-Bunting network nor had he any reservations about constitutional developments. In 1827 he had described Methodist polity as 'having attained such a degree of maturity and perfection, as is not likely soon to admit of any material improvement',[34] and he had expressed no dissent during the Leeds crisis. In opposition it became apparent that, although he was not entirely an involuntary or unwitting agent, he was easily persuaded by stronger personalities to embark on a course of action that left himself as the major, increasingly isolated victim. He lacked the gifts of a controversialist like Everett, and while he was not of the same independent stamp as Beaumont or Galland he possessed little of the organisational ability of Eckett. These serious deficiencies in a prospective agitator were first exposed before he became the figurehead of a lay revolt.

In the period October 1833 to July 1834, when his initial doubts about the appointments to the Institution hardened into outright opposition to the scheme, Warren was greatly encouraged by several of Bunting's ministerial critics, each of whom was sufficiently astute to draw the line between opposition and separation. The Manchester appointment gave ready access to James Everett who was approaching the end of his first period of supernumeraryship (1825–34) and whose local bookshop had become such a recognised centre of intrigue that Newton successfully applied for his return to circuit work. In the District Meeting of April 1834 only Everett and Warren showed any sympathy for Stephens, while a month later both men were in secret conclave with Joseph Beaumont, who had been converted under Warren, and James Bromley 'to deliberate upon and mature a plan for the purpose of curtailing the power of the dominant party in Methodism, whose arbitrary and crooked policy was becoming more and more apparent, by the manner in which they were forcing upon the people and the Funds an expensive Theological Institution'.[35] It was at this meeting in Leeds that Warren almost certainly agreed to lead the opposition in Conference. Everett no doubt outlined a possible speech, since some of the references in the Remarks bore a close resemblance to his own style. The speech itself was drowned by constant disturbances and interruptions in a Conference which for the first time, according to its commentator Joseph Fowler, indulged in marked audience reactions. Both Everett and Beaumont remained silent throughout the debate and soon afterwards dissociated themselves from Warren; by December 1834 Everett was bemoaning the switch in interest from the Institution to the constitution and concluded that Warren had placed himself beyond the bounds of accommodation. Only Bromley, one of the more reckless rebels who rarely failed to bring out the worst in Bunting, continued to support Warren through the disciplinary actions of the next few months.

After the publication of the *Remarks* in September 1834 Warren claimed that he 'knew not how to go forward'.[36] Nevertheless, he betrayed little uncertainty in his initial reactions even if he was unsure of the long term consequences. First, he took the initiative in a personal matter. He was a brother-in-law of Mary Bealey, the head of a large Radcliffe bleaching business and a close friend of the Buntings. The Warren family had benefited by this connection in the form of financial and other assistance, and it was indicative of his preparations for a major crisis that Warren declined any further gifts from this source at the beginning of October. Secondly, he determined the outcome of the Manchester Special District Meeting to which he was summoned, after nine days' notice, on 22 October to answer the charges that his publication was in breach of ministerial confidence and cast unfair reflections on the character of individual ministers. His performance on this occasion was somewhat contrived and his reason for withdrawal lacked substance; he refused to proceed when Bromley, in attendance as a guest, was removed for making a nuisance of himself. Warren was immediately suspended from ministerial duties. Had the meeting run its course, an official censure and a Conference investigation seemed the most likely result; Bunting had recommended this action beforehand, largely because he rightly feared that suspension would provide dissatisfied laymen with a pretext to interfere in the controversy.

Immediately after the Special District Meeting Warren publicly complained that its proceedings were unconstitutional. Yet his main objections could be met by reference to his own handbook, and this became apparent when he challenged his suspension in the courts. His critics maintained that he was forced into legal action by his local supporters, but he had no real reason to oppose the exercise and possibly possessed some confidence as to the result. By the end of 1834 he was drifting further away from any reconciliation with the Wesleyan authorities. Furthermore, he was increasingly influenced by the often ill-judged assessments of his few, close advisers, one of whom was his eldest son, Samuel, an irrepressible publicist and ambitious young man who, like a number of sons of preachers and wealthy laymen, had strayed into the Church. Characterising his father's opponents as 'mean, malignant, and reckless persecutors',[37] Warren jun. evidently believed that a favourable legal verdict was possible if only because the subject of one of his panegyrics for *Blackwood's Magazine*, the Chancellor Lord Lyndhurst, was also a social acquaintance. Besides filial concern, Samuel had other personal reasons for involvement in a court case. Formerly trained in medicine and now a barrister he viewed court action as a means whereby he might be avenged for the treatment meted out to him when his father had declined further assistance from the Bealeys. He had felt the backlash with a demand notice for repayment of a loan made in 1829 to further his studies. It was particularly galling to receive this notice, 'a rude and insolent letter', from the Bealeys' Manchester attorney, Percy Bunting, Jabez's third son. Bunting sen. considered the action ill-advised and regretted 'this mixing up of a personal offence with the Institution'.[38] During the legal conflict both sons figured as chief prompters for counsel, thus providing a minor sub-plot of personal rivalry to the main drama which occurred in the Vice-Chancellor's court between 28 February and 3 March 1835.

The court hearing involved two bills, one filed by Warren against the Oldham Street Chapel trustees and the other filed by four pro-Warren trustees against the remaining ten trustees of the Oldham Road chapel. The prosecution sought to prove the unconstitutional standing of the Special District Meeting, while the defence denied the court's jurisdiction in the matter. There was never much doubt that the bills would be dismissed and the verdict upheld on appeal. Even so, the presence in court of a large number of leading preachers and laymen indicated the significance of the case, and Bunting was so relieved that he burst into tears on hearing the judgement. This legal action virtually ensured Warren's expulsion. At the Conference of 1835 he was granted an opportunity to justify his conduct but only as a special favour. Defence was hopeless at this stage and only Thomas Rowland, who was himself expelled fifteen years later, voted against expulsion. On the conclusion of the court case Warren declared, 'my cause has ceased to be of importance even to myself, merged, as it has become, in the great cause of the people';[39] his cause was in fact increasingly dwarfed by a lay protest movement which had its origins in Manchester.

REFERENCES

[1] T. P. Bunting, *Life of Jabez Bunting, D.D.* (London 1858–1887), i, p. 262.
[2] MSS. J. Riles to J. Bunting 11 October 1825.
[3] MSS. J. Pawson to C. Atmore 26 September 1794.
[4] MSS. I. Wolfe to A. Kilham 9 May 1797.

5 Anon. *Reasons for leaving the Methodists* (Manchester, 1835), p. 26. An eye-witness account of the Band Room meetings.

6 *A statement of facts and observations relative to the late separation from the Methodist Society in Manchester: affectionately addressed to the members of that body, by their preachers and leaders* (Manchester, 1806), p. 23.

7 J. Ashworth, *An account of the rise and progress of the Unitarian doctrine; in the societies at Rochdale, Newchurch in Rossendale, and other places, formerly in connexion with the late Rev. J. Cooke: in ten letters to a friend* (Rochdale, 1817).

8 *Christian Reformer* 1822.

9 See J. Pyer, *Six letters to a trustee of Canal Street Chapel, Manchester in answer to a pamphlet lately published by Samuel Stocks (Jun.) Esq.* (Manchester, 1830); S. Stocks (Jun.), *A reply to the Rev. John Pyer's 'Few plain and indisputable testimonies' explanatory of the affairs of Canal Street Chapel* (Manchester, 1830).

10 MSS. J. Stephens to J. Bunting 1 February 1821.

11 MSS. F. Marris to Lord Sidmouth 11 November 1819 H.O. 42/198.

12 J. Stephens, *The mutual relations, claims and duties of the rich and poor. A Sermon* (Manchester, 1819), pp. 36–7.

13 *Manchester Observer* 25 December 1819.

14 *Ibid.* 22 April 1820.

15 D. K. Royle, *William Royle of Rusholme* (Manchester, 1924), p. 8.

16 J. Betjeman, *First and last loves* (London, 1952), p. 102.

17 MS. Minutes of Grosvenor Street Quarterly Meeting, 1 October 1824, 2 April 1828.

18 B. Gregory, *Sidelights on the conflicts of Methodism, 1827–1852* (London, 1898), p. 105.

19 MSS. R. O. Barlow to C. Prest 1833. See *Rules of the Wesleyan Methodist Local Preachers' Friendly Society* (Manchester, 1833).

20 MS. Minutes of Liverpool Quarterly Meeting 30 March 1809; MS. Mount Pleasant chapel journal 25 January 1819.

21 MSS. W. Myles to J. Bunting 13 July 1825.

22 MSS. J. Riles to J. Bunting 11 October 1825.

23 MSS. J. Scott to J. Bunting 23 January 1829.

24 *Circular* 27 February 1830.

25 MS. Journal of the transactions in the Rochdale Circuit 1829.

26 *Ibid.* 30 June 1830.

27 MSS. J. Hargreaves to J. Bunting 4 July 1834.

28 G. Smith, *History of Methodism* (London, 1864), iii, Appendix G.

29 B. Gregory, *op. cit.*, p. 164.

30 *Methodist Magazine* December 1808.

31 B. Gregory, *op. cit.*, pp. 129–30.

32 S. Warren, *Remarks on the Wesleyan Theological Institution for the education of the junior preachers* (London, 1834), p. 23.

33 *Imperial Magazine* August 1826 Memoir of the Rev. Samuel Warren, LL.D.

34 S. Warren, *A Digest of the Laws and Regulations of the Wesleyan Methodists* (London, 1835), 2nd edn. p. xxi.

35 MS. J. Everett Memoranda 14 May 1834.

36 *Christian Advocate* 27 April 1835.

37 G. Cubitt, *Reply to Dr. Warren's 'Final Answer'* (London, 1835), p. 5.

38 MSS. J. Bunting to T. P. Bunting 4 November 1834.

39 *Christian Advocate* 30 March 1835.

CHAPTER 3

MANCHESTER: THE CONSERVATIVE PROTEST

A recurrent theme of the protest movement in Manchester concerned the imbalance between the original emphases and contemporary accoutrements of Wesleyanism. There existed a widespread belief that only the restoration of pristine qualities could halt the transformation of the extraordinary mission into a vast apparatus for the regimentation of an underprivileged membership. Throughout the struggle the agitators always viewed themselves as the true heirs of early Methodism: 'We are, or would be, primitive Christians, scriptural followers of John Wesley, conservators of Methodism' affirmed one of their leaders whose view was endorsed by another spokesman 'All we want is Methodism in its simplicity, Methodism in its purity. . .'.[1] Such declarations were common enough elsewhere, yet in Manchester the preoccupation with a past golden age signified a predominant concern for the preservation of certain principles and practices rather than an underlying interest in the provision of a necessary basis and justification for sweeping changes. Hence there was considerable resistance when some fellow campaigners in other centres swiftly turned from a defence of allegedly traditional rights to the formulation of a thorough-going reform programme. This development meant that the final settlement was far removed from the resolutions that made Manchester the birthplace of the Association.

These resolutions emerged from the Oldham Street circuit of which Warren was superintendent. At the Quarterly Meeting on 29 September 1834, the first after the publication of the *Remarks*, only lack of time prevented a discussion of four motions concerning the Institution, and the meeting was adjourned until 27 October. Once he received notice of the Special District Meeting, however, Warren brought forward the adjourned meeting to 20 October and obtained substantial support for a set of resolutions which opposed the Institution on the grounds that it had been introduced without reference to the societies, that it jeopardised connexional peace by permitting Bunting to hold two major posts, and that it tended 'to destroy the conservative principles of the Body in respect of its unity'.[2] Towards the end of this meeting, a six-hour marathon, several other motions were submitted but held over until 3 November when yet another adjourned meeting resolved to form a lay association and called on Conference to admit laymen as spectators and to adopt vote by ballot in its proceedings. After his suspension on 23 October Warren could not hope to keep the initiative for much longer. He presided over the second adjourned meeting and clearly believed that the implementation of its proposals would counter-balance the undue influence of the platform party in Conference. But he was largely a spectator when the Manchester and Liverpool leaders formed the Grand Central Association on 6 November, and on the following day a layman chaired the inaugural meeting of the local branch which was held in the David Street Sunday school.

Extraordinary disturbances accompanied these formal proceedings. Four days after Warren's suspension there was pandemonium at a missionary meeting in the Great Bridgewater Street chapel when Captain Thomas Barlow, a Salford local preacher and veteran of Waterloo, proposed a pro-Warren motion. At the adjourned meeting in the Irwell Street chapel three weeks later the police were present to take Barlow into custody when he attempted to overrule the chairman, the redoubtable James Wood. Barlow immediately laid claim to a 'blessed battle fought' and a 'glorious victory gained',[3] and although the trustees did not press civil charges he was put on trial and expelled by a meeting which became so unmanageable that a verdict could not be reached in his presence. Meanwhile Robert Newton had his baptism of fire as Warren's successor. On Sunday 26 October he conducted a noisy morning service at Oldham Street after a police escort through a crowd armed with stones and chanting 'Away with him, away with him'.[4] Further disturbances occurred during the evening service at Oldham Road where the gas was extinguished and Newton, accompanied by friends and police officers, was chased out of the building and pursued by a riotous mob until he took cover in the Oldham Street vestry. During the next week there was a mass exodus from the Oldham Street Leaders' Meeting when Newton arrived to take the chair. The leaders withdrew to the Tib Street Sunday school which was commandeered as the first temporary headquarters of the Association. Newton was effectively barred from the Oldham Street pulpit until the end of November by which time the Associationists were meeting in various Sunday schools and also in the chapels of sympathetic denominations; Warren presided over formal meetings initially concerned with the collection of money, the appointment of officers and the organisation of classes. During the next six months Manchester Wesleyanism experienced the most serious disruption in its history. Membership of the four circuits had increased from 5,955 to 7,488 in the period 1830-4 but fell back to 4,820 in 1835 after which there was an immediate recovery. The Oldham Street circuit accounted for a large proportion of this loss, as its membership was reduced from 2,145 to 650 and congregations at the Oldham Street and Oldham Road chapels dwindled from 2,000 to 400 and 800 to 40 respectively.

In its origins the Association owed much to five individuals: Benjamin Stocks, William Smith, John Hull, William Wood and Ralph Grindrod. Stocks and Smith had much in common in that both were established manufacturers who hankered after a patriarchal role in an independent congregation. Stocks was in business with his brother, the former sponsor of the Tent Methodists, but the partnership was later dissolved and he never belonged to the big league of local manufacturers largely because he lacked what his obituarist described as 'sleepless vigilance' and 'quickness to perceive an advantage'.[5] In chapel affairs, however, he wielded considerable influence; his dramatic exit from the Oldham Street Leaders' Meeting prompted the large-scale defection of leaders. Smith, a Stockport cotton spinner, was no newcomer to controversy; he counted James Everett and Adam Clarke amongst his closest friends and thus received first-hand reports of any Buntingite intrigue. He presided over the David Street meeting and became the Association's first national treasurer. As circuit steward and author of the first rebel pamphlet,[6] Hull played a prominent part in the early organisation but subsequently returned to the Wesleyans. He was no doubt mindful of his business interests as agent for the Bealeys of Radcliffe and certainly he was aware of this consideration when he withheld signatures from one of the early declarations for fear that disclosure of identity would result in loss of employment or business through exclusive dealing. Individuals on both sides suffered such adverse effects. Samuel Grindrod, the proprietor of an academy and one of the few Oldham Street loyalists, had to seek alternative employment when the Associationists withdrew their children, while Everett's bookshop, now managed by his nephew, was first boycotted by the Wesleyans for stocking the *Remarks* and then denied supplies of the publication when the nephew declared for the Wesleyans. The Associationists complained that they were more vulnerable to such pressures especially in the powerful Grosvenor Street circuit, 'The Methodists of Chorlton upon Medlock (the stronghold of the high party) are beginning to awake from their slumber of forgetfulness and apathy; and I have no doubt, if *interest* (for many of them depend upon the high party for their daily bread) were out of the way numbers of them would shake off the galling yoke which, as freemen and men of reason, they begin to feel uneasy'. There is, however, little evidence to suggest that 'the dozens of Methodists of high and low degree', who were employed by large Wesleyan manufacturers like James Wood and Joshua Westhead and for whom the class ticket was a standard form of reference, were greatly affected by this consideration; the more important influence was the prevailing climate of opinion in a particular chapel or Sunday school.[7]

Both William Wood and Ralph Grindrod served as the first national secretaries of the Association. Wood, a woollen manufacturer, had impeccable credentials as a rebel. His father had been identified with the Kilhamites and he himself had kept up a barrage of criticism particularly during the Peterloo period, after which he was temporarily attached to the Tent Methodists. As a keen advocate of disestablishment he publicly supported Stephens, and at the outset of the agitation he denounced the Institution as a sinister agency designed to turn young preachers into Tories. Grindrod had less diffuse interests. His abiding passion was the teetotal movement for which the Association represented little more than a useful platform and a possible recruiting agency. The functions of a secretary were in fact too mundane for a surgeon who was to use his medical knowledge on a celebrated six-year lecturing tour for the teetotal cause during the 1840s.

A number of features distinguished the Manchester situation from other areas. In the first place the common term 'Warrenite' here assumed more than symbolic significance. For while he was soon passed over elsewhere as a nominal leader, Warren attracted much sympathy and attention on home ground and he exercised considerable influence in the purely local policy-making process. The leaders stood by him throughout the court case in which they had a mutual interest, and they met more than their fair share of the £1,800 bill for legal expenses. Moreover they continued to press for recognition of Warren's circumstances, and at the second delegates' meeting they made an unsuccessful attempt to ensure that his restoration to full ministerial status was regarded as a *sine qua non* of any possible agreement between Conference and the Association.

Besides such personal loyalty there was a considerable degree of interest in the precise issue of the Institution. Even some loyal members had initial doubts about the value of the enterprise. William Read, the Oldham Street Quarterly Meeting secretary, claimed that his original objections had been answered by Warren himself, while John Crowther, Warren's junior colleague, had opposed the scheme until October 1834 when his public criticism of the *Remarks* embarrassed the Wesleyan hierarchy, since Warren was still superintendent at the time.[8] Major opposition to the Institution originated in a cluster of attitudes mainly relating to a defence of a revivalist tradition, an aversion to a professional ministry, and a widespread concern for the meaning and application of connexional law.

While revivalism was no longer the staple diet of Manchester Wesleyanism there persisted an inherited or experienced appreciation of its past achievements. There was, too, during the early 1830s an immediate reminder of its potency in the form of the Rev. Robert Aitken, an ordained Anglican curate from the Isle of Man, whose spectacular conversion after sixteen days of continuous fasting and prayer was closely followed by engagements as a freebooting revivalist. His first visit to Manchester in September 1833 drew mixed reactions from Wesleyan circles. Edmund Grindrod, superintendent of the Irwell Street circuit, refused him any accommodation in the Salford chapels, and he failed to appeal to middle class tastes fairly reflected by the wife of James Wood 'I thought I could distinguish very perceptibly an effort in the preacher to produce an animal excitement. . . . I could not divest my mind of the idea of a maniac'.[9] Yet he was welcomed by Warren in the Oldham Street circuit where his preaching style conjured up memories of a fast-disappearing spontaneity and freedom of expression associated with outdoor preaching and band meetings. And as a revivalist who stepped outside the well-marked ecclesiastical boundaries, Aitken lent weight to the belief that a formal organised ministry was an ugly intrusion upon the simplicity of an earlier age. Moreover it was considered inevitable that the Institution would become the graveyard of any aspiring revivalist as academic considerations dulled the call to simple, powerful preaching.

More generally the Institution was regarded as an unnecessary addition to and reinforcing agent of existing patterns of ministry and worship that already displayed objectionable tendencies. Organs, liturgical worship, infrequent pastoral visitation and now an Institution were all of one piece in that they symbolised an alliance between an itinerant order that had lost some of its distinctive qualities and an urban middle class that had undesirable pretensions. Such features seemed symptomatic of a deep malaise and either clashed with early religious experiences or threatened to cloud a particular vision of Wesleyanism as memories of an heroic age prompted the familiar refrain that 'The glory has departed from Methodism'. Thus, one Association leader reached back forty years to his first experience of a class meeting besieged by an angry mob, only to demonstrate that Methodism had flourished without an Institution during the intervening period. An Institution *inter alia* challenged a view of the past and heightened the contrast between the two orders described by one interested observer of the Manchester scene,

Refinement in preaching produces one effect; and plain simple truth, in her russet attire, produces another. An academy among the Wesleyans would work a change somewhat similar to that which we see subsisting between the prim, refined, sickly sentimentality of the city, and the hale, open, rustic simplicity of the country.[10]

Both the complaints and early practices of the Associationists indicated that particular hostility towards the Institution was part of a general protest against the transition from Society to Church. Hence ministers were frequently criticised for their failure to maintain activities associated with the original itinerant system, especially early morning services, outdoor preaching, regular visitation, and society meetings after services. 'Showy chapels', moreover, were declared unsuitable for prayer meetings, lovefeasts and other means of grace which, it was commonly observed, 'are losing their savoury influence amongst a certain class of persons in our society'.[11] Wesleyan apologists argued that some of these criticisms showed no appreciation of the fact of development, for as one of their number observed 'It is quite obvious, that the incidents connected with the working of a regularly established system, must be less striking than those associated with the early progress of a work of religion, amidst difficulties and opposition. . . ' .[12] In the belief that such a change was neither popular nor irreversible, the Associationists emphasised traditional patterns of Methodist life and throughout the controversy there were regular reports of unusually lively class meetings, and inspiring services and lovefeasts. In February 1835 it was noted that 'The people are exchanging boxes of whistles for vocal music . . . forms of prayer for heart worship . . . and splendid chapels for houses, garrets and even factories'.[13] A month later the first wooden tabernacle was erected in Stevenson Square, a pointed contrast to the Wesleyan 'temples' and designed to hold a large congregation which 'had quite got into the old Methodist fashion'.[14] Furthermore, years of pastoral neglect came to an end as full-time preachers took up their duties. John Peters, who was stationed in the town in 1836, commented

The people are greatly pleased in getting a visit from their Preacher. They say it is the good old times of Methodism come back again. Some of them have asseverated that they had been fifteen years members of the Society and never yet had a visit from the Preachers.[15]

Specific constitutional objections to the Institution principally concerned the way in which the project had been foisted on the connexion at large. The enlargement of the preparatory committee was viewed as an infringement of the rule of 1796 which banned any such meetings without the permission of Conference.

There was also strong criticism of the failure to refer the plan
to the societies in accordance with the Leeds Regulations concerning the adoption of new rules. Such gaps between the myth
and the reality of connexional polity intensified general fears
about the workings of the system. In its first statement of aims the
Manchester Association declared that it required nothing new
in the Methodist constitution which it took to consist of the form
of government inherited from Wesley and adjusted by the Plan
of Pacification and the Leeds Regulations. These arrangements
constituted a solemn and binding contract, and they were
analogous to the Magna Carta and Bill of Rights in that they
defined the functions and powers of the respective parties. On
the basis of this contractual view of Methodist government it
was maintained that Conference had denied the spirit if not the
letter of the law and that in doing so it had undermined the
rights of an unsuspecting laity whose deference, trust and ignorance had allowed the preachers to assume authority.

The Manchester Associationists initially substantiated these
charges with fewer, less precise and more local examples than
like-minded parties elsewhere. They might have been hard-
pressed in fact to widen their sights without Warren's prompting
and the ready advice of the Liverpool leadership. Some possessed
only a twilight knowledge of constitutional provisions like many
loyal members who requested the Conference of 1835 to supply
an explanation of the rules, and others sensed rather than
reasoned that perhaps the constitution had been lost by default.
It was not surprising therefore that the occasional revelation,
such as the absence of the Plan of Pacification and Leeds Regulations from the Conference Journal, attracted much attention.
This particular discovery seemed to confirm the worst fears and
reinforced the general impression that the 'laws of usage' had
obscured and distorted, if not supplanted, the original meaning
and intention of the legislators. Much of Warren's case in court
was built on this premiss especially with reference to the small
print of the Oldham Street chapel trust deed and the procedures
of the District Meeting as defined by the Plan of Pacification.
The same point also found expression in the second address
issued by the Central Committee, 'It is against the Laws of Usage,
we protest . . . and we now say again, what is decayed and for-
gotten we would have restored, and what is mystical and in-
definite we would have explained'.[16]

On its appearance in December 1834 this second address indicated the limited perspective of the local leadership. It gave
prominence to the Leeds crisis and made the most cursory of
references to Warren, while the earlier Oldham Street declarations had ignored Leeds and concentrated on local circum-

stances. The same emphasis was apparent in two articles penned by Ralph Grindrod for the *Watchman's Lantern*[17] in which specific grievances were discussed only in relation to the situation in Manchester. Grindrod also argued that a conciliatory gesture by the Special District Meeting might have prevented conflict in the first place; the Liverpool editors, however, were so unimpressed by this view that they cut short his series of articles.

The conservative inclinations of the Manchester leaders found expression in a determination to rescue and, where necessary, to clarify Wesleyan law; 'Our object is to *restore* and not to *destroy*' declared John Hull in a reference to the original proposals and tactics which drew heavily on precedent. At the beginning of the controversy it was agreed to withhold contributions to connexional funds, and the most telling argument in favour of this action instanced the allegedy beneficial effects of a similar proposition in the 1790s. It was argued moreover that the two main aims were not extraordinarily novel. Vote by ballot was no more than the extension of a principle to other matters besides the election of the President and Secretary of Conference. Likewise the presence of laymen in Conference was 'only an enlargement of what has been conceded of late years to the *People* during *one* sitting of the Conference',[18] and in any case, as Grindrod impressed upon his readers, laymen had been admitted to some of the earliest Conferences under Wesley. These proposed remedies and the marked interest in the proceedings of Conference suggested the pale shadow of a neo-Kilhamite movement rather than the radical strains of Free Methodism. As such the original pacemakers soon found themselves on the defensive once different emphases and more expansive demands began to emerge from other centres of agitation. The first meeting with the Liverpool deputation on 6 November saw the start of this process. On this occasion the Liverpool leaders insisted on the abandonment of vote by ballot and subsequently ensured that the proposal was omitted from the first joint address published in Liverpool; they recognised, as did friend and foe alike, that the original proposals were strangely contradictory and half-baked. Although the Manchester leaders formally agreed to this move, they sowed confusion when they included vote by ballot in the second address printed in Manchester, thus leaving the lasting and mistaken impression that this proposal formed part of the Association's original programme.

Within weeks of its formation the Manchester Association came under heavy pressure to identify itself with a more substantial list of grievances and demands. Wesleyan preachers in the town immediately deplored the 'clamours for revolutionary change', yet the original proposals were considered very modest if not entirely irrelevant in other quarters. Three days after the David Street meeting the *Christian Advocate*, given a new lease of life by the controversy, regretted that 'the Manchester Reformers have stopped short of asking the full concession of their rights'[19] and concluded that the only possible advantage to be derived from the programme was the admission of its own reporter to Conference. A month later another editorial queried the consistency and purpose of the two main proposals, while one correspondent drew his own conclusions,

The plan of reform proposed is utterly inefficient. The good men of Manchester are not just the men to lead the aggressive movement against the stronghold of Wesleyan despotism and abuse. Either they are ignorant of the position they ought to take at this crisis, or they are afraid to take it. Dr Warren is hardly the pilot—his professional prejudices and high Tory principles disqualify him from being the champion of popular rights.[20]

At the same time a similar if less extreme message was delivered by John Gordon whose recent resignation from the ministry had been occasioned by the Stephens' case. On a visit to Manchester Gordon warned his audience that their programme was incomplete, and at the first delegates' meeting he helped to shepherd through propositions that made the original aims pitifully weak.

The two delegates' meetings in 1835 brought the Manchester leaders into direct contact with allies whose opinions lacked representation on the Central Committee. In these circumstances the local leaders could not hope to stand on their past record or secure much support for increasingly flimsy aims. The first meeting in April found the Manchester delegates ill-prepared to move as far and as fast towards a precise programme as some of the other participants. When one of their number expressed the hope that any decision would reflect a desire for pacification rather than separation, Robert Emmett, a renegade supernumerary, is reported to have said 'some of the Manchester friends were not disposed to go to the full length which was generally desired; but he believed that they were determined not to rest short of a full scriptural reform in Methodism; though at present they thought it sufficient to lay down general principles'.[21] Apart from other considerations the Manchester delegates attempted to provide a restraining influence because they had made inadequate preparations. The meeting occurred at an inopportune time, only weeks after the end of a court case which had originally 'given a mighty impulse to the cause in this quarter' but now exacted a heavy toll on financial resources and morale alike. The preoccupation with court proceedings and a natural preference for

the recital of grievances meant that little consideration was given
to what might be sought in a national forum. This approach
proved fatal, for it left the field open to more aggressive leaders
who did not hesitate to exploit the uncertain touch of a Manchester leadership headed by Warren.

For Warren the April meeting was a shattering experience and
a foretaste of worse to come. During the course of one of the debates, in fact, he was so rattled by the defeat of one of his motions
that he raised the question of legal costs and indicated his willingness to accept imprisonment if he was forsaken by his supporters. The comment was singularly inappropriate in an assembly that still retained a vital interest in his campaigning
services, even if it refused to allow him to determine policy. 'The
great master', declared Charles Prest a young militant preacher
then stationed in Manchester, 'has become "the mastered spirit
of the faction" ';[22] and certainly Warren's private reservations
and public tergiversation now further weakened his position and
convinced his Wesleyan opponents that he had indeed become
the learned lackey, the hired servant, and the despised tool of a
mob of destructionists.

By the time of the April meeting Warren was still wavering on
the question of lay delegation and initially attempted to divert
attention to other matters. By the end of the meeting, however,
he was plainly annoyed by his failure to secure pride of place for
this proposal in the set of resolutions. The change in his position
resulted from various pressures that became apparent during the
course of the proceedings. First, the Manchester leaders were in
favour of lay delegation and believed that it was a natural extension of their original proposal for lay spectators in Conference. Warren could ill-afford to antagonise this group, particularly since he wished to appear as its major spokesman. Secondly,
Warren had aimed to drive a wedge between the delegates and
the Protestant Methodist representatives led by Sigston and
Johnson. At the beginning of the meeting he proposed that the
Protestant Methodists should vote separately from the delegates.
But once he failed to secure support for this proposal he had to
come to terms with the condition of lay delegation on which the
Leeds leaders chose to align themselves with the Association.
Thirdly, the promotion of lay delegation as the centre-piece of a
reform programme held out the possibility of diminishing the
importance of other resolutions relating to local meetings and
circuit independency. While Warren viewed some of these resolutions as a threat to any connexional system, he maintained that
lay delegation was a 'Conservative principle' which might be
applied to a Conference that had enlarged itself beyond the Legal
Hundred and a District Meeting that already admitted laymen for

certain transactions. The argument lacked much logic, conviction and overwhelming appeal, and the accompanying admission that lay delegation might be impossible 'without abolishing Methodism or reducing it to a ruin'[23] served only to confuse matters. Besides, Robert Eckett, initially regarded by some delegates as a 'Conference spy', was already deploying more powerful arguments which denied the right of any Conference to govern the church, restricted Conference business to the appointment and exclusion of preachers, and rejected lay delegation on the ground that the delegates would be the favourites of the preachers.

The importance of lay delegation in the general programme changed perceptibly between the first and second delegates' meetings. The second meeting in August stopped short of the original unconditional demand and resolved that, if the proposal raised difficulties in discussions with Conference, 'District Meetings and Conference be open to the members of our Society, on some convenient plan to be mutually agreed upon between the two parties'.[24] The willingness to adopt a more flexible approach stemmed from two different assessments of the situation. Some delegates recognised that in view of insufficient support for the proposal throughout the connexion it was premature to press it upon an unwilling Conference. A more prevalent view was that priority should be given to other aims which, if achieved, would render lay delegation less necessary. The Manchester leaders subscribed to the first view with the evident intention to continue the campaign in order to win more substantial support. According to Warren the Manchester members 'would cheerfully prepare for a ten years' campaign',[25] seemingly convinced of their long-term effectiveness as an internal pressure group. The logic of events pointed in another direction, however, after Conference expelled Warren and refused to treat with the delegates. While many of the Manchester members were psychologically unprepared for the impasse of August 1835, the course of the local agitation before and after this period allowed for little optimism, particularly in view of the general attitudes of the local Wesleyan leaders.

Few towns had such a formidable array of Wesleyan ministers and laymen as Manchester. In the ministerial ranks Robert Newton, Edmund Grindrod and John Anderson figured prominently as superintendents who shared a common determination to avoid any semblance of weakness. Newton was undeterred by his reception in the Oldham Street circuit, and he set the course for the rest of his superintendency when he refused to meet a group of Association leaders; like his colleagues, however, he suffered ill-health as a result of the constant strain and he was unable to discharge his duties as Secretary at the Conference of 1836. Similarly

Grindrod felt no inclination to engage in negotiations or to reason with rebellious members. In spite of medical advice to avoid possible excitement he remained as firm as he had been during the Leeds crisis, and he was soon convinced that some new regulations were required 'to diminish the democracy of our Leaders Meetings and Quarterly Meetings, and to protect our Connexion from the frequent occurrence of the unhallowed strifes which now afflict us'.[26] The superintendent of the Grosvenor Street circuit, Anderson, may have lacked the star qualities of the others, but nevertheless his interpretation and meticulous fulfilment of his superintendent's duties excluded the possibility of any concessions. Even if he had been inclined towards a pacific gesture the views of influential laymen in his circuit told against such an action.

A month after Warren's suspension these superintendents spearheaded a swift counterattack in a statement signed by all their colleagues in the district. This uncompromising declaration dismissed all grievances, rejected any demands and aimed 'to put down faction'. In particular it was insisted that complaints concerning the Institution were entirely unjustified, that the Special District Meeting had acted in conformity with the law and in numerable precedents, that the withholding of financial contributions was contrary to Wesleyan rule and moral equity, and that any reform based on the resolutions of the Oldham Street Quarterly Meeting 'would be a curse not only to our own Connexion but to the nation generally'.[27] This statement set the tone for the subsequent controversy and reduced the possibility of a fruitful discussion of differences. It was relatively easy in fact for detailed arguments about the rules to degenerate into highly personal clashes between combative ministers and bristling laymen, as in the Irwell Street circuit where the weighty combination of Grindrod and Prest brooked no opposition from hotheads like Captain Barlow.

The real strength of local Wesleyanism, however, resided in the laity and most especially in what Grindrod was pleased to call 'the intelligent and well-educated portion of our Community'[28] but identified by the opposition press as the inhabitants of Oxford Road 'which is colonised by nearly all the gold, but with little of the knowledge of the Societies here'.[29] In these circumstances a well-organised machine mobilised considerable resources for the defence and implementation of official policy. A local committee of shareholders supervised and largely financed the *Watchman* newspaper which was launched in 1835 as a mouthpiece of the Bunting administration. A substantial proportion of private contributions towards the Institution came from local sources, besides which individual laymen agreed to underwrite the project and also undertook to make up the deficiencies in some of the connexional funds as a result of Association policy. Other demonstrations of financial support were no less impressive. At the height of the agitation Bunting preached at one of the smaller chapels, George Street, and raised an extraordinary Sunday collection of £650. Nor was there any shortage of capable organisers, two of whom, James Wood and Percy Bunting, proved particularly tough campaigners. Wood had long since acquired a reputation for intransigent opposition to agitators, particularly in his capacity as Leaders' Meeting secretary during the Band Room and Peterloo crises. A substantial businessman and first President of the Manchester Chamber of Commerce he was also a life-long friend of Bunting; Percy Bunting, in fact, claimed that his father regarded Wood as dear to him as his own soul. Besides his connexional appointments as treasurer of the Auxiliary and Centenary Funds, therefore, Wood occupied a position to offer advice at the highest level, and it was on his suggestion that Bunting organised a meeting of leading laymen immediately prior to the Sheffield Conference as a striking show of force in the face of the delegates' meeting. Throughout the controversy Percy Bunting orchestrated a comprehensive local campaign and assigned to himself a roving commission that included anything from the preparation of legal advice to the distribution of pamphlets. Such zeal and good intentions clearly distressed his father who initially recommended a very different role 'You are yet young; you have the misfortune to bear my unpopular and hated name—Is it not expedient that you avoid prominency in these agitations. Better to help the preachers privately than as a known and public agent'.[30]

Wood and Bunting represented the distinguished clientele of the Grosvenor Street and Oxford Road chapels which catered for some of the wealthiest Wesleyan families in the country and, in particular, included the Chappell, Fernley, Gray, Marris, Rae and Westhead families. These families formed a tightly-knit group as a result of intermarriage and business partnerships, and they had their equals in neighbouring circuits like the Hooles of Salford and the Burtons of Rhodes. The heads of these households owned some of the largest manufacturing concerns in the area and often put some of their money in other enterprises. During the 1840s the Wood, Westhead, Burton and Chappell families alone invested approximately £200,000 in railways and all lost heavily as a result of the crash in shares of 1847. George Chappell himself confessed at the time that 'the devil has taken me up into an exceedingly high mountain and showed me in flaming letters *Ten Per Cent* and all the glory of it, and I fell down and worshipped—and have lost ten thousand pounds . . .'

Several of these manufacturers had a notorious reputation in radical circles. James Fernley's mill, one of the largest in the town and often the target of arsonists and rioters, was frequently cited by the *Poor Man's Advocate* as an example of the worst features of the factory system. And Holland Hoole, a cotton spinner, attracted strong criticism from Richard Oastler and the working class press for his prominent opposition to Sadler's Factory Bill of 1832, particularly when he claimed that there was nothing in the working conditions of the Lancashire cotton industry which 'ought to be considered outrageous to British feelings or disgraceful to a Christian country'.[31] None of these manufacturers, moreover, took kindly to insubordination, nor did they shy away from a forceful demonstration of opinion. When a leader of the factory operatives sought to intimidate George Chappell, the reply was made in characteristically colourful language 'if any person attempts to molest me, he shall have a button-hole made in his coat, the tailor never made'.[32] In a much more significant and earlier incident the Burton family, one of whom led the Oldham Street chapel trustees in Warren's court case, called in the military to deal with rioting amongst their Luddite operatives; seven of the rioters were killed in an action that not only proved to be the bloodiest Luddite affray in the country but also indicated where the sympathies of the Wesleyan leadership lay in the social divide.

These manufacturers often viewed the Associationists as tiresome turn-outs who withheld contributions to connexional funds in much the same way as the operative struck for higher wages. Their official response was formally and tersely expressed by the Grosvenor Street Quarterly Meeting which 'pledges itself to renewed exertion of faith and prayer in furtherance of the work of God in connexion with Wesleyan Methodism as now constituted'.[33] In effect neither negotiation nor compromise was possible with the rebels, and nor should Conference feel obliged to introduce new measures that might be interpreted as a sign of weakness. At the Sheffield meeting Bunting was urged to stand firm and to introduce only minor changes. Chappell expressed a fairly common view when he remarked 'I am afraid of Dr Bunting's making concessions to clamour, not to necessity'. Wood was even more apprehensive about the possibility of major innovations, and somewhat inconclusive evidence, a report in the *Christian Advocate*, suggests that he persuaded Bunting to abandon several of the more liberal proposals which were considered in the context of new legislation. Although Wood retained strong objections to the undefined composition of the Quarterly Meeting which meant that 'Any Leader or Local Preacher of seventeen exercises a right to attend and vote who may have the gift of the gab', he and the other Manchester leaders recognised that the new rules effectively confirmed their power and influence in the chapels.[34] Against this type of opposition the Associationists had to yield to superior force or accept the possibility of separation. In the expectation of a temporary withdrawal the site of the Stevenson Square tabernacle had been secured for six months only, yet after August 1835 even the most optimistic of assessments suggested that a long siege was in prospect. On 1 November a new and more substantial tabernacle, 'winter quarters', was occupied on a site opposite the old building. During the same month the first chapel was opened in Oldham Road but collapsed two months later, curiously presaging the fate of the new organisation. The beginnings of a chapel-building programme effectively sealed the choice in favour of independence. Shareholding schemes were introduced to finance the main chapels which were opened in Bury Street (Salford), Grosvenor Street, and Tonman Street in 1836 and in Lever Street two years later. With the exception of Bury Street competitive siting close to Wesleyan rivals gave lasting effect to the division and usually worked to the advantage of the parent body. Furthermore, the formation of four circuits in 1838 followed the Wesleyan pattern; the First or Lever Street circuit had 1,255 members and covered the Oldham Street circuit, the Second or Grosvenor Street circuit had 869 members, the Third or Tonman Street circuit had 507 members and covered the Great Bridgewater Street circuit, and the Fourth or Salford circuit had 346 members. The provision of permanent accommodation was a necessity in view of a membership of 3,092 in 1836 but it proved extravagant in extent twenty years later, by which time the membership had been almost halved (1,624 in 1856), Lever Street had a debt running into thousands of pounds and Tonman Street had suffered closure. Similarly although the existence of four circuits had administrative advantages and no other branch was large enough to justify such a measure, weaknesses soon became apparent in this arrangement. Tonman Street, in particular, was always a costly prestige symbol and, but for a short period in the late 'thirties, it had the lowest circuit membership largely due to the fact that the Great Bridgewater Street circuit sustained the smallest net loss of members, 214 in 1834–5. Moreover the circuit division was the result of disagreement rather than well-conceived plans, for as one of the leaders observed 'it had never been intended but to have one circuit in Manchester. However, the various leaders' meetings passing resolutions of a conflicting nature, rendered a division absolutely necessary'.[35]

The long-term decline of the Association may be traced to this early period when the shifting sands of dissentient opinion exposed a crisis of identity. At the outset the prospect and reality of independence accentuated differences of opinion and caused a steady stream of losses. Some members balked at the idea of secession and renewed their Wesleyan affiliations, usually because their principal objective had always been to reform rather than to leave the connexion. Others took flight to non-Methodist denominations as an inspiring crusade degenerated into a series of squabbles in official meetings where, as John Peters noted in a short, comparatively trouble-free period, 'it is truly astonishing to see what harmony there is among those who evidently possess great warmth of temper if not restrained by the grace of God'.[36] During the course of the controversy new leaders emerged to take the place of some of the original spokesmen who, it was complained, had proclaimed the loudest against Conference misrule and had been the first to abandon the cause. Several of these leaders like John Greenhalgh, a schoolmaster, and William Souter, a draper, had undergone a formal trial and expulsion that prejudiced any hopes of reconciliation, while others like Thomas Taylor, a watchmaker, and Joseph Lees, a salesman, represented disgruntled elements amongst the local preachers who were dubbed 'local talkers' by one Wesleyan. These leaders soon discovered the limits of their authority and popularity, even though they had the assistance of financial backers like John Kirkham, a timber merchant, who erected the first tabernacle and Robert Lowe, a cotton manufacturer, who later purchased the Grosvenor Street chapel for the continued use of the Association.

Developments in the Lever Street circuit demonstrated some of the major difficulties, and the leaders who had once boasted that no aristocratic neglect or priestly intolerance could roll back the ark of freedom were soon on the defensive as various agencies, including a neighbouring circuit, sought recruits at their expense and as some members were lost to the world during the commercial depression of the late 'thirties. Susceptibility to the proselytising zeal of the denominational underworld became evident as early as 1835 when competitors as dissimilar as the Quakers and Aitken's Christian Society appealed to an Associationist audience. For the Quakers a well-timed anonymous publication by a former Manchester Wesleyan, *The Light of Christ Exalted* (1835), had the desired effect, much to the consternation of one leader who reported that an undisclosed number of members had joined the meeting-house. Certainly the publication raised the sort of questions that bothered the Associationists, particularly its enquiry as to whether Methodism had abandoned all primitive strength and vigour for organs and prayer books.

Aitken's Society plagued the Association throughout its early existence; individual members and sometimes entire classes were attracted to this cause, and on several occasions the leaders mounted unsuccessful rescue operations.[37] Further damage was inflicted by the Mormons in 1840. The Lever Street leaders were so concerned by this threat that they seized every opportunity to deflate some of the claims concerning the 'gift of tongues'. Their campaign reached a climax with an elaborate experiment involving a former member of the Association as a subject. The performance of this semi-literate cotton operative provided convincing evidence of spurious claims, and the leaders were delighted to announce that their subject had failed to speak fluent Hebrew or to improve on 'some eight or ten half-stifled snorts, or grunts . . .'.[38] The damage had been done, however, and this event scarcely reversed a considerable leakage to the Mormons, principally involving the rank and file but including leaders like Thomas and John Brotherton, silk manufacturers and cousins of Edward Brotherton (author of a book on Mormonism), who eventually joined the New Jerusalem Church after a disillusioning visit to Nauvoo. Both Aitken's Society and the Mormons benefited by a strong sense of disappointment, for the dull, shapeless style of the Association failed to satisfy certain emotional needs and also suggested that early Methodism had not been resurrected after all; the Assembly Address of 1839 might well enquire 'O where is that primitive zeal . . . that burning energy, for which the first Christians were so remarkable . . . that quenchless love for perishing sinners, by which the early Methodists were so distinguished?'[39]

The other circuits fared little better than Lever Street during this period. In 1838 the Salford circuit almost disappeared after the resignation of its promising young preacher, David Rutherford, who saw no future in a system that failed to guarantee representation for the preachers in the Assembly and also denied the preachers exclusive right to the chairmanship of circuit meetings. The newly-appointed preacher, Henry Breeden of Derby Arminian Methodist fame, arrived to find himself locked out of the preacher's house and surrounded by leaders who not only shared Rutherford's objections but also decided to dissolve the circuit. Breeden's lively preaching saved the situation and indeed Salford was the only circuit in the area to increase its membership in later years. On his next appointment in 1840 Breeden faced another, less critical situation when he entered the Grosvenor Street circuit only to discover that his predecessor had departed with a minority of members to form an independent congregation; his efforts here temporarily reversed the general decline in membership.

The troubled state of affairs in Salford was directly related to the developments that caused Warren himself to retire from the Association. After April 1835 the crucial debate on the relative merits of central authority and local independency found Warren and his local supporters forever on the defensive in the highest councils. At the first Annual Assembly in 1836, which was held in Manchester and at which he was elected President, Warren was once again confronted by substantial support for proposals that virtually demolished his case for a strong connexional system. The main challenge to his position took the form of an adopted resolution 'that every Circuit have the right and power to govern itself by its Local Courts, without the interference of any Yearly Meeting, as to the management of its internal affairs'.[40] The only chance of modifying, if not overturning, such arrangements now lay in union with other Methodist connexions and, in particular, with the Methodist New Connexion. Warren thus secured the appointment of a committee under his chairmanship to explore this possibility. Association and New Connexion representatives entered into negotiations in October 1836 and continued to meet periodically until March 1837, by which time there was majority support for a proposed scheme within the Association committee. Throughout these proceedings Warren was greatly assisted by the fact that Manchester had the largest number of representatives on the committee, most of whom held to a less modified form of connexionalism than some leaders elsewhere and were also encouraged by their press ally, the *Manchester Times,* to seek such a union. The Assembly of 1837, however, rejected the scheme and strongly criticised the committee for its willingness to reach an agreement on largely New Connexion terms. In effect the committee had proposed a uniting Conference with an excessive amount of legislative authority.

The defeat of this scheme was in fact a foregone conclusion once the Assembly had completed its major deliberations on constitutional provisions. Warren and his supporters were outvoted at every point in the course of these debates. On the controversial issue of the Assembly's composition the adoption of free representation quashed an alternative proposal designed to ensure representation for the preachers. The Lever Street Quarterly Meeting had resolved to press for a system whereby circuits with fewer than 1,000 members appointed one preacher to the Assembly and other circuits sent two preachers. The Manchester preachers, Warren and Peters, supported this proposal on the ground that an itinerant ministry constituted a distinct agency and therefore deserved the same representation and protection in a central body as the membership enjoyed in local meetings. Defeat on this point was closely followed by failure to secure the exclusive right of preachers to chair local meetings; it was decided that this function could be performed by itinerant or local preachers. Most of the Manchester representatives were as dissatisfied with these decisions as Warren himself, and one of their principal spokesmen, Joseph Lees, who had been one of the secretaries of the first Assembly, voiced their common concern when he expressed his reluctance 'to labour amongst a people who pointed out their preachers as men to be guarded against —as despots whose every proceeding must be carefully watched'.[41]

After this Assembly Warren was even less inclined to compromise himself any further and in October 1837 he tendered his resignation. His entry into the Anglican ministry eighteen months later produced predictable reactions in Wesleyan quarters. His critics had assumed that it was impossible to improve on his past inconsistencies, and even though they had largely exhausted their scorn for such a pitiful character they did not hesitate to quote some of his memorable remarks, not least of which was his statement at the Conference of 1834 that 'I shall lift up my voice most solemnly against our taking one step towards the Church'.[42] Some of his local followers, however, continued to support his new ministry, most notably two former members of the Central Committee, William Smith and Jabez Sanderson, whose respective financial resources and organisational ability helped to establish his new church in Every Street, Ancoats where he laboured for the next twenty-five years. Ancoats had of course defeated better men than Warren and the name of his church, All Souls, proved apt in view of the poor attendances. Moreover this unusual example of Associationist support for an Anglican venture was given an ironic twist when William Read, the resolute loyalist of the Oldham Street Quarterly Meeting, also entered the Anglican ministry at a later date.

Neither the constitutional settlement of 1837 nor the withdrawal of Warren convinced some of the Manchester leaders that their cause was lost. Consequently, they fought a rearguard action at the Assembly of 1838. Eckett, the chief architect of the constitution, was well-prepared to meet the challenge. At the outset he complained that the Manchester leaders had divided the circuit without the consent of the Assembly; there was in fact no specific provision governing such actions and a measure was immediately introduced to close the loophole. In his opposition to any further dealings with Warren he was even more critical of the local leaders, John Hull and William Souter, who had 'trifled with' the Assembly in their self-appointed role as mediators and who now wished to send an official deputation to Warren with a view to possible reconciliation. Eckett argued that the deputation should only inform Warren that he was *persona non grata*, but

on this point at least he relented in the almost certain knowledge
that an agreement was unlikely at this late stage. There was no
room for compromise, however, on substantive constitutional
matters, particularly when the Grosvenor Street representatives
recommended the formation of a special committee composed of
an equal number of laymen and preachers with responsibility
for the examination of the preachers. In support of this proposal
Hull claimed that he only feared for the preachers and that his
main intention was to safeguard their status and interests. But
Eckett interpreted the move as a disguised attack on the constitution and as a means whereby Warren might be persuaded
to return to the fold. The proposal was thus rejected and the
defeat of the Manchester leadership was complete when Thomas
Taylor, a Lever Street officer, failed to secure re-consideration of
the principle of free representation in favour of an Assembly
evenly divided between preachers and laymen.

The cumulative effect of these developments became apparent
during the 1840s when the Manchester Association displayed the
signs of a flagging cause. Anxious discussions and frequent ex-
hortations accompanied the decline in membership, but all to
little avail. In a reference to a few conversions in 1845 the comment of one of the preachers summed up the depressing state of
affairs, 'Oh, how pleasant it is to have fruit! Such reward as this
does indeed sweeten labour, and more than counterbalance the
crosses of a Methodist Association preacher's life'.[43] During the
next ten years the rate of decline in membership began to slow
down as some benefit was derived from the spill-over effect of the
Wesleyan Reform controversy.

The Manchester Reformers opened their campaign with a
threat 'to shake the powers that be to their very foundation'[44]
but eventually developed only a smaller version of the Association. The leadership mainly consisted of a post–1835 generation
of local preachers whose appeals for the restoration of the primitive character of Methodism were combined with protests against
the partnership of the ministry and the influential laity. Frequent
criticisms of the gross disparity between prosperous suburban
chapels and poor preaching rooms were advanced with choice
examples of the pastoral neglect of working class areas; thus
general opposition to the ministers in some of the downtown
chapels and poor preaching rooms was reinforced by reports
that students at the nearby Didsbury College were far too busy
seeking marriage into wealthy families to visit poorer households.

While the membership of the Manchester circuits declined
from 6,578 to 5,558 between 1849 and 1854, the Grosvenor Street
and Irwell Street circuits accounted for a substantial proportion
of this net loss, 455 and 281 respectively. Grosvenor Street was

worst affected for much the same reason as Oldham Street had been reduced in 1834. The division of the circuit in 1846 meant that the wealthy leaders of the new Oxford Road Circuit lost their substantial interest and influence in the old circuit; they were succeeded by the officer class of the Reform party which was mainly drawn from the shopkeeping and artisan ranks of the nearby township of Hulme. The Reformers established their first preaching room in Grosvenor Street and subsequently erected their only chapel in Chapman Street, Hulme. In the Irwell Street circuit they secured support at the Irwell Street and Gravel Lane chapels, both of which had long since suffered from the drift of prosperous members to the suburbs. Elsewhere in the circuit considerable gains were made amongst the smaller societies at Swinton, where the Wesleyans secured a court injunction to prevent the occupation of the chapel by the Reformers, and at Pendleton, Pendlebury and Patricroft. In each case the infrequent visits of the minister and the use of preaching rooms were contrasted with the lavish conditions at the Higher Broughton chapel, the wealthiest in the circuit and second only to Oxford Road in its fashionable congregation, 'A gaudy temple can be speedily enlarged and extravagantly decorated at Broughton and become the embodiment of Christianity; but these simple people have not souls half so valuable as the aristocratic Wesleyans . . . '.[45]

There was, however, a considerable difference between rousing semi-literate and sometimes quasi-rustic audiences against the urban citadels and exploiting class differences on a large scale. This was particularly so in a town which had passed through the period of extreme social tension by the early 1850s. The change in the climate of opinion was in part reflected in the attitude of Wesleyan leaders who were now less inclined to deal with agitators at one fell swoop. The Reformers indeed ascribed their lack of progress to the soft approach adopted by most superintendents with the notable exception of George Osborn in the largely untroubled Oxford Road circuit. And while it was reported that apathy increased as the former haughty demeanour of the preachers gave way to great mildness, some of the influential laymen proved less uncompromising than on past occasions. In 1851 Percy Bunting was prepared to support a more liberal ruling on memorials. This was a modest gesture yet it foreshadowed a personal reappraisal of connexional polity that resulted in his support for the admission of laymen to Conference twenty years later; the appearance of his pamphlet *Laymen in Conference* (1871) curiously coincided with the foundation in Manchester of the first Free Methodist Institute for ministerial training. There was, too, more recognition of the ruinous consequences of the social barriers within and, more importantly, between chapels. George Chappell, now the doyen of the Oxford Road congregation, was reported as saying 'There was one thing which he would recommend to his more wealthy lay-brethren, and that was to make themselves more acquainted with their brethren; he would not say poorer brethren, for no man was really poor . . .'.[46] Certainly the Reformers made least headway where a chapel contained a fairly wide social mix or where business leaders were also astute managers of chapel affairs as were Eli Atkin, a manufacturing chemist, at Red Bank, Samuel Russell, publisher of the *Manchester Courier*, at Cheetham Hill, and George Whyatt, the owner of a large dyeworks, at Openshaw.

The scale of the conflict was also limited by the character of the Reform leadership. It was always a matter of surprise to the Reformers' newspaper, the *Wesleyan Times*, that 'even in Manchester' there were signs of decisive action. In February 1850 one correspondent declared 'Do not think the Manchester Methodists are dead to reform', yet two years later there was still only the promise of 'a general outbreak' with the acknowledgment that 'In the majority of cases here, Reform takes the moderate phase'.[47] A divided and largely undistinguished leadership failed to consolidate support for the organisation. At the first delegates' meeting in 1850 two of the Manchester delegates, Richard Hardman, a tradesman and treasurer of the local committee, and Josias Browne, a commission agent, disagreed over policy towards the expelled ministers and subsequently withdrew from the campaign. The principal local spokesman, William Martin, was a dominant figure on the public platform but eventually found himself in a minority on the General Reform Committee, meeting the same obstacles as Warren when he pressed for union with the New Connexion. Once it became apparent that an arrangement with the Association was more likely by the end of 1854, he resigned from the organisation, attacked the committee and decamped to the New Connexion.[48] Few of the local Reformers followed his example, and instead a large majority was already opting for the Association on the opening of formal negotiations. For besides mutual sympathy and common concerns both groups shared a large degree of social homogeneity.

The Free Methodist leadership was drawn from a few small manufacturers and a larger body of skilled artisans and shopkeepers. The social composition of the Association in particular was so uniform that one of the officers observed 'We have no class interests amongst us; but are "cemented in one" '.[49] Apart from several notable and often fleeting exceptions, the occupations of the uppercrust only marginally differed from those of most members, at least in comparison with what was perceived as the wider gap between the skilled artisan and the semi-skilled operative or unskilled labourer. The trust of the Association's York Street chapel was representative of the entire leadership and included the following occupations: flour dealer, engraver, wood turner, tool manufacturer, agent, plumber, printers' block cutter, corn merchant, salesman, horse dealer, starch manufacturer, and embosser. The occupations of new members, noted in the Lever Street records of 1836,[50] typified the standing of the rank and file: four tailors, two shopkeepers, spinner, labourer, shoemaker, wire drawer, turner, police officer, smallware dealer, bleacher, weaver, and chair bottomer. The bulk of the membership belonged to a static, if not declining, social group which often feared for its status and standard of living. The Oldham Street rebels especially had daily reminders of the fact that they resided in a locality now consisting of neglected property, labourers' habitations, Irish immigrants and the flotsam and jetsam of society. As first generation immigrants in a town full of the same, they struggled to maintain their standing as part of a self-employed class often engaged in occupations of pre-industrial origin and always determined to stave off the possibility of factory employment. They had no contact with the working class politics of the neighbourhood, nor did they lend their support to particular causes. In 1838 the Lever Street leaders declined the use of their premises for a service conducted by J. R. Stephens on behalf of the Factory Short Time Committee, and at the same time they strongly supported one of the young preachers, John Roebuck, who conducted a much-publicised series of debates with Robert Owen. A plainly dressed and largely self-educated people, they smacked of a Dickensian shabby genteel class and looked 'more scholarly than they were' according to one of the preachers. Very few improved their skills or increased their fortunes; a comment in the obituary of Thomas Taylor also applied to most of the other leaders 'while he laboured other men entered into his labours and reaped the fruit of his sowing. Still, he was a man who did not unduly repine, and always valued high principle more than wealth'.[51]

The attitudes of such individuals towards industrialisation and urbanisation often betrayed a longing for an uncomplicated rural society which became more idyllic as they were further removed from their origins. This feeling found expression in several ways as for example in 1837 when a group of Association leaders, no doubt immediately influenced by the effects of commercial depression, contemplated the formation of a joint stock company with a view to purchasing land in Canada for a settlement of artisans and farmers. More generally it was significant that the real growth points of the Association lay outside the town in artisan suburbs and villages like Moston, Blackley and Newton

Heath. In these circumstances the Village Missionary Society, established in 1836 with three full-time agents, attracted a larger body of supporters and won more recruits than any evangelistic enterprise in the courts and alleys of Oldham Road or Angel Meadow. It was obviously the correct strategy to enter areas almost bypassed by other religious agencies; equally clearly the move was in keeping with a predisposition to maintain contact with a fading society popularly associated with independent, non-deferential and individualist attitudes. In these surroundings, it seemed possible to recapture the ethos of early Methodism that had vanished from the town chapels and left a system whose worst feature was organisation from above rather than from below.

Throughout the conflicts in Manchester smouldering discontent fed on resentment at the way in which the Wesleyan hierarchy, itself a beneficiary of upward social mobility, appeared to neglect or, worse still, discriminate against members who found themselves trapped in an increasingly inhospitable environment. The protesters were of the same stock as the supporters of multifarious reform movements, but in this instance upbringing and a preoccupation with chapel life determined that Wesleyanism bore the brunt of hitherto unspoken grievances and anxieties. For many Associationists, however, rebellion and secession rarely signified a brave, determined and conscious effort to fashion a new system of church government. Nor did events take on the same meaning as for younger and more radical figures elsewhere. A mainly sober, middle-aged leadership sought an outlet for an accumulation of diffuse frustrations and not an exit from Wesleyanism, even when the disorderly proceedings and violent behaviour of certain individuals suggested otherwise. Constant appeals to the past not only bore witness to what was disliked in modern Wesleyanism but drew attention to the fear that neither the present nor the future offered much hope for a reversal of fortunes. Warren grieved over his unrecognised talents in much the same way as his supporters deplored their loss of influence; both hesitated to embark upon an independent course, for therein lay the way to greater obscurity.

In common with other causes fathered or supported by their social peers the Associationists and Reformers demonstrated that their own struggle had more than a purely instrumental function. In effect the public campaign satisfied certain deep-seated needs and gave importance to an otherwise anonymous group. Uneventful lives were lent colour, drama and excitement by a range of activities that permitted extravagant gestures and expressions. Formerly insignificant characters discovered that the public platform had many uses. When an Association leader, George Hughes, related to one of his audiences the details concerning the expulsion of a friend, the pathos was unrestrained,

I was present when that dread sentence was passed. . . . Oh! my friends, if you had been present on that occasion—if you had beheld the consternation of that meeting—if you had heard the sighs and groans which resounded through that assembly, and had witnessed the bitter scenes of distress—if you had seen the flood of tears trickling down our dejected cheeks, and which bedewed the forms on which we knelt when at prayer,—had you, I say, beheld this touching scene,—a scene such as I never beheld before, and such as I hope I shall never behold again,—I am sure you would have been ready to 'weep your spirits from your eyes'.[52]

Good or bad theatre, the language evoked memories of the old class meeting and band room, and it had a powerful and instantaneous effect in the different circumstances of a large public meeting. Emotions ran high in such an atmosphere and often quickly subsided to leave a question mark against the real meaning of the performance. Certainly, Hughes and his friends had justification for their complaints, yet they failed to reconcile their conservative inclinations with present realities; had they done so they might have been the real makers of the Association with a vision of the future rather than a view of the past. As it was, they were ill-equipped to mastermind the transition from an internal reform movement to an independent body.

REFERENCES

[1] *Watchman's Lantern* 14 January 1835.

[2] *Resolutions and Propositions passed at the Quarterly Meeting of the First Circuit* (Manchester, 1834).

[3] *Captain Barlow's narrative of the blessed battle fought, and glorious victory gained at the Wesleyan Missionary Meeting* (Manchester, 1834).

[4] *Manchester Guardian* 1 November 1834.

[5] *United Methodist Free Churches' Magazine* July 1863.

[6] J. Hull, *A short and plain answer to the statements in Mr. William Read's 'Candid Address', with a few brief remarks on the recent 'Declaration'* (Manchester, 1834).

[7] *Christian Advocate* 15 December 1834; T. Champness, *True Tales* (undated), p. 9.

[8] W. Read, *A candid address* (Manchester, 1834); J. Crowther, *Defence of the Wesleyan Theological Institution in reply to the Remarks of Dr. Warren* (Manchester, 1834).

[9] *Select letters of Mrs Agnes Bulmer with an introduction by Rev. W. M. Bunting* (London, 1842).

[10] J. Everett, *The Disputants* (London, 1835), p. 64.

[11] *The Second Affectionate Address of the United Wesleyan Methodist Association* (Manchester, 1834), p. 12.

[12] *Illuminator* 4 November 1835.

[13] *Watchman's Lantern* 4 February 1835.

[14] *The Corrected Report of the Debates and Decisions of the Adjourned Meeting of Wesleyan Methodist Delegates* (London, 1835), p. 6.

[15] MS. Diary of Rev. John Peters, 5–6 February 1836.

[16] *The Second Affectionate Address of the United Wesleyan Methodist Association* (Manchester, 1834), p. 16.

[17] *Watchman's Lantern* 14 January 1835, 4 February 1835.

[18] *Resolutions and Propositions passed at the Quarterly Meeting of the First Circuit* (Manchester, 1834).

[19] *Christian Advocate* 10 November 1834.

[20] *Ibid.* 15 December 1834.

[21] *Ibid.* 27 April 1835.

[22] *Illuminator* 27 May 1835.

[23] *Christian Advocate* 27 April 1835.

[24] *The Corrected Report of the Debates and Decisions of the Adjourned Meeting of Wesleyan Methodist Delegates* (London, 1835), p. 36.

[25] *Ibid.* p. 21.

[26] MSS. E. Grindrod to J. Bunting, 2 March 1835.

[27] *Statement of the Preachers of the Manchester District on the case of Dr. Warren* (Manchester, 1834), p. 13.

[28] MSS. E. Grindrod to J. Bunting, 2 March 1835.

[29] *Christian Advocate* 17 November 1834.

[30] MSS. J. Bunting to T. P. Bunting, 4 November 1834.

[31] H. Hoole, *A letter to the right honourable Lord Viscount Althorp M.P., Chancellor of the Exchequer: in defence of the cotton factories of Lancashire* (Manchester, 1832); See also *Parliamentary Papers*, 1833, vol. xx D.2, p. 99; R. Oastler, *A letter to Holland Hoole in reply to his letter to the Right Hon. Lord Viscount Althorp M.P., Chancellor of the Exchequer in defence of the cotton factories of Lancashire* (Manchester, 1832).

[32] MS. J. Everett, Memoranda, 7 November 1838.

[33] MS. Minute Book of Grosvenor Street Quarterly Meeting, 31 December 1834.

[34] B. Gregory, *op. cit.*, p. 189; *Christian Advocate* 12 October 1835.

[35] *Christian Advocate* 6 August 1838.

[36] MS. Diary of Rev. John Peters, 11 January 1836.

[37] See MS. Minute Book of Lever Street circuit Leaders' Meetings, 1836–7.

[38] T. Taylor, *An Account of the Complete Failure of an ordained priest of the 'Latter Day Saints'* (Manchester, 1840).

[39] *Minutes of the Fourth Annual Assembly of the Wesleyan Association* (London, 1839), p. 27.

[40] *Minutes of the Annual Assembly of the Wesleyan Association* (London, 1836), pp. 14–15.

[41] *Christian Advocate* 7 August 1837.

[42] B. Gregory, *op. cit.*, p. 158.

[43] *United Methodist Free Churches' Magazine* April 1861.

[44] *Wesleyan Times* 25 February 1850.

[45] *Ibid.* 7 October 1850.

[46] *Wesleyan Vindicator and Constitutional Methodist* August 1851.

[47] *Wesleyan Times* 7 June 1852.

[48] W. Martin, *Words of explanation and warning to the Wesleyan Reformers* (London, 1855).

[49] *Wesleyan Methodist Association Magazine* November 1849.

[50] MS. Minute Book of Lever Street circuit Leaders' Meetings, 1 February – 5 December 1836.

[51] *United Methodist Free Churches' Magazine* February 1880.

[52] *Christian Advocate* 16 February 1835.

CHAPTER 4

ROCHDALE: THE RADICAL MOVEMENT

'If an answer be given to Rochdale, it must be a rebuke'[1] declared
Bunting in reply to the critical address which the Rochdale leaders dispatched to the Conference of 1829. Six years later and after
further reprimands, however, only a court order thwarted the express purpose of a majority of trustees to occupy the Union Street
chapel for a public meeting. The date of the proposed meeting,
1 October 1835, marked the point at which mounting internal
dissension was superseded by a process of separation. During the
next few months the largest circuit membership in Lancashire was
reduced by sixty per cent and the town acquired its most impressive Nonconformist body. The new seat of Methodist influence,
Baillie Street chapel, boasted a congregation of exceptional talent
and wealth which retained its position as a Free Methodist stronghold throughout the nineteenth century. In its origins and early
development the Rochdale Association was the product of a particular locality rather than the embodiment of a national movement. Its special features consisted of a radical critique of
Wesleyan polity and a resolute advocacy of new social interests,
and no acceptable degree of toleration could finally contain this
explosive mixture within a Wesleyan framework.

In view of the prolonged agitation over the Leeds conflict, the
Rochdale leadership delivered a predictably prompt and hostile
judgment on the Conference decisions of 1834. As early as 1
October 1834, three weeks before the resolutions of the Oldham
Street circuit, the Rochdale Quarterly Meeting welcomed the publication of the *Remarks* and expressed its opposition to the Theological Institution. By December the general controversy was
deemed so serious that it was agreed to press for a special meeting
of the Legal Hundred; the circuit offered to pay all expenses. The
President of Conference rejected this unusual proposal and recommended a formal address which was eventually composed and
submitted to the Quarterly Meeting on 1 July 1835. On this occasion, however, the superintendent refused to put the address to
a vote. A majority of the trustees immediately summoned a meeting of all the officers, and on 15 July fifty-eight of the sixty-six officers voted in favour of a major declaration.

The July address was a comprehensive statement of the causes
of discontent; it was arranged under twelve headings. First, the

subject matter of earlier memorials was repeated in a reference to the unconstitutional interference of the Special District Meeting in the Leeds conflict. Secondly, there were objections to the introduction of a test concerning the doctrine of eternal sonship and the consequent expulsion of one of the ministers. This was a veiled and inaccurate reference to Adam Clarke's retirement from circuit work. An outstanding scholar and preacher, Clarke was viewed by the Buntingites as an unsound and disruptive influence in large part because he denied the eternal sonship of Christ but also because he was regarded as an obstacle to Bunting's connexional policies. Prior to the Conference of 1831 Bunting expressed the fear that Clarke might be elected to the Presidency for a fourth time and that 'his triumph would be in some degree that of the people who do not love Methodism as it is. . .'.[2] Clarke was in fact manoeuvred into a supernumeraryship against his will. Thirdly, the pro-Stephens resolutions composed but withheld earlier in the year at last received an airing, and it was asserted that 'Conference's erroneous views on the Union of Church and State question' had caused considerable offence. The Theological Institution and Warren's trial naturally figured as two further causes of discontent, although Warren himself was hardly known in the town and possibly only remembered as an unsuccessful volunteer for the nearby Bury circuit in 1832. Edmund Grindrod was convinced that the 'very corrupt' Rochdale leaders had no interest in Warren except in so far as he served their party purposes.

Certainly Warren's plight paled into insignificance in comparison with the disputed role of the preachers in local meetings which produced three specific grievances. First, the preachers had assumed the power to prevent free discussions in Quarterly Meetings and to refuse a vote on resolutions as in this instance. Secondly, members had been expelled in opposition to a majority of the Leaders' Meeting, and thirdly the preachers had so altered the rules that officers could be dismissed regardless of majority opinion within local meetings. Furthermore, the controversy was also related to the way in which Conference treated memorials in a 'disrespectful manner', omitted the Plan of Pacification from its journal, and reserved to itself the management of many connexional funds. While the memorialists thus measured the gap between their own understanding of connexional law and official interpretations, there was no mistaking their assessment of the fundamental cause of discontent which was 'the total exclusion of the laity from all the legislative, and from all or nearly all executive power'. No return to first principles nor restoration of rules would make good this deficiency; the only acceptable solution lay in 'the immediate admission of the people to such a share of power in the government of the church that their express concurrence shall be necessary in all important matters, especially those of legislation, finance and administration of discipline'.[3]

Parts of this address drew heavily on outrages elsewhere, for while other circuits had been torn assunder by this time the Union Street cause was still intact with no evidence of disciplinary measures. The comparatively belated division was largely due to the conduct of the superintendent and the attitudes of the dissident leaders. It was always likely that the local leaders would choose the subject matter and timing of a contest with limited reference to events elsewhere. The developments of 1834-5 took place in a remarkably self-contained town that was about to lose much of its obscurity but few of its unusual aspects. G. J. Holyoake's hyperbole 'Human nature must be different in Rochdale from what it is elsewhere'[4] was but one attempt to emphasise the peculiarities of a town that raised John Bright, produced the Pioneers, turned radicalism into a respected and reasonable force, avoided sharp conflicts between employer and employee, and joined a strong sense of individualism to the cause of collective action. Independence and self-help were so embedded in local culture that the advice or demands of an external body rarely went unchallenged and often encountered strong resistance.

An increasingly centralised connexional system fitted awkwardly in these circumstances and neither Conference's writ nor leadership overawed the rank and file. Pulpit personalities rarely visited or took up appointments in the town, while unwanted Conference directives were set aside if they happened to conflict with local practices; the Sunday school regulations of 1827 met such a fate. Moreover it was quite easy to browbeat some of the less well-known preachers stationed in the town, as one superintendent, Bernard Slater, discovered to his cost when his handling of objections to the Leeds case was censured by Bunting 'Brother Slater has erred in mistaking the law, and in thinking you could conquer the Radicals. He went with them one mile, and the devil compelled him to go with them twain. The Rochdale devil has conquered'.[5] Bunting evidently believed that the Rochdale leaders were in the same league as the Leeds dissentients and that no compromise was possible with such a party. His judgment, however, gave little indication of how a preacher of modest ability and fearful disposition should respond to a hostile majority in a local meeting, especially when the opposition included substantial businessmen who might have figured amongst the 'lay lords' in a different setting. The same problem arose in a more acute form in 1834 when one of Slater's successors, Philip Garrett, reacted in such a way as to postpone the climax of the agitation.

At the outset Garrett lacked the will-power to discipline the opposition, and as a result he was soon caught between charges of irresolute conduct and the gratuitous commendations of his opponents. Appointed to the town in 1834, he had voted against the Institution in Conference and he was therefore prepared to listen to local objections. But once he permitted a vote on the resolutions of 1 October 1834 and these were published contrary to a private agreement, he was in a weak position that was further undermined by his failure to take action when a large number of officers and members decided to join the Association on 18 November. Although the ringleaders were persuaded to reverse their original decision to withhold contributions to connexional funds, some Wesleyans quickly concluded that Garrett was mishandling the situation; 'Surely their preacher allowing such proceedings will be as bad as they are' commented John Burton in a letter addressed to James Wood of Manchester on 21 November, alerting the connexional leaders to what were described as the very deep designs of the Rochdale people. At the same time Garrett was advised by one of his junior colleagues, Richard Heape, to summon a Special District Meeting in order to expel the members of the Association. As a local man, Heape was undeterred by the fact that some of his closest friends and relatives, including his brother Samuel, were amongst the chief offenders. Yet this course of action was an uninviting prospect for Garrett, and Heape soon despaired of any positive lead 'Mr. Garrett, as I expected, has been overpowered by the violence of the opposition . . . his mind has been distracted and bewildered. . .'.[6] It was clear that the tormented superintendent, whose son was apprenticed to one of his main adversaries, was losing control of the situation and that Conference had to remove him at the earliest possible moment. In the meantime, however, he denounced the Association yet complied with the requests of the leaders, tamely agreeing to submit the proposal for a special meeting of the Legal Hundred after declaring that sooner than lend his name to the Association he would sign a paper to decapitate all children in the town.

In their instructions to Garrett, the leaders showed a determination to place Conference in the worst possible position. The apparently innocent request for an extraordinary meeting of the Legal Hundred was little more than a provocative gesture based on the certain knowledge that this assembly would not meet out of season. The July address was presented in a similar manner, since it was virtually unanswerable in terms of precise, satisfactory concessions; and its parting shot 'we most respectfully, yet firmly, require to be effectually reformed', was likely to elicit one response. In addition, particular enquiries were usually designed to unearth evidence of skulduggery in high places, as when Garrett was forced by 'men who seem to be on the look out for something to find fault with'[7] to request information concerning Missionary Society finances.

Immediately after the Conference of 1835 rejected the July address and appointed a new superintendent, John Sumner, the authors of the address convened a meeting on 19 August to decide on a course of action in the event of disciplinary measures. It was resolved that any preacher responsible for expulsions should be threatened with a trial by trustees and that all efforts to clear the chapels should meet formidable resistance. These contingency plans displayed a profound contempt for any interpretation of connexional law, and there was no attempt, nor could there be, to justify such measures on any grounds other than the power and independence of local meetings. Notwithstanding the judgment in Warren's court case, the disaffected leaders dared to hope that they might secure the Union Street property, into which they had recently sunk approximately £2,000. Sumner had to avoid such an eventuality at all costs, and at a Society meeting on 13 September he announced that unless officers and members submitted themselves to certain tests 'he would hold no communion with them'.[8] This ultimatum convinced ten of the fifteen Union Street trustees that the time had arrived to contest control of the pulpit, and accordingly they arranged a public meeting for 1 October. The ostensible reason for this meeting was to explain 'matters to the People; as to prevail on them if possible to continue with us as hertofore',[9] but in fact, as the numerous placards promised, the organisers intended to publicise the principles of Wesleyan reform. Although he was a stronger character than his predecessor, Sumner was ill-equipped for singlehanded management of a crisis that hastened his death two years later. After consultations with the Manchester preachers he secured the professional services of Percy Bunting whose intervention incensed the trustees, one of whom threatened to throw the attorney into a nearby canal. The trustees refused to cancel the meeting, and the deadlock was only broken on the morning of 1 October when Bunting arrived in the town with a court injunction which banned any public meeting on Wesleyan premises unless conducted by one of the preachers. The transfer of the meeting to other premises heralded separation, for within a few weeks the trustees resigned their posts and by the end of the year their supporters were preparing to meet for public worship in a warehouse which was opened on 8 January 1836.

In Lancashire, only the Oldham Street circuit exceeded the losses at Rochdale as the membership fell from 1,911 in 1835 to 745 in the following year, 'the Exodus of a whole people rather than the withdrawment of a portion' commented one observer.[10]

The difference between this net loss and the Association membership of 1,710 in 1837 was largely due to the fact that the new circuit included Bury and Bacup, both of which were separate Wesleyan circuits and reported a combined net loss of 200 members in 1836. The Wesleyan leadership was decimated by the withdrawal of the ten trustees and at least two-thirds of the class leaders and local preachers, while a large majority of Sunday school teachers also elected to join the seceders after a controversy concerning the organisation and status of the schools.[11] Amongst the twenty-five chapels and preaching rooms in the circuit some of the most serious devastation occurred in the surrounding villages where popular class leaders invariably exercised far more power and influence than the preachers; one such leader, who supervised six classes in several villages, was largely responsible for the defection of 100 members, and the preachers were naturally 'loth to part with him, as he brought so much money to the board'.[12] The Bagslate Moor, Whitworth and Spotland societies almost disappeared as a result of Association gains, and for several years afterwards the Wesleyans struggled to maintain class meetings. There were also extensive losses at Smallbridge, Healey Stones and Lowerplace while the chapel at Pottery, a private foundation hitherto exclusively served by Wesleyan preachers, was placed at the disposal of the Association. Since most of these village causes consisted of handloom weavers, earthenware workers, and colliers, the major financial consequences were most apparent in the town. At Union Street itself a majority of the pewholders abandoned the building to a congregation which was initially small enough to assemble in the vestry; the annual income from pew rents, £423 in 1835, was sharply reduced and even after a measure of recovery only £176 was collected in 1838.[13]

The management of the Association was mainly confined to a small group headed by the trustees, two of whom, John Petrie and George Ashworth, emerged as the dominant personalities. Petrie, an engineer of Irish descent, was chairman of the first Quarterly Meeting and his subsequent activities impressed both the denominational historian, Matthew Baxter, who considered him the outstanding Free Methodist layman of his generation and John Bright a life-long friend who regarded him as a guarantee of the reality of religion. Ashworth, a woollen manufacturer, was a leader whose loyalty to the new cause always remained in doubt, yet his opinion carried much weight as the first president of the Baillie Street trustees and the chapel's leading shareholder. Four of the other trustees were also particularly active and influential. Thomas Booth, a chemist, was closely involved in the Sunday school dispute as superintendent; James and John Hoyle, corn merchants, opened up their warehouse as the temporary headquarters of the Association; Samuel Heape, a merchant, belonged to a large established local family which was divided in its loyalties like several other families;[14] and John Howard, a wool-stapler who held the position of Chief Constable on two occasions, was one of the wealthiest trustees, and his marriage to Anne Heape was but one example of the inter-marriage between these families. The rest of the dissident trustees, John Ormerod a leather merchant, Samuel Standring a tailor, and James Turner a rope manufacturer, played a less prominent role in the proceedings, although they too formed part of the new Baillie Street trust which also included Abraham Tweedale and Thomas Booth jun., cotton manufacturers, and Stephen Broad a wool-stapler.

Besides these major financial supporters the Association also included a considerable number of young leaders like Oliver Ormerod, Edward Taylor and John Ashworth, who all became local celebrities. Ormerod, a leather merchant, had no business ambitions to interfere with his career as a gifted polemicist and leading advocate of nonconformist liberalism. After an early campaigning partnership with Bright in the Temperance and Literary and Philosophical Societies, he acquired a reputation as a dialect writer, pamphleteer and newspaper editor before he secured his most influential position as the first editor of the liberal *Rochdale Observer*. Taylor, a chemist, was amongst the most radical of the Baillie Street set; he first attracted attention for his denunciation of the local church and tory network, subsequently became an outstanding devotee of municipal socialism, and eventually earned formal recognition as the first freeman of the borough. Ashworth, a painter by trade, embarked upon his public career as the founder of the Chapel for the Destitute and in time he emerged as the local pioneer of the later nineteenth-century social gospel; he became more widely-known, however, as the author of the highly popular *Strange Tales from Humble Life*. Each of these men found wealthy patrons within the Association. Petrie financed Ashworth's major publication, Taylor owed more to George Ashworth than he ever cared to admit and Ormerod's journalism was largely financed by the Petrie and Ashworth families. Moreover they all contributed to and benefited by a rapidly changing society. They belonged to a rising social group that prospered and advanced only as a result of a formidable challenge to existing institutions and vested interests. A character sketch of John Ashworth noted 'You do not stop because there are impediments in the way, but appear to be inclined to put forth strong and vigorous efforts to achieve an end',[15] and the observation applied with equal force to the other leaders, for whom a change in denominational loyalties coincided with a major adjustment to the opportunities of a new, provincial society.

Few if any of the local churches rivalled the Association in its identification with the novel and subsequently prevailing forces that transformed the town and incidentally turned Baillie Street into the unofficial civic church. In so far as secession was an ecclesiastical manifestation of widespread social changes it was engineered by men convinced of the need for a range of instruments firmly within their control and expressive of their own values. Both economic interests and social aspirations helped to fashion this general attitude. Much of the wealth of the Association's leaders was derived from an industrial economy of which they were the pioneers. Rochdale had traditionally served as a centre for the finishing and distributive processes of a woollen trade based on domestic industry. The advent of the cotton industry towards the end of the eighteenth century and the later mechanisation of the woollen industry saw the rise of a new group of manufacturers. Of the various denominations Wesleyanism attracted the largest number of these first generation businessmen. Abraham Tweedale was amongst the earliest cotton manufacturers in the area and his Spotland mill was one of the major local establishments. In 1814 Petrie opened a small foundry and soon developed the largest engineering works in the town; his firm produced the first steam engines in the area and subsequently thrived on a growing export market. George Ashworth, born in 1799 and eight years younger than Petrie, commenced operations as a woollen manufacturer in 1820 and soon afterwards introduced power loom weaving to the town. This last innovation foreshadowed much else besides the disappearance of the handloom weaver, for the new employers aimed to sweep aside the civic leadership of the church and tory families and to define themselves as the new *élite*. The transfer of power was already far advanced when Ashworth himself maintained public order as magistrate during the plug plot troubles of the early 1840s, and it was completed twenty years later when his eldest son, who was also magistrate, organised the Cotton Famine Relief Committee.

It was during the 1830s, when the conflict between old and new Rochdale became most marked, that a number of prosperous, ambitious and often young Wesleyans entered public life. Several organisations owed much to their leadership and support. The first temperance society, founded in 1832, was dominated by Union Street members, while a year later the formation of the Literary and Philosophical Society drew a disproportionately large number of its radical young-bloods from the same source

as did the Reform Association on its creation in 1834. The prospective Associationists sought the outlines of a new political
and social order through such ventures. It was almost inevitable
that their Wesleyan sympathies should be questioned and found
wanting in the light of early findings. Exclusively local management of flourishing societies bred the necessary confidence to
resist and eventually to overthrow a Wesleyan system of government that failed to recognise new skills and status. Furthermore,
it was always unlikely that Wesleyanism could be permanently
associated with the plan of campaign that emerged from the
fountain-head of middle class radicalism in the town, the Literary
and Philosophical Society. It was in this setting that general
opposition to established authority crystallised in a programme
to oust the tories from local government, to abolish all traditional
privileges, and to emphasise the interests of the industrial classes
over and against other interests. The commitment of the Associationists to these aims found many expressions, not least of which
were a number of short-lived journals like the *Vicar's Lantern*
(1842–3) and the *Pilot and Rochdale Reporter* (1847) which were
edited by Taylor and the *Spectator* (1844–5) which was produced
by Ormerod. Insofar as these publications were critical of the
Church, they reflected one of the factors responsible for the
secession of 1835, for by the early 1830s conventional Wesleyan
restraints were commonly regarded as serious obstacles to a proposed alignment with militant Nonconformity.

Nonconformist inclinations required little encouragement in
nineteenth-century Rochdale. Church and chapel dominated the
field and the Roman Catholics were few in number on account
of the absence of an Irish population. The Church itself, however, palpably failed to cater for a growing population. By the
'thirties there were only three churches in the town, none of
which provided facilities to supplement formal, public worship.
Under a particularly unpopular vicar, W. R. Hay of Peterloo
notoriety, the parish church moreover often presented itself as an
agency primarily organised to defend its property rights and
financial privileges. Such features easily provoked radical criticism
and allowed burgeoning nonconformist causes to fill the vacuum.
Thus the religious census of 1851 reported that nonconformist
causes attracted 75 per cent of all attendants at public worship;
the Association alone accounted for 25 per cent of nonconformist
attendants and almost equalled the number of Anglican attendants. Amongst the Associationists there was little understanding
of or sympathy for the ambivalent Wesleyan attitude towards the
Church. Whether by virtue of age and upbringing or recent admission to the swelling Wesleyan ranks, few members had long-
standing links with any religious organisations and even fewer

could trace an eighteenth-century Methodist ancestry that combined Church and Society. Consequently, they viewed themselves as members of the Nonconformist community and they were welcomed as such in October 1835 when the proposed Union Street meeting was in fact transferred to premises belonging to the Baptists and Lady Huntingdon's connexion.

Before October 1835 the Association's leadership made few explicit references to an alternative ecclesiastical system in the event of a division. Yet the difference between declared grievances and proposed measures in the July address indicated that radical changes had a greater appeal than any likelihood of the proper observance of the rules by Conference. At the same time there was little more than guarded interest in the national agitation; the six local delegates remained silent throughout the debates of the first delegates' meeting and only two observers attended the second delegates' meeting after they had made individual efforts to lobby Conference. It was clearly intended to safeguard the local character of the movement and to avoid hasty adoption of a programme that failed to remove the offensive features of Wesleyan government. Immediately after the division, the actions of the leaders were largely influenced by local considerations. Most of the early decisions coincided with the eventual constitutional framework of the Association. This was a measure of the inherent strength of a local leadership that supported Robert Eckett in the Assembly. Eckett observed more than the diplomatic niceties when he wrote 'From personal acquaintance with many of our Rochdale friends, I entertain feelings of the highest respect and esteem for them. . . . They have, deservedly, considerable influence in the administration of the affairs of the Association'.[16] Such influence was almost entirely beneficial in Eckett's estimation, for on key issues like the authority of local meetings and the role of the Assembly he shared the decided views of the Rochdale leaders.

The Rochdale Association held its first Quarterly Meeting on 1 January 1836. During the next few months a formal organisation was fashioned in accordance with the principle of circuit independence and on the basis of the Quarterly Meeting as the highest authority in the circuit. 'From Rochdale' declared Eckett by way of a well-chosen example to overwhelm his opponents 'it was stated that the Quarterly Meeting was the highest authority in the circuit . . .',[17] and in all formal respects at least it was this meeting that managed circuit affairs and tolerated no external interference. Hence when the Middleton and Oldham Associationists applied to join the circuit they were admitted on condition that they conformed 'to the rules and usages of the Association as practised in this Circuit'.[18]

While this assertion of circuit authority postulated a different kind of national organisation from the Wesleyan model, there was no immediate desire to abandon connexionalism in favour of independency. The value of the full-time preacher was an important consideration in this respect. Local support for an itinerant system was in part due to the fact that antagonism between preachers and people was not so marked as in other places; both Slater and Garrett had yielded to local pressure and even Sumner could be excused as the cat's-paw of the Manchester preachers. Furthermore, the leaders were not prepared to subsist on a diet of local preaching. Significantly only one of the ten trustees was a local preacher. A general preference for the services of the itinerant preacher soon became evident as local preachers were virtually excluded from Baillie Street, much to the annoyance of some of their number.[19] Only a connexional system, however, could guarantee a steady supply of preachers. In the period before the Assembly formally undertook this task there were several attempts to secure preachers but on each occasion negative responses emphasised the difficulties involved in local initiatives. At an early stage both David Rowland and James Bromley declined invitations; the former was unable to convince the Liverpool Quarterly Meeting of his suitability for the itinerancy and the latter could not contemplate such a precarious existence.

Support for an itinerant system was also a measure of the new controls designed to check the growth of ministerial power on a Wesleyan scale. The Quarterly Meeting had such confidence in these arrangements that it proposed to ensure some form of representation for the preachers in the Assembly; each circuit with two or more preachers would be compelled to elect one of this number to the Assembly. This proposal produced a rare disagreement with Eckett who argued that it undermined the principle of circuit independence. Unlike the Manchester leaders whose support for mixed representation was influenced by New Connexion sympathies, the Rochdale leaders simply recognised the limited influence of the Assembly and refused to contest Eckett's argument, 'For such a task I have not the requisite ability, leisure or inclination'[20] concluded George Ashworth who was the main spokesman on this occasion. In any case the circuit was still at liberty to make its own choice of representatives and it became established practice to elect at least one and usually two of the preachers to make up a party of three representatives. This local balance in favour of the preachers was also apparent in connexional bodies by the 1850s when the preachers normally constituted a majority in the Assembly and Connexional Committee.

The Rochdale leaders were disinclined to dispute the value of free representation largely because they had every reason to present a united front with Eckett on the eve of the Assembly of 1837. Developments during the preceding eighteen months indicated that both parties shared the same views concerning the general purpose and powers of the Assembly. The local leadership was determined to circumscribe the functions of the Assembly and to reject any scheme that unnecessarily veered towards central controls. The possibility of a union between the New Connexion and the Association raised the issue in an acute form. It was of little consequence that Warren was able to muster majorities in the committee appointed to examine the matter when his opponents exercised substantial influence elsewhere. At one of the committee meetings on 5 December 1836 only four of the twenty-one members objected to a uniting Conference with considerable legislative power, yet two of the four dissentients, Eckett and Ashworth, recognised that they could reverse this decision by other means. The proposed union in fact was dealt a telling blow by the Rochdale Quarterly Meeting which, two months before the Assembly of 1837, declined to entertain such a plan 'so long as the Conference of the Methodist New Connexion possesses and is determined to retain the "General and Legislative Powers".'[21] No amount of argument could prevail against this point of view, particularly since Rochdale raised £482 of £813 contributed to the Home Mission and Connexional Fund in the period 1836–7. This financial interest also persuaded the Assembly to appoint Petrie as connexional treasurer in 1838. He accepted the post 'with much hesitancy' but remained in office until 1854; Ashworth and himself agreed to meet any deficit.

Between 1836 and 1840 the attention of the Rochdale leadership was divided between the workings of the national organisation and the progress of a local building programme based on a shareholding scheme to meet the cost of Baillie Street Chapel. Set in an undeveloped part of the town and opened in January 1837, this chapel was the largest in the area and also in the Association; its financing revealed some of the main intentions of its founders. The shareholding scheme was approved early in 1836 on the basis of its proprietorial and financial merits. First, shareholding ensured that full control over the chapel was vested in a local body so that no itinerant preacher could prevent use of the chapel by trustees and shareholders 'to discuss matters pertaining to their religious liberty, the inherent birthright of every British subject'.[22] Furthermore, it was stated that any itinerant preacher could be suspended or expelled by the Quarterly Meeting. This unqualified provision had an entirely radical character in the wider context of the reform campaign, because it came perilously close to a declaration of complete circuit independence. On this basis the Assembly would be reduced to a stationing committee with no control over the fate of its preachers. This extreme position was eventually abandoned after it was realised that a powerful circuit required no disciplinary authority to remove an unpopular preacher. First-hand experience of local influence was gained in March 1837 when the Quarterly Meeting disagreed with one of the two preachers over his proper place of residence. The dispute was referred to the Connexional Committee which clearly sympathised with the preacher but accepted that his immediate suspension and removal were 'necessary in behalf of the peace and prosperity of the Rochdale Circuit and of the Association generally'.[23] The preacher received no further appointments and the Rochdale leaders willingly accepted the Assembly's exclusive right to expel a preacher.

The second declared advantage of shareholding lay in the opportunity to overcome common money-raising problems without the undue influence of wealthy members in the management of the chapel. In particular it was maintained that shares would be held 'in many hands' and that their popularity would permit a reduction in the 'extravagantly high' pew rents of other leading chapels. Equally important the project offered a safe investment and a reasonable return on capital with annual dividends to be fixed not in excess of $7\frac{1}{2}$ per cent. These anticipated benefits largely failed to materialise in the course of the next few years. Shareholding proved no more successful in securing funds than the more familiar means that had been employed to meet the financial outlay on the new Union Street chapel in 1826. The total cost of the Baillie Street complex was £6,200, of which £2,457 was met by shares. Also contrary to public expectations if not private assessments, share ownership was concentrated in a minority of members; there were approximately 120 shareholders (including children) and one-half of the shares belonged to the Ashworth, Booth, Hoyle, Petrie and Tweedale families.[24] Nor was there a reduction in pew rents at least in comparison with Union Street charges. Fragmentary evidence suggests that, if anything, rents were higher at Baillie Street, where all of the 981 private sittings were let before the opening of the chapel, than they had been at Union Street. Both chapels contained almost the same number of private sittings, 1,191 (Baillie Street) and 1,100 (Union Street) according to the religious census of 1851. Yet Baillie Street income from pew rents, £272 in 1837, more than accounted for a reduction of £247 in the annual income from Union Street sittings during the period 1835-8. Moreover the promised dividend on shares was greatly dependent on income from pew rents, so it was always likely that initial hopes of cheap seating accommodation would compete unsuccessfully with attempts to offer a satisfactory dividend.

This form of private enterprise remained in existence until 1841. By this time the attractions of the new connexional model deed outweighed the diminishing benefits of a system that had begun to encounter sales resistance and to yield declining dividends. In 1839 there had been a disappointing response to a new issue of shares designed to finance the extension of seating accommodation. As dividends fell from 5 per cent to $2\frac{1}{2}$ per cent in the period 1837–40, worsening economic conditions limited the amount of additional funds and also imposed economies in other areas of chapel life; the number of preachers was reduced by one in 1840 and the Quarterly Meeting agreed to end the provision of pipes and tobacco out of Society funds. In the light of these circumstances and in view of the fact that shareholding excluded a financial appeal to the general public, it was decided to abandon the system and to persuade shareholders to relinquish their shares without compensation. Despite intensive canvassing a loan of £1,000 was necessary to pay off the unrelinquished shares.

The shareholding system fully exposed the social character of the Association in that it appealed to the manufacturer, the substantial shopkeeper and the more prosperous sections of the skilled artisan class but shut out the factory operative and handloom weaver by virtue of its financial demands and the impact of economic depression. Only a much more modest plan like that of the Pioneers in the next decade, 3d. weekly for a £1 share, could attract the bulk of the working class. The Baillie Street scheme was based on the purchase of a £1 share by means of a 5s. deposit and a minimum monthly instalment of 2s. 6d. The purchase of a share secured admission to the shareholders' meeting where voting rights were restricted to church members. Ultimate responsibility for all matters rested with the trustees who had to possess ten or more shares and one of whose functions was to fix the annual dividend. The trustees were elected by the shareholders who were themselves divided into grades in strict accordance with the number of shares held by each individual. Approximately twenty shareholders had a substantial controlling interest, since voting rights in the shareholders' meetings depended on the number of shares; twenty or more shares bought four votes while five or less qualified for one vote with two intermediate categories. The main shareholders were also in a position to determine the allocation of pews which ranged from first class pews for holders of one hundred or more shares to fifth class pews for holders or nine or less shares. Non-shareholders applied to individual shareholders for a private pew.

The hierarchical character of the shareholding system was extended to the management of other affairs as far as possible. The democratic procedures of the Quarterly Meeting, open membership and ballot voting, suggested otherwise, whereas in fact the displacement of rank and wealth by popular controls was more apparent than real. Some of the trustees opposed the introduction of open membership in 1837, yet their influence was scarcely lessened by this measure. Under Petrie's direction the leading families eventually managed to secure the abolition of ballot voting in 1846. The Leaders' Meeting was also dominated by members of the same group, all of whom had several interests in its disciplinary function. For besides common cases of sexual misdemeanours, abusive language and violent behaviour, there were charges arising out of commercial misconduct such as 'the taking of an unchristian advantage in a trade transaction' and 'the falsification of accounts'[25] which prompted serious investigation by a business class intent on the maintenance of certain standards and the protection of its reputation.

The shareholding scheme was remarkably fair in the light of current business practices, yet it was redolent of the 'forties freehold and the £10 household enfranchisement. Both the scheme and the general organisation tended to institutionalise or, at least, to accentuate social divisions hitherto largely concealed within the parent body. The accompanying display of wealth and status made Baillie Street a microcosm of part of a society which was brash, outspoken, slightly arrogant and possibly intolerable to those persons of insufficient means to enjoy the rewards of independence. One of the earliest casualties of the venture recalled 'I became a teacher there and remained in it about two years, but never felt at home, for the leaders were not social; ideas of caste ran high, and a poor man was almost overlooked even if he was intelligent and devout'.[26] Unlike some Associationists for whom the influence of wealthy Wesleyan laymen was a matter of grave concern, the Rochdale leaders were far more inclined to believe that Wesleyanism had failed to attune itself to the needs of a new, radical and provincial middle class.

During the two decades after the secession the Baillie Street leadership gave practical effect to its own understanding of the proper functions of a religious organisation. While particular attitudes towards the devotional and missioning aspects of chapel life often signified a disregard for earlier Wesleyan experiences, both the business of official meetings and varied dealings with the poor were shaped by the interests of the dominant social group. Few leaders showed any urgent desire to recapture some simple, revivalist emphasis of early Methodism. The rapid growth of Wesleyan membership between 1825 and 1834 encouraged a policy of consolidation with a view to the formation of settled and respectable congregations. Before 1835 Union Street displayed some of the probable elements in such a development, for it had become a fashionable place of worship where according to one participant, who lamented the absence of serious religion, 'the congregation was gay, and fond of dress'.[27] And when an organ was installed in Baillie Street in 1844, only a small minority of the rank-and-file viewed the innovation as a sure sign of arrested spiritual growth. Meanwhile, some of the traditional agencies of Methodist life had a declining appeal as class and band meetings struggled to attract large numbers. 'Met the few who weekly assemble for prayer and band meeting' noted one of the preachers in 1839, and the situation had scarcely improved twenty years later when one of his successors referred to the common problem of thinly-attended classes.[28] Some members were so engrossed in public affairs that they had little time for these meetings, while others evidently felt most uncomfortable in such circumstances: 'It's no use;' explained one of Petrie's daughters excusing herself from further attendance at class 'the moment Mr. —— turns his eyes upon me, with "Well, sister, how is it with you today?" I am just a lump of ice in a volcano – a dumbstock'.[29] In effect attendance at class was becoming an irksome ritual associated with stereotyped expressions and 'compulsory' speaking. In the 1850s, the Baillie Street leadership began to organise mutual improvement societies which, as elsewhere, were regarded by many members as an acceptable alternative to the class meeting.

Mission work fared little better than some of the weekday meetings, once initial enthusiasm had become a spent force. It did seem as though a circuit with thirty chapels and preaching rooms by 1838 was poised to break new ground, but these facilities were designed to serve existing members rather than the unevangelised masses. Rare outbursts of revivalist activity normally affected a few persons besides those already within the organisation, and on one such notable occasion it was reported that 'Fathers, mothers and teachers shed tears of joy when they saw their sons, daughters and scholars "bending before the cross and offering the publican's prayer" '.[30] It was clearly possible to maintain a substantial cause by virtue of recruitment from large households; Petrie and Ashworth alone raised ten leaders of the Association. Expansion beyond these limits, however, was restricted during the 'forties and the 'fifties when membership sometimes fell as low as 1,100. The formation of three new circuits, Bacup, Bury and Heywood, largely accounted for losses while the absence of major gains was regularly explained by the circuit authorities in terms of the lack

of 'a deeper work of piety amongst the members', and the official
agency for evangelistic enterprises – the Foreign and Home Missions Committee – frequently reminded members of their duty
'to diffuse the gospel among their perishing fellow creatures as
widely as possible'.[31] Yet the leadership was mainly responsible
for this deficiency in view of its distaste for any recruiting scheme
that involved personal sacrifices or rode roughshod over social
pretensions. A preference for the unexacting yet productive
labours of the professional evangelist was evident in the contrasting treatment meted out to John Guttridge and James Caughey.
Guttridge, one of the Association's popular preachers, was appointed to the town in 1851 after a considerable division of
opinion within the leadership. Opponents of the appointment
were mortified when he invited all and sundry to organise camp
meetings and to undertake the tasks of the street missionary.
Caughey, an American Methodist evangelist, received a much
friendlier reception than Guttridge, for his visit in 1860-1 not
only resulted in an unprecedented influx of 500 new members
but made few demands on his sponsors who had been anxious
to hire his services for some time.

Besides supervision of the membership, much of the business
of official meetings concerned arrangements for the promotion of
various causes. While trustees deliberated on how to provide
chapel accommodation for meetings of the Literary and Philosophical Society, the Anti-Corn Law League or the Temperance
Society, the Quarterly Meeting frequently discussed the means
whereby congregational support might be secured for the Religious Freedom Society, the Peace Society or the Good Samaritans.
The Association provided a large number of leaders for such
organisations, and individual members engaged in extensive
charitable services as in the case of the Good Samaritans whose
main purpose was to impart religious instruction to the recipients
of relief. Baillie Street itself, however, offered little encouragement to the poorer sections of the community especially the disreputable poor. Relief from chapel funds was restricted to members of at least twelve months' standing, while a proposal to increase the number of free sittings, one-fifth of the total number
of sittings, prompted no response in 1847. The opening of a
Chapel for the Destitute in 1858 served as a commentary on some
of the preoccupations of the chapel leadership. John Ashworth
first contemplated such a venture in the early 1850s when he recorded the reactions of some of his fellow Associationists,

'What', says one 'are you going to teach the poor that our churches
are not open to them? We have plenty of room; why do they not
come?' 'What', says another 'are you going to widen the distance

betwixt rich and poor, by opening for them separate places of worship?—you will do more harm than good'.[32]

Ashworth postponed the project on account of these objections and the lack of assistance. But even though his critics were unwilling to tolerate doubts concerning a particular understanding of social cohesion and self-help, they could not deny that their own efforts had palpably failed to attract a substantial section of working class support. Ashworth recognised that Baillie Street was managed by and catered for the successful and that consequently there was no alternative to an independent enterprise.

Unlike the Association, post-1835 Wesleyanism made systematic use of lovefeasts, open-air services, class meetings and band meetings. Moreover there was no demand for the services of the professional evangelist, if only because there was local talent of sufficiently persuasive powers such as Abraham Lord, the Bagslate revivalist and subject of one of Ashworth's *Strange Tales*, and Thomas Garfitt, a brush manufacturer, whose journeymen and apprentices formed the nucleus of his regular outdoor meetings. By such traditional means some of the losses of 1835 were made good to yield a membership of 1,310 by 1849. During the same period the Union Street trust, originally so depleted that trustees were drafted in from other towns, was transferred to local members. Conciliatory preachers were also appointed to keep the peace after 1835. Daniel Chapman (1837–9) believed that the Association had been born out of intolerance on both sides and he later maintained an equivocal position in the Reform controversy; Richard Felvus (1839–41), the biographer of Philip Garrett, took the view that dissatisfied members could be accommodated without resorting to disciplinary measures;[33] and Thomas Rowland (1843–6) was always prepared to support the liberal, anti-Buntingite party in Conference.

The new Wesleyan leadership supervised an unpretentious cause whose membership was primarily chapel-orientated, rarely influential in civic life and generally working class in composition.[34] Much support was concentrated in surrounding villages and townships like Castleton Moor where most members were factory operatives and Healey Stones or Bagslate where handloom weavers formed the bulk of the congregation. Differences of background and temperament usually separated the Wesleyan leaders from their Association counterparts. Three of the prominent leaders, James Booth, Henry Cartwright and Benjamin Hartley, had spent much of their early life beyond the close confines of the town. Booth was educated in Manchester and subsequently joined his father, Thomas, in a business partnership that survived the troubles of 1835. Cartwright, a native of Spilsby, was an insurance

agent who removed to the town in 1828. Hartley, a woollen manufacturer, was a patriarchal figure who had joined the Wesleyans
in the 1790s and whose personality traits, 'essentially a peace-
maker and catholic minded', were shared by the other leaders.
Unlike some of the big guns in the Association such individuals
lacked a combative disposition and they never attracted the kind
of comment made in a highly sympathetic obituary of George
Ashworth jun., 'perhaps his principal infirmity was that from the
very intensity of his opinions he might not make sufficient al-
lowance for the equal sincerity of those who differed from him'.[35]

The modest recovery of Wesleyan strength during the 1840s
was temporarily halted by the outbreak of the Reform controversy. The Reformers failed to cause the same havoc as their predecessors. During the critical period 1849–52 the circuit membership was reduced by two hundred. This comparatively small loss,
however, included a disproportionately large number of officers
and it was spread unevenly amongst the societies, some of which
had remained intact in 1835 but were now plunged into bitter
disputes; the hitherto trouble-free Milnrow society was almost
wrecked by the withdrawal of members and Sunday school
teachers and scholars, sufficiently large in number to justify the
opening of the only Reform chapel in the Rochdale area. Moreover, somewhat inflated membership figures reflected a common
concern of the preachers to avoid extensive pruning of the lists.
During his second appointment to the circuit at this time Richard
Heape proved far more accommodating than he had been in 1834,
even though it was possible to secure majorities for formal expulsions on this occasion.

The Reformers scarcely established an independent organisation before they merged with the Association. The Milnrow
seceders successfully applied to join the circuit in May 1853, by
which time many of the town members were gravitating towards
Baillie Street. Two of the principal organisers and delegates to
national meetings, Joseph Dickin and Thomas Watson, demonstrated a considerable measure of affinity with the young activists
of 1835. Dickin was a public speaker who attracted attention as
a result of his campaign on behalf of the Lancashire Public School
Association and his conduct of a series of debates with G. J. Holyoake. At his trial before the Leaders' Meeting he denounced the
superintendent as 'Accuser, witness, juryman, judge and execu-
tioner' but soon discovered that a large majority of the meeting
was quite prepared to assist his passage out of the society. As a
protagonist who 'rarely failed to catch the time to speak, but was
not always observant of the time to keep silence',[36] Dickin had
more in common with assertive Associationists than docile Wesleyans. Watson arrived at the same conclusion, for soon after he

took up residence in the town in 1846 it became clear that his political views, social aspirations and economic interests made continued membership of a Wesleyan cause on the periphery of public life a far less attractive proposition than identification with the highly-esteemed Baillie Street congregation. New denominational ties suited his rapid progression from young employee in 1849 to sole owner of a successful silk manufacturing concern thirteen years later and also furthered political ambitions that resulted in his election as the first Free Methodist Member of Parliament in 1885.

The Association welcomed these recruits at a time when it was itself recovering from an internal crisis which ended in the formation of an independent cause and a net loss of ninety members in 1852. After 1835 most leaders viewed secession as a final act and accordingly sought to avoid perpetual discord; they were separatists and not schismatics argued Oliver Ormerod, the chief apologist, who was mindful of the ugly connotations of schism and aware of the fact that the Association had no more power and less moral authority than the Wesleyans to prevent further disruptions.[37] A small minority of leaders, however, evidently believed that the events of 1835 had merely opened a debate in which judgment was reserved until the appearance of a fully-developed system. They had so little liking for subsequent measures that they were prepared to abandon the Association when certain family squabbles reached a climax.

It was a long-standing feud between the families of George Ashworth and John Hoyle that precipitated this division. Embittered relationships assumed critical proportions when James, second son of George Ashworth and husband of one of John Hoyle's daughters, involved himself in a legal battle over the will left by his father-in-law in 1845. As one of the beneficiaries under this will Ashworth was determined to effect an immediate sale and division of the property, but he was steadfastly opposed by the four trustees who were all Baillie Street leaders acting with the approval of the other beneficiaries. By 1851 Ashworth was so irritated by the stalemate that he applied for a court ruling and at the same time charged the trustees with misappropriation of money. This move turned a private action into a matter of public concern. Between July 1851 and January 1852 the Baillie Street Leaders' Meeting investigated the dispute, found Ashworth guilty of 'antichristian conduct', and concluded that he would have undergone formal expulsion if he had not already removed himself from their company. Since he had expressed lack of confidence in a meeting that was neither competent nor impartial, Ashworth clearly expected little sympathy from most leaders and none whatsoever from the Hoyles who alleged that his deplorable behaviour had hastened the death of his wife.[38]

Throughout these proceedings Ashworth was supported by his father and also by his four brothers who resigned from the Association in December 1851. Besides personal conflict other factors were responsible for this withdrawal of one of the leading families. George Ashworth himself had become disenchanted with the Association. By this time he laid claim to few formal ties, since he was not bound by membership and his period of office as trustee was marked by repeated requests to be relieved of the post. In view of his initial refusal to sign the new trust deed it is probable that the transfer of the Baillie Street property from the shareholding scheme to a connexional deed was effected without his support and that he demanded compensation for the return of his shares. Although he continued to exercise influence through official channels and on one occasion insisted on the expulsion of his brother, he found himself at odds with particular developments in relation to Sunday school policy.

Both the purpose and management of the Sunday schools attracted considerable attention after 1835. The official view was that the quasi-independent status of the schools should give way to a more distinctly denominational identity and system of control. Schools would then be unable to harbour rebels beyond the range of church discipline. Moreover, the present curriculum, which included instruction in writing, would be given more religious content. It was thus hoped to encourage the recruitment of new church members, and individual schools made specific arrangements for this purpose; the teachers' meeting in the village of Brimrod, for example, resolved that 'Superintendents take every class into the vestry at least once a quarter for the purpose of speaking to them in a more special manner about their souls'.[39] The Quarterly Meeting acted on these considerations in 1843 when it formed a circuit school committee consisting of circuit and school representatives as well as the itinerant preachers. The main function of this committee was to co-ordinate the activities of some 5,000 scholars and 700 teachers.

Initial opposition to this measure and also to the consequent abolition of instruction in writing was principally associated with a new school and preaching room at Sudden Brow. These premises had been made available by James Tweedale, a wealthy cotton spinner, who used his own resources and the Association's name and personnel to provide educational facilities for his employees. Tweedale was not a member of the Association nor did he readily recognise its jurisdiction until some years later. Meanwhile the school offered refuge to any teacher who refused to serve under the new committee. It had a particular appeal for teachers who were not members of the Association and who were therefore unable to serve on the committee; approximately one-fifth of the teaching force was in this category and the figure was even higher in some of the villages like Bagslate where only 20 of the 44 teachers belonged to the Association in 1838. At the outset the Ashworth family sympathised with this opposition and expressed interest in the general idea of a factory enterprise; one of the family, Edmund, who later became the first chairman of the Rochdale School Board, was appointed school librarian at Sudden Brow in 1844. After conflict between Tweedale and the circuit authorities flared up again in 1850–1 and after the saga of Hoyle's will had run its course, the Ashworth family seized on the issue of the circuit school committee to pull out its supporters from Baillie Street. Twenty-one teachers promptly withdrew their services and joined a number of members and scholars to form an independent body that held its first service at the Ashworth residence in June 1852. Two years later, after the number of scholars had increased from 30 to 400, George Ashworth utilised some of his Holland Street factory property to construct ten classrooms and a place of worship, while a lecture room, reading room and library were added in 1861.

The Holland Street project fulfilled several purposes of its sponsor. The educational functions of the Sunday and weekday schools expressed Ashworth's lifelong interest in intellectual and moral development. In childhood he had ventured to enlighten neighbouring children in early morning lessons and as an employer he showed his appreciation of the practical advantages of such endeavour when he hired the Baillie Street chapel for the weekday instruction of his factory children. The new custom-built premises provided a more comprehensive system of education than was on offer in comparable local establishments. The range of facilities had much in common with a factory community and clearly confirmed Ashworth's position as one of the leading members of the local public service aristocracy, the head of a firm 'distinguished for its liberality towards its workpeople'.[40]

This extension of philanthropic concern also increased the means of social control at the disposal of the Ashworth family. On the opening of the chapel Edmund Ashworth observed 'When a vessel is launched, there is a host of questions put about it, so it is with this. Who built it? Voluntaryism. Who works it? Voluntaries'.[41] Most of these voluntaries, who were spared the expense of collections and pew rents, were employed in the family's woollen mill, so that a foreman like John Milne, co-superintendent of the Sunday school with Ashworth's eldest son, had good cause to support his employer's withdrawal from the Association. In return for the provision of various facilities, therefore, the Ashworths were assured of a degree of influence over their labour force at a time when working class organisations and suburban development threatened to widen the gap between employer and employee. In this respect the Association had proved an unsatisfactory instrument on account of its size, structure and social character, whereas a small integrated unit facilitated close supervision of the membership. It was possible to concentrate on certain functions at Holland Street, since recruitment from the factory constituency reduced the number of activities associated with the large denomination and also limited losses in the often disastrous transitional period between school and church membership. Furthermore, the Ashworths were now in a position to determine policy. Their strong support for voluntaryist principles was frequently declared in their opposition to any proposal for State interference in education, but it was also evident in other matters such as the sabbatarian controversy. Unlike the Associationists who campaigned against Sunday opening and objected to the particular provisions of Walmsley's Bill of 1856, the Ashworths resisted any legislation that protected 'the Sabbath or any other religious ordinance'[42] on the grounds that they opposed all State control of religion. This liberal attitude formed a marked contrast to what they acknowledged as the acceptable standards of social morality. At Baillie Street they had been the sternest defenders of a moral code that emphasised *inter alia* the evils of smoking, alcohol, gambling and theatre-going. Some of these habits caused greater offence than others and evidently attendance at theatres was common enough for the Ashworths to raise the matter at several official meetings; on one such occasion they secured the standard admonition but only after 180 of the 200 members had vanished during the course of the discussion. At Holland Street, however, the family had a captive audience and it was able to impose its standards on a company that was regarded 'as somewhat puritannical in its outlook'.[43]

Besides its factory connections Holland Street was also the product of a fifth column element in the Association that had always hankered after independency. By the early 1850s this body of opinion despaired of an organisation that had turned full circle to produce a connexional leader like Eckett whose conduct raised the spectre of Buntingism. And when local meetings set aside complaints about a particular policy as in the case of the Sunday Schools, it seemed that neither a reformed connexional system nor a strengthened circuit authority adequately safeguarded individual interests. Hence some of the more radical Baillie Street leaders elected to join the Ashworth camp; John

Scowcroft, a warehouseman whose father had been one of the founders of the Pioneers and who was himself an active member, became one of the principal teachers at Holland Street, while John Meadowcroft, a radical shopkeeper who had frequently disagreed with the Baillie Street leaders, also volunteered his services. Besides the Ashworths, Edmund Taylor was the most prominent defector. A thoroughgoing Nonconformist, Taylor considered that the continuous process of schism, so characteristic of local church life, was a vital expression of the absolute freedom of religious thought; thus, he welcomed the troubles that beset the Wesleyan, Association and Congregational bodies in the period 1849–52. Holland Street offered ample accommodation for Taylor's idiosyncrasies, for his staunch advocacy of popular education and aversion to creeds and denominational ties were easily tolerated in an enterprise that stressed the social benefits of practical religion by means of moral rather than theological expositions.

The emergence of an independent congregation reflected both the strength and weaknesses of the parent body. The Association had far too many leaders for its own good, some of whom were often intolerant of opposition and all of whom knew enough of each other's frailties to indulge in disputes that strained personal relationships to breaking point. In the absence of strong ministerial leadership or some such guardian angel, there was no mechanism to ensure that differences of opinion caused minimal damage, nor could any aggrieved party appeal to a higher tribunal to reverse the decision of a local meeting. Trial and judgment by one's peers, therefore, could arouse as much if not more antagonism in a time of crisis as any measure of discipline by a Wesleyan minister or Conference. Divisive influences, however, never effectively undermined the impressive solidarity first revealed in the secession and subsequently displayed in a more general context. Neither the continued spectacle of an unreformed Conference nor the negligible public importance of the Union Street cause was required to assuage any doubts about the original decision in favour of secession. An unusually confident leadership benefited by a hospitable social milieu in which it was possible to maintain unity and to extend influence in a common struggle against both the bastions of the old order and the adverse features of the new society. By 1857, therefore, when it received the uniting conference with the Wesleyan Reformers, the Rochdale Association still enjoyed an uncommon degree of prosperity as the largest circuit in the country. Yet this success was no guide to the progress of the same cause in the different circumstances of Liverpool.

REFERENCES

[1] B. Gregory, *op. cit.*, p. 86.
[2] MSS. J. Bunting to E. Grindrod, 2 March 1831.
[3] *Address to the Wesleyan Conference* (Rochdale, 1835).
[4] G. J. Holyoake, *The History of the Rochdale Pioneers* (London, 1893), p. 1.
[5] B. Gregory, *op. cit.*, p. 83.
[6] MSS. R. Heape to J. Bunting, 28 November 1834.
[7] MSS. P. Garrett to R. Alder, 2 July 1835.
[8] H. Howarth, *A brief account of Baillie Street Sunday school* (Rochdale, 1883), p. 21.
[9] MS. Minute Book of Union Street Chapel Trustees, 17 September 1835.
[10] *Christian Advocate* 6 August 1838.
[11] See Chapter 6.
[12] *Christian Advocate* 22 February 1836.
[13] MS. Seat Rents Account Book of Union Street Chapel, 1835–8.
[14] C. and R. Heape, *Records of the family of Heape* (Rochdale, 1905).
[15] A. L. Calman, *Life and labours of John Ashworth* (Manchester and London, 1876), p. 54.
[16] *Christian Advocate* 10 July 1837.
[17] *Ibid.*, 7 August 1837.
[18] MS. Minute Book of Baillie Street Quarterly Meeting, 26 September 1838.
[19] *Wesleyan Methodist Association Magazine* January 1845.
[20] *Christian Advocate* 17 July 1837.
[21] MS. Minute Book of Baillie Street Quarterly Meeting, 12 June 1837.
[22] *Proposals for the erection of a Methodist Chapel and School Room in Baillie Street, Rochdale in shares of one pound each* (Rochdale, 1836).
[23] MS. Minute Book of Baillie Street Quarterly Meeting, 29 March 1837.
[24] MS. Baillie Street Chapel Cash Book, 1836–9; *Baillie Street Chapel Share Certificates* (Incomplete set).
[25] MS. Minute Book of Baillie Street Leaders' Meeting, 1845–55.
[26] R. Standring, *Sunday Schools among the mountains as they were fifty years ago* (Rochdale, 1874), p. 21.
[27] *Ibid.*, p. 19.
[28] MS. Diary of Rev. John Peters, 14 December 1839; *United Methodist Free Churches' Magazine* April 1861.
[29] I. Mills, *Threads from the Life of John Mills* (Manchester, 1899), p. 55.
[30] *Wesleyan Methodist Association Magazine* April 1853.
[31] MS. Minute Book of Rochdale Wesleyan Association Foreign and Home Missions Committee, 1842.
[32] A. L. Calman, *op. cit.*, p. 59.
[33] J. Grose, *Memorials of Rev. Daniel Chapman* (London, 1862); R. Felvus, *The Methodist Preacher: or recollections of the late Rev. Philip Garrett* (London, 1864).
[34] MS. Union Street Chapel Marriage register, 1850–63; MS. Seat Rents Account Book of Union Street Chapel, 1824–44.
[35] *Rochdale Observer* 9 August 1873.
[36] *United Methodist Free Churches Magazine* 1873.
[37] H. C. March, *The writings of Oliver Ormerod* (Rochdale, 1901), p. 320.
[38] MS. Minute Book of Baillie Street Leaders' Meeting, 1851–2; MSS. Correspondence between Baillie Street Leaders' Meeting and James Ashworth.

[39] MS. Account Book of Brimrod United Methodist Sunday school, 27 November 1853.
[40] *Rochdale Observer* 9 August 1873.
[41] *Rochdale Sentinel* 14 January 1854.
[42] *Manchester Guardian* 20 February 1856.
[43] *Rochdale Observer* 12 September 1942.

CHAPTER 5

LIVERPOOL: THE DISSIDENCE OF DISSENT

Mid-nineteenth century Liverpool Methodism afforded ample proof of the prolonged and generally adverse effects of internal conflict. In the period 1801–34 Wesleyan membership increased from 1,712 to 3,795 while the population of the town rose from 82,295 (1801) to 201,751 (1831). By 1851, however, there was a smaller membership, 3,209, based on the same circuits which now covered a population of 375,955. At the same time the early development of Free Methodism was confirming the worst predictions of its critics, for after two secessions jointly responsible for a net loss of 2,000 members barely 200 members were still attached to the cause by 1857. This absolute and relative decline in numerical support reflected both the disappearance of favourable conditions in the town at large and the emergence of a problematical set of domestic circumstances. During the early decades of the century Methodism expanded as a result of extensive recruitment amongst English immigrants. In the second quarter of the century, however, increasing numbers of non-English immigrants flooded into a town that lacked the standard features of an industrial class society. It soon became apparent that Methodism was at a competitive disadvantage in this situation and that further growth depended on success in a sharp struggle for the allegiance of a fairly small section of the population. In effect the Methodists were unable to tap the reservoirs of support which continually swelled the ranks of diverse groups like Ulster Orangemen in the Church, Irish Roman Catholics, Scottish Presbyterians and Welsh Baptists. Moreover the Wesleyans were limited to the status of the largest nonconformist denomination in a town where the combined weight and rivalry of Anglicanism and Roman Catholicism relegated nonconformity to a decidedly inferior position; the religious census of 1851 reported that only 26·8 per cent of the attendants at public worship were nonconformists, the smallest percentage of any town in the country.

During the early 1830s at least Liverpool Wesleyanism was in a particularly buoyant condition, apparently overcoming the setbacks of the previous decade. The five main chapels and twenty-five other preaching places scattered across the two circuits recorded a net increase of 500 members in the period 1830–4. There was, too, a determined effort to reduce the heavy debts on the large chapels, and a special appeal in 1830 raised the extraordinary sum of £3,500. In spite of continuing disagreements, moreover, it seemed possible that internal criticism could be contained, particularly when both circuits carried resolutions against the *Circular*. By July 1834 in fact one leading layman claimed that the principal troublemakers had been 'neutralised if not extinguished . . .',[1] yet this assessment proved extremely optimistic as developments in Manchester immediately confounded hopes of lasting peace.

On 17 October 1834 twenty-seven local laymen addressed a letter to Warren in which they complained of accumulated grievances and irresponsible authority. Three weeks later a large deputation attended the inaugural meeting of the Association in Manchester and on 10 November a local branch was formed by a committee of twenty-eight members. A week after the first public meeting on 21 November a series of trials and expulsions commenced and continued for the next five months. By April 1835 the physical separation of the two bodies was virtually an accomplished fact, and the Association now engaged a full-time preacher to assist with the regular public services first organised at the beginning of 1835 and held in the Music Hall, a large and favourite haunt of propertyless religious sects. The course and outcome of the agitation revealed considerable differences between and within the two circuits. In the period 1834–6 the membership of the South circuit declined from 2,145 to 1,562 but recovered its former strength by 1838, whereas the larger reduction in the membership of the North circuit, 1,650 to 980, was followed by a slow and partial recovery during the next twenty years. The impact on individual chapels was even more varied. In the North circuit Brunswick escaped almost unscathed while Leeds Street was so devastated that it was replaced by a new chapel in Great Homer Street in 1839. In the South circuit Stanhope Street was largely unaffected and actually increased its number of class leaders from 23 to 29 during the controversy, Mount Pleasant conceded some losses, and Pitt Street suffered extensive damage. The Association membership, first officially recorded as 1,406 in 1837, was largely drawn from these chapels.

The rapid and uneven process of division was the result of a combination of influences. Initially the Association leaders justified their actions by reference to ministerial disregard for disciplinary procedures, the unauthorised character of the Leeds Special District Meeting, the improper composition of exclusively ministerial District Meetings, the irregular introduction of the Theological Institution and the restrictions on the right of memorialising Conference. These specific grievances soon formed the basis of general strictures on priestly domination that frequently prompted Roman Catholic analogies and also rested on root and branch opposition to particular sections of the laity. Sweeping condemnations were readily publicised by two fort- nightly publications: the Association's *Watchman's Lantern* (December 1834–November 1835) and the pro-Wesleyan *Illumi- nator* (January 1835–March 1836). The first uncompromising editorials of these papers were couched in typically extravagant language; the Association paper aimed to ensure that 'the acts of those "who love darkness rather than light", for a reason which shall be nameless, shall henceforward have the cloak of conceal- ment torn from them . . .',[2] while the *Illuminator* described its rival as 'nothing more than the inflammable vapour produced from the putrefaction and decomposition of those substances with which swamps and bogs abound . . .'.[3] This trade in insults quickly polarised opinion, and in the second issue of the *Illumi- nator* on 21 January 1835 John Stamp, the editor and also junior minister in the South circuit, declared that there was already sufficient evidence to indicate the necessity for a division. This view was largely supported by recent proceedings in one of the chapels.

In its origins the Association was mainly identified with Leeds Street leaders whose suspected connections with the *Circular* and frequent objections to ministerial supervision had caused Bunting to complain of a 'bad radical faction ever on the alert to seize any occasion of annoying us'.[4] This party was so well-organised and extensive that it swamped official meetings and forced super- intendents to adopt questionable expedients to maintain their control. In the period 1827–35 there was a marked difference in character between the suprintendents of the two circuits, which in part accounted for the more turbulent elements at Leeds Street. Successive superintendents in the South circuit had no wish to embroil themselves in disputes; Robert Newton was preoccupied by connexional affairs, William Henshaw had known doubts about official actions in the Leeds crisis, and David McNicoll was primarily concerned to allay the fears of disgruntled mem- bers. Moreover the new superintendent in September 1834, the scholarly and experienced George Marsden, evidently hoped for a peaceful appointment especially in view of the recent death of his wife, and throughout the controversy he hesitated to expel the rebel leaders and always sought to limit the loss of members so as to promote a rapid recovery.[5] In the North circuit, however, the altogether sterner leadership of Scott, Bunting and Jackson only intensified the opposition. The Leeds Street leaders never forgave Scott for his handling of their Leeds memorial, nor did they conceal their dislike for Bunting particularly when he threatened to appoint wealthy Brunswick stewards to supervise their affairs. In 1833 Bunting was succeeded by Samuel Jackson, a young and impetuous individualist who had no wish to govern a troubled circuit and who originally believed that Bunting had been too severe in his judgment of the Leeds Street leaders. Although he steadfastly refused to sign the loyal declaration drafted by the London preachers in reply to the *Remarks,* Jackson acted without compunction once it was clear that these leaders were the chief organisers of the Association.

Jackson first took decisive action on 11 December 1834 when he expelled one of the ringleaders without the support of the Leaders' Meeting and on the ground that a jury of accomplices was not a fit tribunal. This decision drew a protest from twenty-two of the twenty-seven leaders who re-assembled a week later only to discover that Jackson was no longer prepared to tolerate their company and ordered them to vacate the Leeds Street premises. During the next few weeks both parties engaged in a series of cloak and dagger operations usually designed to secure property, funds and members alike. On Sunday 21 December the leaders occupied the chapel until Jackson called up 'a strong detachment of *Brunswickers* . . . to overcome the disaffected plebeians at Leeds Street'.[6] During the following week the Brunswick leadership feared retaliatory action at their missionary meeting and thus ensured that the platform was flanked by police officers. Meanwhile the Association leaders began to issue counterfeit class tickets in order to extend their support and to retain control of class money. Such tickets also served to confuse the loyal stewards who were appointed to man the barricades in the aisles of the Leeds Street chapel and to inspect all tickets before admitting members to communion. It was not legally possible to exclude some of the pewholders from the premises, because one of the peculiar features of the chapel was that a number of pews had been put up for public auction and successful bidders thus gained freehold possession. Although the Wesleyan authorities were unable to shift and eventually forced to compensate such pewholders, the chapel was abandoned by the bulk of the congregation in the weeks following the first love feast at the Music Hall on Sunday 28 December.

The Leeds Street leaders displayed unrestrained opposition towards the ministerial and lay hierarchy. It was commonly alleged that certain officers, members and institutions had long suffered as a result of a marked disparity in the wealth and influence of societies and individuals. Local preachers were singled out for special attention and often portrayed as despised and neglected toilers whose value was rarely acknowledged by the ministers. Moreover their services were rejected by the prosperous Brunswick and Stanhope Street leaders who were held to believe that untutored and socially inferior laymen were incompetent 'to hold forth the word of life in the ears polite of the refined congregation. . . .'[7] Some of the young local preachers were the principal opponents of the traditional arrangement whereby ministers occupied the main pulpits while outlying stations were served by themselves; by June 1835 the Association had eleven such preachers, only three of whom were amongst the thirty-three local preachers listed on the circuit plan for 1825. Besides their preference for ministers, liturgy and organs, wealthy laymen were also criticised for their inattention to standard Methodist requirements, for it was frequently alleged that some were not members of society and that many more failed to attend class and prayer meetings. Furthermore they were charged with outrageous discrimination against poor members who lost their free sittings as trustees made further provision for a paying congregation whether at Brunswick where sixty-seven free sittings were turned over to private use in 1833 or at Mount Pleasant where private sittings increased from 487 to 590 in the period 1815–50.

The ministers were represented as the chief supporters of such powerful congregations, and their neglect of the preaching rooms and of the undistinguished members was adduced as evidence of a strong class bias and of an increasingly chapel-oriented ministry. Consequently, the Associationists made one or two striking gains amongst some of the small causes. They replaced Wesleyan preachers in the pulpit of the Floating Chapel, an ex-battleship which had been fitted out by the Bethel Union for religious services, and also in the pulpit of the Herculaneum Pottery Chapel which had been erected by the owners of the pottery works for their employees and which was served by local preachers who understood the dialect of the immigrant potters from North Staffordshire. The Association also won over some of the Welsh Methodists whose defection neither surprised nor disappointed the Wesleyan authorities long accustomed to their disruptive activities. In 1818 the Welsh Independent Methodist Society had arisen from conflicts over the Poor Fund,[8] and this Society merged with the Association in 1838. During the 1820s the Welsh contingent in the Quarterly Meeting sided with the Leeds Street leaders and so far failed to make adequate contributions to the funds that a separate Welsh circuit was formed in 1826. Although one or two Welsh leaders joined the Association, this circuit was most seriously affected by the Reform controversy.

General support for the Association was governed by the social composition of individual congregations. The mercantile, manufacturing and professional class at the Brunswick and Stanhope Street chapels displayed intransigent opposition towards the agitators. The Brunswick laymen were led by Thomas Crook, an accountant, who publicly welcomed the possibility of a secession as a form of blood-letting, Thomas Kaye, a Tory newspaper proprietor, who organised the publication of the *Illuminator*, and Thomas Sands, a merchant, who ranked second only to Jackson as a leading opponent of the rebel leaders. At Stanhope Street laymen like Michael Ashton, an ironfounder, and Thomas Wilson and Richard Crook, attorneys, were no less active and usually appeared as the chief prosecutors in disciplinary proceedings, always urging the reluctant Marsden to expel dissident members.

In contrast to these spokesmen the leaders of the Association represented the much more modest social standing and resources of members who, according to one Wesleyan assessment, 'are not the most experienced or elderly, or intelligent, or spiritual. Nor are they, by any means, the most respectable and wealthy . . .'.[9] The leaders were mainly drawn from a group comprising the shopkeeper, artisan and petty clerk whose employment was usually precarious rather than productive of an improvement in status and remuneration. They delighted in the title of 'proletarian rebels', yet they had no real roots in the working class society in which they found themselves. Leeds Street chapel, indeed, was regarded as an embattled community not only because any assertion of independence was likely to conflict with the conventions of the Wesleyan hierarchy but because the building was now situated in a developing dockland area with the concomitant features of decrepit property and an unskilled population. A similar situation existed at Pitt Street which had lost most of its wealthy patrons and was already beginning to decline in the face of a hostile working-class neighbourhood. Of the five main chapels Mount Pleasant still attracted a congregation of exceptional social diversity, largely because of its location between a working class district to the west and the fashionable Abercromby Square area to the east. Several rebel leaders, including the chairman of the committee, belonged to this chapel, but they were amongst the least prosperous members in view of the fact that income from pew rents was only reduced from £296 to £281 in 1834–5.[10]

While the Association exhibited a large measure of social homogeneity, it was also based on a comprehensive albeit unstable coalition of interests. One set of protesters, distinguished by personal features as much as by particular views, included some of the most prominent and garrulous of the Leeds Street leaders, two of whom, David Rowland and James Picton, typified this

restless and unreliable element. Both of these leaders clearly enjoyed controversy and often betrayed a largely negative if not
anarchic attitude towards the ultimate purposes of the campaign.
Essentially publicists and professional agitators, they shared an
inflated view of their own importance in a town so preoccupied
by more consequential disputes that Wesleyan disturbances had
limited interest. Rowland was the older and more experienced of
the two men, and after the disciplinary case of 1825 his home became the recognised headquarters of the Leeds Street cabal.
Predictably he was the first leader to undergo expulsion at the
hands of Jackson; any other role might have sorely grieved him,
for he reacted to the sentence with a sigh of relief 'Brethren, I
feel a sweet, a delightful sense of God's love and favour' and evidently he relished the prospect of ensuring that 'These acts of
ecclesiastical cruelty and injustice shall be proclaimed from one
end of this land to the other.'[11] His incorrigible braggadacio, however, always concealed an element of inner timidity whether
evidenced in his failure to vote against Bunting's appointment in
1830 after lobbying to this effect or illustrated by his short-
comings as a national leader when he sometimes recoiled before
the consequences of his mob oratory and intriguing. Much of his
strong criticism of the ministry was in part a consequence of disappointed hopes. If he had been presented with the same opportunity as his brother, Thomas, it is likely that he would have
abandoned a largely undistinguished succession of posts (ship-
broker, tea-dealer, secretary to the Liverpool Pilots' Association
and book-keeper) in order to enter the ministry. Certainly his unsuccessful candidacy for the Association itinerancy in 1836 only
intensified his frustrated ambition.

While Rowland mainly addressed himself to connexional politics, Picton was far more expansive in his expression of anti-
clerical and republican opinions. Unlike Rowland he was on the
threshold of a comfortable career as an architect, and his
secretaryship of the local Association combined with his editor-
ship of the *Watchman's Lantern* demonstrated a determination
to enter public life. But this particular episode scarcely advanced
his claims and he later regretted some of his literary effusions
which he ascribed to youthful excesses. As an editor he held the
view that practical advice was secondary to a long diatribe against
a Conference whose irresponsible actions were unparalleled in
ecclesiastical history and threatened the liberties of all Englishmen. The *Circular* had always blurred the distinction between
restoration and reform just as it had invariably avoided any
examination of courses of action in the event of a division. Likewise the *Watchman's Lantern* singularly failed to include any
systematic discussion of constructive proposals; cursory editorial

comment on the proceedings of the two delegate's meetings confirmed the general preference for invective.

It would be misleading to explain the controversy simply in
terms of Rowland's platform performances and Picton's writings
or the wayward leadership of these and other generally young
rebels like William Byrom, a schoolteacher, who contributed a
number of inflammatory articles to the *Watchman's Lantern*,
Thomas Bew, a builder, whose obituarist reported that 'he could
always discover any unpleasant clanking in the machinery, and
was ready with some advice to remedy it,'[12] and Henry Pooley,
a grate manufacturer, who could be as melodramatic as Rowland:
'we are treading in the steps of Martin Luther' he announced on
his expulsion. The Association encompassed a wide variety of
opinion that ranged from conservative and revivalist inclinations
to reformist and more extreme emphases. A note of conservative
protest was generally struck by the older members; sixteen of the
twenty-eight members of the local committee had been Wesleyans
for more than twenty years. The Leeds controversy and the disciplinary measures of a superintendent like Jackson figured high
on their list of complaints. Sometimes personal recollections of
the constitutional debates of the 1790s lent considerable weight
to the expression of grievances as in the case of John Russell,
the octogenarian figurehead of this body of opinion. Russell was
one of the few leaders shocked by the treatment meted out to
Warren who was one of his former class members, and he was
obviously dismayed by the methods used to silence dissentient
opinion. The brutal administration of discipline also induced
otherwise loyal members to join the Association; Robert Thorpe,
one of the few leaders to survive the mass exodus of later years,
was initially reluctant to join the movement and only did so in
the wake of expulsions which he believed to be equally as
illegal as the Association itself'. Such leaders actively sought a
peaceful settlement and evidently hoped that Conference might
recognise the error of its ways as it had responded to popular
protests against the disciplinary measures of 1825.

The revivalist element accepted much of the conservative
diagnosis of the crisis. Both parties maintained that the authentic
voice of Methodism was being drowned by the organs and liturgy
of the wealthy chapels. There was, too, a common impression
that ministers and rich laymen alike despised the rough speech
and simple homilies of the poor, pious, laborious, independent
local preacher and class leader. But whereas the conservatives
argued over disputed points of connexional law, the revivalist
order was scarcely attracted by such an exercise. Shortly after his
expulsion William Sanderson, a tailor and one of the leading
representatives of this body of opinion, engaged in outdoor

preaching instead of denominational polemics, and many of his fellow prayer leaders at Mount Pleasant, who also joined the Association, acknowledged that their main aim was purely revivalist in character, 'It is our glorious object to roll the tide of war into the heart of the enemy's territory, shouting "Victory, victory, through the blood of the lamb. . . .' This call to arms was by now foreign to the pew-holders of the nearby Stanhope Street chapel, for whom the missioning of benighted parts of the town was best left to either agencies like the interdenominational Town Mission or persons who felt peculiarly called to such an undertaking. Some loyal Wesleyans were obliged to seek alternative outlets for their militant evangelism. Edward Sunners, the 'cabmen's bishop', only became a popular street preacher as a full-time agent for the Town Mission,[13] while George Pennell, a feather merchant and local preacher who had some sympathy for the reformers, later financed a number of mission halls and full-time agents, became one of the most important local figures in the Second Evangelical Awakening, and eventually joined the Primitive Methodists.

If conservative and revivalist spokesmen originally aimed to refurbish a battered Wesleyan tradition, reformist and radical opinion partially or completely dismissed any historical justification for certain proposals. Initially the reformers professed support for the constitutional settlement of the 1790s but they soon shifted their position to campaign for changes. Richard Farrar, a coffee dealer and chairman of the local committee, articulated the views of this predominant group in various statements that plotted the change in direction. At the beginning of the agitation Farrar disclaimed any intention of seeking constitutional innovations. In his second major speech in January 1835 he countered the suggestion that the Association wanted changes by maintaining 'I still say that substantially we do not'. This qualified statement inadequately summarised the current situation, because the initial demands for a disavowal of the power exercised by the Special District Meeting and the restoration of the disciplinary and memorialising functions of the local meetings had now been joined by a request for some safeguard, possibly lay delegation, against future conflicts between ministry and laity. Three months later at the first delegates' meeting Farrar completely broke the back of his original argument when he supported the key resolution in favour of the members' right of interference in the regulation of all affairs. Meanwhile radical leaders spurned appeals based on precedent. They held the view that Wesleyanism had systematically opposed the concept of religious liberty. Picton was most representative of this young, radical element in that he was not only wholly inspired by certain forms of current political dogma but endowed with limited experience, if not knowledge, of Methodist polity. Passing judgment on past and present reformers, he maintained that the delegates of 1797 had merely allowed Conference 'to varnish their chains' and that extensive debates on the unconstitutional activities of Conference generally wasted time and resources. In effect Picton virtually admitted that, as Wesleyan upholders of the Pastoral office insisted, the authority of the preachers had been unimpaired by the Regulations of 1797; 'The great error of the preachers' concluded Picton 'is that they strive to perpetuate a government suited only for the commencement of the system. In no religious communion but that of the Conference Methodists could so illiberal system have survived so long'.

Besides disciplinary action the Wesleyan response to dissentient opinion initially involved a concerted effort to expose the shabby character and limited influence of the rebel leaders. It was not difficult to dredge up damaging details of personal misdemeanours. Before 1834 some of the leaders had been privately restrained by such means. Russell for example was effectively silenced by one of the minsters 'communicating to him a gentle hint respecting a certain part of his conduct . . .'.[14] In its first issue the *Illuminator* alluded to a case of immorality in which Rowland had been involved as a youth. Farrar disposed of the incident as one solitary sin committed in haste, and as hastily repented of, yet the publicity clearly embarrassed the leadership and partly accounted for Rowland's subsequent failure to become an Association preacher. Moreover Farrar himself provided damning evidence of personal instability, for in the course of an address to a Leeds meeting he was so irritated by the interruptions of W. Gilyard Scarth, a well-known local Wesleyan and close friend of Bunting, that he challenged Scarth to a duel. References to other leaders included caustic comments on the excessive drinking habits and 'bacchanalian associates' of Henry Pooley and constant ridicule of the vulgar company that frequented the premises of Anthony Barnes, a publican and one of the senior Leeds Street leaders. The advantages of such character assassination, however, were outweighed by a largely counterproductive emphasis on the lowly social status of the rebels. When the management of the *Watchman's Lantern* was dismissed as 'those scribblers as ignorant as untutored Hottentots' the comment only amplified protests against a Wesleyan establishment insensitive to the impact of its social dominance. The Associationists were denounced as anarchists and petty despots, but when they chose to call themselves 'men, Britons and followers of Christ' they had an instant appeal in those quarters least accessible to the influence of the Wesleyan leadership.

The substance of the Wesleyan answer to the Association involved the rejection of the proposed programme and the defence
of existing institutions. As an unrivalled local exercise in Wesleyan apologetics the *Illuminator* indicated the major objections
in one of its earliest and comprehensive articles, a counterblast
to the first delegates' meeting. The outcome of this meeting only
confirmed the original suspicion that the rebels had always intended to press beyond the redress of grievances in order to
agitate for changes. It was further maintained that the claim to
the right of intervention in all church affairs not only wrongly
presupposed the existence of such a scriptural right but sought
to make the ministry subservient to the passions of the people.
The argument was essentially that developed by Bunting,
Beecham and Watson, only here expressed more forcefully to
counter a ranting and haughty democracy and to prove that any
denial of the authority of a divinely-commissioned ministry was
bound to lead to heresy and anarchy. Wesleyan purity and freedom could not be subjected to the ephemeral and worldly designs
of the agitators: 'The Association indignantly ask—may we not
be trusted? We reply—no, you may not. Others have been led
into this bog, and why may not this be your call'.[15] This terse
warning of dire consequences had scarcely been issued before it
was confirmed by events. Wesleyan spokesmen always maintained
that their opponents would be temperamentally unsuited for the
management of an independent organisation and that enthusiasm
would wane once the Music Hall spectacular, based on a
succession of public speakers and 2,000-strong audiences, was
replaced by the mundane chapel service. The role of local personalities in the national campaign soon indicated the deficiencies
of the leadership while the interaction of diverse elements eventually undermined the fragile unity of the movement.

The Association leaders adeptly exploited grievances in their
own locality, yet they were less impressive in the major debates
concerning a general programme. They started with a considerable advantage only to find their influence curtailed by the
emergence of new leaders. In early dealings with their Manchester
partners they proved more seasoned campaigners as they vetoed
vote by ballot and permitted only perfunctory references to
Warren in formal statements. Farrar fairly reflected local opinion
in his expression of thorough contempt for the ballot and his
assertion that 'The Association was formed for the general good;
the case of Dr Warren furnished an opportunity, merely, for its
operation'.[16] There were also fewer references to the issue of the
Theological Institution in Liverpool than in Manchester,
although Rowland put the opposition case as succinctly as anyone
when he declared that the preachers would be sent to college

'to be taught the art of church government, to be instructed in
the practices of Jesuitism, to be taught how to manage your
meetings, how to slight independent men, how to pass by the
man who has the honesty, manliness, and Christian courage to
avow his sentiments in open day'.[17] The composition of the Central Committee was heavily weighted in favour of the Liverpool
leaders who occupied fifteen of the twenty-four appointments
despite the fact that their branch was less than half the size of
the Manchester organisation. This predominant position, however, was soon weakened by differences of opinion. At the first
delegates' meeting the principal spokesmen agreed that the
authority of local courts was a more important issue than the
composition of Conference. Farrar considered lay delegation 'a
detail, not a principle' and Rowland regarded the measure as
unnecessary. But confusion reigned amongst the local delegates
at the second meeting when William Johnson advanced lay
delegation as a necessity, Rowland now believed that such a
policy amounted to a scriptural right, Farrar was still unmoved
by this general argument, and Barnes was disinclined to discuss
any proposal with a Conference committee likely to consist of
'Jesuits'.

This type of disagreement was compounded by various forms
of inconsistency. In August 1835 Rowland finally admitted that
he had never been hopeful of a positive response from Conference
and yet he insisted that further agitation would result in success,
notwithstanding all local evidence to the contrary. Only by the
continuation of the controversy, in fact, could he reinforce his
own position and retain some semblance of unity, and these
underlying purposes soon betrayed contradictory and obstructive
designs. By 1837 Rowland was advising his audiences to avoid
extremes in their attitudes towards the ministry, while Farrar
was expressing the hope that nothing would be done to outrage
Wesleyan feelings or to degrade the Christian ministry. These
moderate statements formed an odd contrast to the belligerent
expressions of 1835 when, incidentally, these same individuals
had not hesitated to sack their first full-time preacher, James
Lamb, after only a few months' service. Such views scarcely
betokened a serious reappraisal of policy by a more mature leadership but rather constituted a highly personalised attack on Robert
Eckett. At the Assembly of 1837 Rowland's new-found respect for
the ministry was revealed in his unsuccessful attempt to delay
the introduction of free representation, but this move was
primarily intended to unseat Eckett rather than to consider the
merits of the case. Farrar was equally opposed to Eckett, although
less able than Rowland to conceal personal animosity; at the
Assembly of 1838 he seemingly forgot his earlier indifference to

Warren when he rebuked Eckett for hostility towards the former leader, but on his own admission his main purpose was to demonstrate that he himself 'feared no man, no, not even Mr Eckett, whose influence was in everybody's mouth . . .'.[18] By this time the bold and usually negative declaration had become the trademark of leaders who found themselves at odds with each other once they exchanged the role of agitators for that of church leaders.

The transition from protest movement to independent organisation was increasingly accompanied by disorderly proceedings in official meetings. It was indeed a rare occurrence for the first itinerant preacher John Peters, who was stationed in the town between 1836 and 1839, to comment after one meeting 'Passed over peacefully, thank God'.[19] A few of the more agreeable leaders were driven to despair by ruinous conflicts that soured personal relations and paralysed the organisation. Robert Thorpe reflected on these troubled experiences 'So much was there of sin, and selfishness, and strife of words, and grasping at power in the new Church, that my soul might truly be said to dwell among lions'.[20] Bizarre conduct was all too possible in this situation as for example when one of the minor leaders opposed a number of proposed rules, called a meeting attended only by himself, adopted an alternative set of rules, and elected himself delegate to the Assembly.[21]

This contention resulted in substantial losses. In the first place some of the revivalist members discovered an outlet for their energies shortly after the Rev. Robert Aitken intervened in the agitation as a self-appointed arbitrator in June 1835. It had been planned to hire Aitken as full-time preacher at the Music Hall but he was evidently appalled by the speed with which it was proposed to terminate Lamb's contract. In any case he was more concerned to advance his application for admission to the Wesleyan ministry, and his review of the controversy was generally unfavourable to the Association, 'I love your souls, but I will oppose your measures. I pity your case, but I abhor your conduct'. Once his overtures failed to impress Conference, however, Aitken formed the Christian Society in December 1835. Based on an amalgam of Anglican and Methodist polities as well as an unusual mixture or evangelicalism and tractarianism, this Society claimed 1,500 members spread across seven towns by 1837. Aitken had his largest following in Liverpool where he built Hope Hall as his headquarters in 1836. Known locally as Jumpers or Ranters, his supporters attracted attention mainly because of their frenzied revivalist activities in the vaults of the Hall; it was standard practice for members of the congregation to rise up, dance and caper about the room, jump over the forms, tear their hair and clothes, and throw themselves on the floor. As early as January 1836 several Association leaders went over to the Society and they were joined by a number of members until the collapse of the Society in 1840. In the intervening period there were attempts to limit these losses by means of a merger, and the attendance of two of the Society's representatives at the Assembly of 1837 seemed to increase this possibility. But there was a considerable difference between the conventional Association service and the uninhibited expressions of the Hope Hall set. Furthermore, any hopes of union were finally dashed by the bad publicity that the Society began to receive as a result of the investigations of Samuel Warren Jun. who ironically had cause to comment on 'the wild, irrational, indecorous and even impious proceedings' of a congregation which included some of his father's former albeit nominal supporters.[22]

Some of the other members of the Association eschewed such excesses but they were also disappointed by the dull formalities and restrictions of the new body. The first full-time circuit missionary, William Sanderson, soon encountered opposition from leaders whose refusal to endorse unconventional ventures seemed to perpetuate the worst forms of Wesleyan respectability. In 1839 Sanderson campaigned for an itinerant preacher possessed of 'zeal and holy energy' but his candidate, Joseph Woolstenholme whose appointment three years later coincided with a rare increase in membership, was passed over in favour of James Molineux whose stylish preaching drove away 'most of the zealous labourers from the Society'. Sanderson himself resigned from the Association a year later and subsequently pursued an independent ministry that resulted in the formation of the Free Gospel Church in the town.[23]

The second and most conspicuous group of deserters consisted of some of the young leaders whose maverick-like features found varied expressions. With the exception of Rowland these leaders currently or subsequently enjoyed a higher social status than the rest; their withdrawal and denominational loyalties often reflected this difference. By the early 1840s both Pooley and Byrom had returned to the Wesleyans. Pooley made his peace with the same Brunswick leaders whose designs 'to gratify the rich man' had previously caused him such offence but now seemed in keeping with a respectable businessman whose early operations as a grate manufacturer had given rise to an engineering works which was about to manufacture a world famous weighing machine. Byrom was even more fickle in that he later emerged as one of the most active Wesleyan Reformers after which he joined the Anglicans; in the meantime he abandoned his school duties for a flourishing business as an accountant and estate agent. Wilson

Ledger, a former member of the Central Committee and a self-styled gentleman, joined the Independents, while Charles Rawlins, scion of a substantial mercantile family and founder of the local Mechanics' Institute, was always more loosely connected with the Association than the rest of this group and had lost all interest in Wesleyan disputes by the time he joined the Unitarians in 1839. Finally, Picton began to sever his connections in 1845 and successively attached himself to the Baptists, the Independents and the Anglicans. Evidently disillusioned by the way in which the 'grand liberal talk of 1835' had degenerated into the 'vulgarity, ignorance, narrow-mindedness and cant of humdrum sectarianism', Picton was clearly aware that his thriving architect's practice, which had commenced with a commission to design Association chapels, permitted him to make new social acquaintances and to embark on a more extensive public career.[24]

The serious effect of such losses was apparent in the almost uninterrupted decline in membership from 1,406 in 1837 to 452 in 1852. This reduction meant that initial financial commitments pressed heavily on diminishing resources and that there was a continuous struggle to maintain the four chapels: Bispham Street, Pleasant Street, Heath Street and Scotland Road which were opened in 1836, 1839, 1842 and 1843 respectively and which were joined by Gill Street (Welsh Association) and Grange Road (Birkenhead) in 1847. Neither avoidance of direct competition with Wesleyan rivals nor easier access to public worship than existed at the Music Hall guaranteed the prosperity of any of these chapels. The largest and most central chapel, Pleasant Street, had a Grecian design that was welcomed by the local press but seemed an inappropriate style for the critics of Wesleyan 'temples'. In any event the chapel soon became a declining cause that had no contract with distant middle-class settlements and little impact on the working-class in the vicinity; the religious census of 1851 reported that less than one-sixth of its 1,400 sittings were occupied by adults. The plight of Bispham Street and Scotland Road was even more desperate by this time. Both chapels were situated in the north of the town and suffered severely as an area of varied craft industries was turned over to a predominantly Catholic population of unskilled labourers. On census Sunday Bispham Street had an adult congregation of fifteen, merely the worst example of widespread decay now compounded by unrelieved chapel debts in the region of £6,000. It was against this background that a dispirited religious community was plunged into a disastrous controversy in the early 1850s, when dissident leaders made common cause with the new advocates of Wesleyan reform.

The Reform controversy lacked much of the drama of the

previous agitation. There was no headlong rush into a public campaign marked by strident protests, and while one superintendent observed that the Reformers' 'proceedings are languid, and their counsels are distracted . . .'[25] friendly observers frequently bemoaned the failure to filibuster official meetings. The authorities were never embarrassed by hostile majorities in the vestry, and most of the principal organisers chose to resign rather than to undergo disciplinary proceedings. The campaign was largely managed by leaders like John Burrows, a medical practitioner and talented public speaker, Peter McTaggart, the owner of a large hosiery business and the first circuit steward, John Smith, a hide merchant and secretary of the organisation, Edward Parnell, a ship broker who acted as treasurer, Thomas Lloyd, a timber merchant who presided over most of the public meetings, and William Byrom the national finance agent. Although these middle-aged leaders enjoyed a more respectable standing and were imbued with less social antagonism than their predecessors, they drew their grievances and support from the same sources as the Association. Unsuspecting laymen were warned that 'the priests are too artful, too well trained', while loyal officials were contemptuously dismissed as 'yesterday stewards, the creatures of the ministry only . . .'.[26] Local preachers once again played an active role. Burrows, Byrom and Lloyd represented this element and the major clashes often occurred in their meetings. Since 1835 there had been attempts to improve training facilities for the local preachers, but although the North circuit formed an Improvement Society for this purpose in 1843[27] there were still complaints that an assertive professional ministry refused to recognise the proper status of the local preachers. Similarly there were familiar grumbles about discrimination in the administration of discipline; one local correspondent noted that poor members were frequently reprimanded or expelled for bankruptcy, marriage to the unconverted, and irregular attendance at class, while influential laymen remained in office despite such misdemeanours.

At their first public meeting on 9 November 1849 the Reformers resolved to press for an open Conference and also expressed sympathy for Everett, Dunn and Griffiths. Like Warren, however, the expelled ministers had no personal following in the town, and local opinion was influenced far more by the fact that Joseph Beaumont was once again at odds with the connexional leadership. Beaumont had acquired a local reputation as a result of a particularly active ministry in the South circuit during the early 1840s. He had been appointed against the advice of the stewards but was strongly supported by reformist leaders who welcomed both his efforts to assimilate Wesleyanism into the

Dissenting community and his enthusiastic reception for the American evangelist, James Caughey, whose 'machinery of revival' including the use of decoy penitents so offended the Buntingites. The Reformers' concern for ministerial rebels, however, was secondary to a detailed programme first publicised in July 1850 and incorporating four demands: the unrestricted right to memorialise Conference, the nomination of officers by local meetings, the replacement of an absent or recalcitrant superintendent by an elected chairman, and a revision of connexional law by a committee of ministers and laymen. It was thus proposed to restore a past order by such means, for according to Lloyd, an officer of forty-two years standing, the Reformers were conservatives in the strictest sense of the word, as they wished to fall back on their original purity, their original rule and discipline.[29]

The South circuit bore the brunt of the agitation and reported a net loss of 400 members in the period 1849–51, while the North's membership remained fairly stable. The circuit suffered as a result of the same social conditions and ministerial attitudes that had previously affected its neighbour. With the exception of Stanhope Street the circuit now contained downtown chapels which had become isolated in the wake of population movements. Between 1831 and 1851 the Pitt Street membership declined from 838 to 327, the Mount Pleasant membership was reduced from 543 to 430, while Stanhope Street increased its membership from 394 to 645.[30] Situated in an overwhelmingly Irish neighbourhood, the Pitt Street chapel was saddled with heavy debts and, like Mount Pleasant, was largely managed by small tradesmen and artisans who combined a sense of neglect with a heightened feeling of independence. The membership of both chapels was reduced by one-third as a result of the controversy, and the first Reform preaching room was opened in the vicinity of Mount Pleasant. The circuit also covered a large proportion of the outlying village societies which were susceptible to the influence of a dissident leader; thus the Old Swan and Windsor societies were badly affected, while the entire membership of the small cause at Aigburth declared for the Reformers. The North circuit was less vulnerable to controversy on account of its predominantly middle class congregations, although the Reformers, none of whom belonged to the leading Wesleyan families, did make some gains at Brunswick where a fall in pew rent income of £120 in 1850–1 induced some apprehensive mortgagees to call in their loans. By this time, however, Brunswick had been eclipsed by the more prestigious Great Homer Street chapel where pew rents exceeded £400 p.a. and an affluent congregation could afford to employ doorkeepers, pew-openers and choristers. The Reformers attracted neither support nor fierce lay opposition from this quarter. Some of the old war-horses had fallen on hard times. Business failures were a fairly common occurrence amongst the local leaders; both Sands and Ashton went bankrupt during this period. Some of the other veteran leaders like George Heald, brother of the Wesleyan Member of Parliament and formerly an active supporter of financial demonstrations of loyalty, now pleaded reduced circumstances in the face of connexional appeals and informed Bunting in 1850 'I am not in the passing acceptation of the phrase "one of your rich men".'[31]

Most leading laymen were in fact prepared to leave the conduct of the campaign to ministers whose diverse personalities accentuated the differences between the two circuits. The superintendent of the North circuit in the period 1848–51, William Stamp, was willing to reason with rebellious members when he was not distracted by current disclosures of financial scandals involving two relatives who had embezzled local and connexional funds. His colleagues, William Illingworth and Samuel Hall, had no taste for controversy, and Hall actually won the respect of the Reformers for his refusal to accept the case for the disciplinary measures of 1849. Peter McOwan, superintendent of the South circuit between 1847 and 1850, had no such reservations and he rejected the Reformers' demands as 'unconstitutional and revolutionary'. His successor, Robert Newton, was equally opposed to any suggestion of appeasement and was strongly supported by his colleague, Robert Newstead, whose warning to Bunting in November 1850, 'the troublemakers *must* soon be dealt with firmly', was closely followed by several expulsions and a spate of resignations.

The Reformers formed an independent organisation in the early months of 1851 when they opened their headquarters in the Royal Assembly Rooms and organised public worship in five other preaching places. By the end of the year they had a membership of 350 served by ten preaching rooms and divided into twenty classes of English and Welsh composition. The Welsh circuit had prospered as a result of large-scale immigration during the 'forties, but the membership of 630 in 1849 was halved in the course of the agitation. The difference between the size of the Reform membership and total Wesleyan losses indicated a failure in organisation that became even more apparent as a result of an ill-fated union with a group of ex-Associationists.

Paradoxically the Reform crisis had its most devastating effect on the Association in the form of a lengthy conflict between a large section of the local organisation and the connexional leadership. Much of the public debate involved two interrelated issues: an Association-Reform union and ministerial discipline. As connexional editor Eckett fired the first shot in this contest with an

article which condemned both the *Fly Sheets* and Conference yet
maintained that the latter 'has not exceeded the limit of its legal
power or authority, as recognised by the laws of Conference
Mehodism . . .'.[32] Moreover Eckett viewed the expelled ministers
as unsuccessful engineers of a palace revolution rather than as
exponents of constitutional changes, and he warned the Reformers to avoid personal attacks and to act on the best of motives.
This assessment immediately irritated a number of Reformers
and no doubt contributed to the mutual antipathy between the
first President and the first Secretary of the U.M.F.C. Eckett had
no liking for the suspected author of the *Fly Sheets*, and Everett
was characteristically caustic in his first impressions of the Association leader, 'It was difficult to get rid of the feeling that you were
in the presence of a man with an evil eye, a sinister look, a brazen
meretricious leer and a braggart impudent face . . .'.[33] While
Everett confined this observation to his diary, some of the Liverpool leaders were soon saying much the same thing in public.

The Liverpool Associationists expressed unqualified support for
the Reformers at the beginning of the agitation. Pleasant Street
chapel was made available for public meetings; Rowland yet
again regaled audiences with tales of the ecclesiastical atrocities
of yesteryear; and various leaders found a new lease of life as
putative pioneers of an Association-Reform union. At the outset
Eckett was regarded as the principal opponent of such an alliance
particularly in view of his identification with the hateful practice
of 'question by penalty', and it was one of the Liverpool
preachers, James Carveth, who first publicly denounced Eckett.
Carveth was appointed to the town in 1849 after a ten-year
ministerial career distinguished by an unusually rapid succession
of appointments which opponents attributed to his mediocre
preaching ability. Yet while only one circuit had retained him
for a second year during this period (appointments invariably
lasted two and often three years), he arrived in Liverpool to find
that his failings were overlooked and often shared by the local
leaders. Carveth already bore a grudge against Eckett whose
savage review of one of his political tracts appeared in the Association magazine in April 1849.[34] Eckett was unable to commend
this publication largely because it consisted of strong language
and rehashed Chartist proposals, and he refused to publish a
second letter from Carveth in reply to his criticism. This rebuff
immediately suggested to Carveth that the management of the
magazine was based on 'an editorial exclusiveness as complete
as can possibly exist', and soon after his removal to Liverpool
he broadened the attack in a pamphlet that deplored Eckett's
attitude towards the Conference of 1849.[35] Throughout these
exchanges Carveth had the backing of a majority of local leaders.

At the Assembly of 1850 the Liverpool representatives attempted to obtain a vote of censure against Eckett, and while they managed to dissociate the Assembly from his private views they bitterly contested the accompanying decision to make no reference to this resolution in the official minutes. Two months later the Liverpool Quarterly Meeting endorsed the views of its representatives and prepared for a further struggle to expose Eckett as a devotee of Buntingism and as a leader whose control of the Book Room, command of the Assembly platform and influence in the Connexional Committee were designed, according to one of the representativs, 'to enslave the minds of the Travelling Preachers . . . and to crush the lay-influence of the circuits'.[36]

After the Assembly of 1850 it was clear that the best means to mount a national agitation on these lines was to concentrate on the issue of ministerial discipline and, in particular, 'question by penalty'. Several of the northern circuits like Leeds and Carlisle called for official condemnation of 'question by penalty', while other circuits were equally interested in the issue but were less inclined to rally round the Liverpool leaders; significantly the Rochdale leader, Oliver Ormerod, suggested that the persistent decline in the Liverpool membership was hardly surprising in view of the activities and manifest ill-will of the local leaders. Eckett himself was determined to secure clear guidelines so as to deal with Carveth. Throughout the first half of 1851 Carveth called on all local meetings to condemn 'question by penalty' and, by implication, to oust Eckett. The conflict reached a climax in the Assembly of 1851, and after a four-day debate it was resolved that any minister was obliged to explain his conduct and to undergo interrogation on the basis of the evidence. In effect the Assembly was prepared to deal with recalcitrant ministers in the same way as Conference.

This decision amounted to a crushing defeat for Carveth and the Liverpool leaders who immediately campaigned for the abrogation of the resolutions and for the destruction of 'cliqueism' within the Connexional Committee. Rowland bitterly complained that the Assembly had thus 'raised up an embankment over which the Reformers would not climb, and created a chasm they would not venture to pass . . .'.[37] This was also the view of the *Wesleyan Times*, which had earlier warned its 'excellent friends at Liverpool' that hopes of union were premature and now added that acceptance of the principle of inquisitorial process made the possibility even less likely. A large majority of Associationists saw no sufficient cause for further controversy and instead there was increasing pressure to discipline the Liverpool leaders who were sliding into independency. At the Assembly of

1852 Carveth was brought to trial on the ground that he had presided over an illegally-constituted circuit meeting. He was suspended from ministerial duties after he refused to co-operate in the investigation, whereupon the Liverpool leaders renounced all connections with the Assembly, recalled their representatives and appointed a circuit committee.

Neither the general impact of the Reform agitation nor the particular issue of ministerial discipline entirely explains these events. Throughout this period the prominent role and troublesome personality of Rowland meant that statements of principle often served only to obscure personal motives, and particular incidents merely provided the occasion rather than the cause of controversy. There developed, in effect, an unequal struggle for power between Rowland and Eckett. By 1850 Rowland had consolidated his position in local affairs as a result of earlier defections and the removal of certain key leaders; Farrar, for example, had long since emigrated to South America. But his leadership of a crumbling circuit now carried less weight in connexional affairs, and he failed to secure any of the highest offices after his election as President in 1840. Continued membership of the Connexional Committee offered little consolation, particularly since he always boasted of his status as one of the founding fathers. Yet while he reminded his audiences that 'the Association had its birth in the parlour of my house', he found himself increasingly overshadowed by Eckett. During the 'forties, Eckett established an unassailable position and occupied the posts of President for three years, of Secretary for five years, and of Connexional Editor for the whole period. By 1850 he commanded sufficient influence to issue idle threats of resignation, and it was from this position of strength that he isolated Rowland within the Connexional Committee. Rowland effectively lost the battle months before the Assembly of 1851. At a meeting of the Connexional Committee in February he replied to merciless criticism from Eckett by inviting the members of the committee 'to look me in the face, to look at my bald head and white hair, to call to mind their intimate knowledge of my position and character in Liverpool, what I had sacrificed of time, labour, health and property for the Connexion . . .'.[38] This appeal elicited no sympathy precisely because the audience was much too familiar with the wiles of the veteran agitator and recognised his ability to injure others while still presenting himself as the injured party. It was now common knowledge that Rowland was stage-managing Carveth's campaign, that he was publicly dismissing the committee as a hostile faction, and that he was principally intent on dislodging Eckett whose contemptible depotism he compared unfavourably with the gentlemanly and dignified despotism of Dr Bunting.

Prior to the Assembly of 1852 Rowland frequently denied any intention of forming an independent movement, yet few observers were surprised when he promptly organised such a body after the Assembly. The Liverpool division exacted a heavy toll on an already enfeebled cause. The circuit was only saved from extinction by a hastily-arranged salvage operation, largely financed by a special national appeal which drew heavily on Rochdale funds. A sharp reduction in membership from 425 to 267 in the year 1852–3 was accompanied by the loss of three chapels, Pleasant Street, Herculaneum Pottery and Grange Road, none of which had been settled on the model trust deed. While the seceders took possession of these chapels, the threatened sale of the other chapels presented the grim prospect of a disinherited denomination. The handling of this difficult situation was entrusted to an emergency committee chiefly comprising the President of the Association, Thomas Bayley, who was appointed to the circuit in August 1852 and who probably concealed some of the membership losses, Robert Thorpe, one of the few survivors of the original leadership, George Quail, an accountant, and Richard Lloyd, the last holder of the hereditary office of port gauger and father-in-law of Silas Hocking, the United Methodist minister and author. These leaders avoided any public controversy with Rowland, for as Bayley dryly observed 'we prefer leaving strife to those who love it'.[39] Their immediate concern was to secure alternative accommodation and to prevent the sale of the remaining chapels; an unpretentious central chapel was acquired in Russell Street while the Scotland Road and Heath Street chapels were withdrawn from the market. It proved more difficult to arrest the decline in membership which reached its lowest point at 214 in 1857. But the Association had managed to survive whereas the seceders had meanwhile passed into the nethermost regions of the denominational underworld.

The rapid collapse of the seceding body exposed all the weaknesses of independency under an unstable leadership. Initially there was considerable optimism as the rebel Associationists managed to persuade a majority of the Reformers to form an organisation whose membership, although never officially disclosed, was probably in the region of 400 according to an estimate based on a local religious census of 1853.[40] Rowland believed that he now headed a mighty movement which had sunk the local Association without trace, and he maintained that the actions of the Assembly had shocked the Christian feeling and intelligence of the Liverpool population. Only his trusted admirers like John

Bridson and Richard Sharpe, both of whom had been committee members in 1834, really shared such illusions.

Fatal differences of opinion soon materialised largely because Rowland tolerated no rivals in his supposedly liberal system of government. Although financially supported by the seceders, Carveth was increasingly disenchanted by his subordinate role. He had served the purpose of his paymasters only to find himself denied former status and regular employment. Moreover his advocacy of a more balanced relationship between ministry and laity than existed in the Wesleyan and Association connexions appeared increasingly irrelevant to laymen who had altogether discarded the idea of a professional ministry in favour of their own preaching and organisational abilities. While Carveth eventually withdrew from the cause, the most serious defections occurred amongst the Reformers. They had agreed to union because Rowland had supported their activities and not only offered to save them the expense of a chapel building programme but gave an assurance of exemption from any financial liability. Respected leaders like Burrows, however, quickly realised that they had been inveigled into an impossible situation. They were horrified by the way in which Rowland dominated the Pleasant Street services and indulged in vehement addresses that disregarded any proper distinction between the pulpit and the public platform. Dismay turned into unyielding opposition when Rowland went back on his original promise and demanded that some of the leaders should become trustees. He met with a blank refusal to which he responded by closing the chapels. By 1856 Pleasant Street had been sold to the Anglicans, the Herculaneum Pottery had reverted to the Association, and Grange Road had been purchased by the Roman Catholics.

Most of the Reformers dispersed to other churches and usually joined the Association. Until 1860 Rowland and a handful of supporters maintained a short-lived existence in Hope Hall which was the graveyard of many obscure sects and, appropriately, the former centre of the first set of disillusioned Associationists, the revivalist supporters of Aitken. Both of these parties bore a heavy responsibility for the internal contradictions and defects of the Association. In their respective ways both failed to appreciate, and in such an unfavourable social milieu could ill-afford to ignore the fact, that the tradition from which they had deviated had been dependent on sustained evangelism and an ordered form of government. In a review of local Wesleyan problems over thirty years, one of the superintendents commented in 1857 'We have been the prey of many dividers and stealers',[41] and in this locality at least controversy had given rise to a peculiarly unconstructive alternative to Wesleyanism.

REFERENCES

1 MSS. T. Kaye to J. Bunting, 9 July 1834.
2 *Watchman's Lantern* 17 December 1834.
3 *Illuminator* 7 January 1835.
4 MSS. J. Bunting to E. Grindrod, 2 March 1831.
5 MS. Diary of Rev. George Marsden, vol. 8, 1834.
6 *Watchman's Lantern* 31 December 1834.
7 *Ibid.*, 1 July 1835.
8 MS. Minutes of Liverpool Quarterly Meeting, 1 January 1818.
9 *Illuminator* 1 April 1835.
10 MS. Mount Pleasant Chapel Pew Lists, 1834–5.
11 *Watchman's Lantern* 17 December 1834.
12 *United Methodist Free Churches' Magazine* 1877.
13 S. Johnson, *Edward Sunners – the Liverpool Cabmen's Missionary* (Liverpool, 1886).
14 MSS. J. Beecham to J. Bunting 1 April 1830.
15 *Illuminator* 27 May 1835.
16 *The Corrected Report of the Debates and Decisions of the Adjourned Meeting of Wesleyan Methodist Delegates* (London, 1835), p. 12.
17 *Watchman's Lantern* 18 February 1835.
18 *Christian Advocate* 6 August 1838.
19 MS. Diary of Rev. John Peters, 2 October 1838.
20 *United Methodist Free Churches Magazine* October 1867.
21 *Christian Advocate* 20 August 1838.
22 R. Aitken, *An address to the preachers, office-bearers and members of the Wesleyan Methodist Societies* (London, 1835), p. 31; *My first circuit: Law and facts from the North. In a letter to Christopher North Esq. From an old contributor* (London, 1838); *Laws, Regulations and General Polity of the Christian Society, in connexion with the Rev. R. Aitken, being the substance of the minutes of their first general Convocation, held at Liverpool on the 27th day of October 1836* (Liverpool 1836); *Liverpool Review* 20 June 1903.
23 W. Sanderson, *Life and labours of William Sanderson* (Wigan, 1899).
24 J. A. Picton, *Sir James A. Picton: A biography* (London, 1891).
25 MSS. P. McOwan to J. Bunting, 11 January 1850.
26 *Wesleyan Times* 29 July 1850.
27 MS. Minutes of Liverpool North circuit Local Preachers' Meeting, 1 September 1843.
28 *Christian Witness and Church Members' Magazine* March 1847.
29 *Wesleyan Times* 29 July 1850.
30 MS. Minutes of Liverpool South Quarterly Meeting, 1831, 1851.
31 MSS. G. Heald to J. Bunting, 26 November 1850.
32 R. Eckett, *The Fly Sheets and Conference condemned* (London, 1849), p. 4.
33 MS. J. Everett, Memoranda 6 June 1855.
34 J. Carveth, *A new and practical scheme of reform developed; or the way to political equality and equitable taxation made plain* (Manchester, 1849).
35 *Wesleyan Methodist Association Magazine* August 1849; J. Carveth, *Recantation demanded and refused: or a rejoinder to 'An Appeal to facts', contained in a pamphlet recently issued by the Rev. Robert Eckett, relative to the prerogative exercised in the expulsion of the Rev. James Eckett* (London, 1850).
36 *Wesleyan Times* 14 October 1850.

[39] *Wesleyan Methodist Association Magazine* November 1852.

[37] D. Rowland, *An appeal to members of the Wesleyan Methodist Association relative to certain arbitrary proceedings of the Connexional Committee and Annual Assembly of 1851* (London, 1851).

[38] *Wesleyan Times* 19 April 1852.

[40] *Liverpool Mercury* 25 February 1853.

[41] *Wesleyan Times* 23 March 1857.

Chapter 6

POLITICAL ASPECTS OF SECESSION

Political attitudes separated conflicting groups in nineteenth-century Wesleyanism as a growing consciousness of corporate strength and individual preferences increased the problems of connexional management. However much evangelical tenets promised protection from the divisive character of secular affairs, only a strictly exclusivist or other-worldly position offered any possibility of freedom from political tensions. Since such extremes were avoided albeit occasionally in favour of the different phenomenon of quietism, some kind of rapport with political life became a necessity. Upholders of Wesleyan spirituality might declaim against worldly distractions and insist that Conference 'cannot "come down to wallow in the mire" of secular politics',¹ but few leaders lacked or suppressed normal political instincts and even fewer failed to appreciate the political implications and potential of Wesleyan expansion. There existed different levels of opinion throughout the connexion. Conference defined and defended a number of interests as the ruling body. Laymen were affected by such interests and also by other considerations, so that the extent to which purely denominational emphases and influences account for their behaviour can be gauged only by reference to a particular social milieu. In many cases internal dissension assumed political significance partly as a result of the directives and advice of Conference and partly because local leaders chose to articulate views concerning the desirable structure and functions of secular and ecclesiastical government.

The nature and consequences of the early process of Wesleyan politicisation have been variously explained in terms of counter-revolutionary activities or stabilising influences with a pronounced tendency towards conservatism. A series of guidelines, known collectively as the 'no politics rule', expressed the official attitude towards political affairs. By this expedient it was intended to prohibit the use of connexional premises and platforms for political purposes and to warn members of the detrimental effects of excessive involvement in politics. More generally and as a product of the turbulent 1790s the rule aimed to demonstrate loyalty to the established order and to allay fears of any alleged association with radicalism. Properly and comprehensively implemented, this provision could serve to prevent unnecessary conflict and its value was recognised by other Methodist connexions in their turn; the membership of the Association, for example, was advised by the Assembly of 1839 'Whatever may be your political opinions, never introduce them into the Church of Christ, nor suffer them to interfere with your religious duties, or unduly to occupy your attention'.[2]

Against a changing background of increasing and diverse political interest, however, the rule became a major bone of contention as its practical effect was seen to favour a certain outlook. During the course of the debate on the Stephens' case, Bunting observed 'Some say a strong arm must be laid on the Tory side. They tried to catch me in order to fry me, but they failed. I wish they had not caught one on the liberal side'.[3] It was usually the case in fact that liberal or radical spokesmen fell foul of the rule, while others escaped with impunity and often explained away any apparent infringement of the rule by locating certain issues within the realm of 'Christian politics'. The accompanying distinction between religious motives and political action was dismissed by opponents as a thinly-disguised form of political engagement or what Daniel O'Connell described as 'the sanctimonious hypocrisy of your malignant piety' in his virulent attack on the Orange prejudices of the Manchester Wesleyans.[4] The concept of Christian politics was so elastic that much could be subsumed under this heading to the point where the rule was devoid of meaning. During his stormy Manchester ministry (1838–41) William Bunting viewed his political sermons as a necessary antidote to the secularisation of politics and, more especially, he saw no reason to exclude his Orange politics from the pulpit. Yet he invoked the 'no politics rule' when he happened to disagree with a particular cause, thus declining an invitation to participate in a Manchester meeting of dissenting ministers, which was convened in 1841 to discuss the Corn Laws, on the ground that 'I am not able to bring within the range of those purely Christian politics, with which it is the peculiar duty of Christian ministers to interfere, a much disputed fiscal question. . . .'[5]

Prior to the 1830s special causes and denominational concerns characterised much official involvement in political affairs whether in opposition to Lord Sidmouth's Bill or in support of the abolition of slavery. The mobilisation of rank and file support for such purposes demonstrated the growing importance of a religious community whose inclinations were noted by politicians. Political influence was further increased by the extension of the franchise and the consequent appearance of a sizeable Wesleyan electorate after 1832. This new feature also meant that the hitherto apparent innocence of the 'no politics rule' and of the major crusade now faced more problematical circumstances in which

party loyalties might weaken any official lead or, worse still, bestir certain members to challenge what they regarded as the prevailing political bias.

The first parliamentary election under the Reform Act of 1832
revealed strong Wesleyan support for the Whigs in each of the
three towns.[6] While the slave question had an adverse effect on
Tory calculations, the absence of any other major issue encouraged
an uninhibited expression of political views. In effect it proved
possible for the layman to make a choice as an independent voter
rather than as an individual unduly conscious of and responsive
to denominational pressures. Nevertheless, the general pattern
of voting behaviour scarcely obscured the Tory sympathies of a
select band of Manchester and Liverpool laymen, most of whom
like Wood, Burton and Bunting in Manchester and Crook, Sands
and Kaye in Liverpool figured as protagonists in the disputes of
1834–5. These Wesleyan Tories subscribed to a political philo-
sophy based on a hierarchical view of society and a patriarchal
attitude towards authority. They derived their political education
from the narrow confines of an evangelical faith rather than
through contact with secular schools of thought, and neither their
background nor current events inclined them towards the spon-
sorship of new or revived forms of political dissent. On the contrary, both foreign and domestic revolutionary disturbances
confirmed their worst suspicions of social forces that threatened
the very fabric of Church and State. Moreover their highly-
developed conservative theology and understanding of the human
condition worked against any notion of beneficial changes arising
out of a restructuring of society.

On most occasions the Wesleyan Tories explained their behaviour by reference to religious as opposed to political motives.
They discountenanced political strife and invariably fought shy
of party labels, mainly because they saw politics in the one-sided
terms of a Tory establishment which, by virtue of its peculiarly
native and time-honoured qualities, rendered unnecessary an
alternative form of government. Hence party politics were usually
stigmatised as the creation of an unruly and irreligious opposition which could be counteracted only by needful duty and un-
sullied principles. The importance of personal qualities, religious
principles and denominational considerations often seemed to cut
across the grain of political bitterness and in-fighting which invited sordid compromise and petty intrigue. Scornful of the seamy
side of political life, Wesleyan leaders liked to boast that they
neither made enemies nor lost friends as a result of their public
engagements, and as one of the anti-Association pamphlets declared, 'The Connexion fears no democratic rage, and courts no
aristocratic smile; the friend of all, the enemy of none'.[7] Such

professions and apparently exemplary conduct were viewed otherwise by opponents who claimed that the facade concealed a minor political machine for the exclusive use of one party. A Manchester correspondent sought to expose the dissembling character of the local Wesleyan Tories when he remarked 'And yet you and your friends are no party politicians – not you indeed, your sublimated spirits cannot breathe in so murky a region. . . . It is a notorious fact that there are among you some of the most devoted, hardy and active politicians to be found in the country'.[8] Although they were party activists, most of the outstanding members of this group failed to become influential figures in their own right. Often they lacked sufficient breadth of interest or experience to appeal to a wide public, as James Wood discovered when he contested the Ashton-under-Lyne parliamentary election in 1837. During the Manchester election campaign of 1832 Wood had been proposed as a possible candidate at the head of a radical working class-Tory manufacturer coalition, but this was always an unlikely arrangement for one who had so ruthlessly opposed working class leaders during the Peterloo period. At Ashton, Wood evidently hoped to seek revenge for the way in which his rivals, Joseph Stephens and Charles Hindley, had been associated with recent Wesleyan disputes; Hindley, a radical millowner, had lent assistance to the Association. Neither his intentions nor his programme won popularity. And in Liverpool the character of local politics and society told against any Wesleyan figure who aspired to join the upper echelons of the Tory establishment and yet found himself in no man's land surrounded by hostile faces or, at best, lukewarm friends.

In the familiar surroundings of the chapel, however, the Tories enjoyed more promising conditions for exercising power and influence. They had been accustomed to little more than sporadic opposition in this situation and even in troublous times they overwhelmed dissentient opinion and produced an impressive set of loyal addresses. The seemingly natural identification of personal views with the general good almost disguised the projection of a particular political image, at least until serious internal conflict threatened to undermine their authority and induced them to play a more overtly political role. Previously latent influences now became manifestly partisan as battle-lines were drawn according to political opinions. For although each party disclaimed any political motives and generally attributed such to its antagonist, the case for a certain church order owed much to contrasting political values. In the belief that the opposition was grounded on misguided and intolerable political principles, the Wesleyan Tories often employed three main arguments. First, they insisted that Methodism was not responsible for party and antipatriotic politics but was instead the victim of such external influences. Thus the Kilhamites had attempted to import French revolutionary thought into the chapels just as later reformers were infected by a form of independence that was sweeping aside all subordination and control in society. Secondly, there was a broad attack on the democratic notions and levelling principles of the agitators. The so-called 'fungus of democracy' signified a complete disregard for legitimate authority and a denial of mixed government in favour of rule by one class; on these grounds appeals for liberty merely concealed the despotism of the multitude. Thirdly and most importantly reformist propositions betrayed a fundamental misconception of the ties between ministers and people. It was maintained that the reformers, whose 'brains teem with ideal pictures of constitutions, laws, churches, governments . . .', singularly failed to appreciate that the relationship between ministers and people had an entirely different character from relations between civil governments and people. For besides the voluntary basis of a religious community, the particular responsibility of the Wesleyan minister could not be likened to secular arrangements, since the Pastoral Office 'is not conferred at the hustings, and renewable at the will of the constituency conferring it'.[9]

The political sympathies of the Free Methodists were evident before the polarising effects of agitation. In the parliamentary election of 1832 the prospective Associationists gave solid support to the Whig candidates, and the Wesleyan Reformers also belonged to the body of Gladstonian liberals in the making. In both cases there existed a critical attitude towards any institution or measure which undermined religious and civil liberties or strayed far from the dissenters' emphasis on the primacy of conscience in religion and politics. Clashes with the Wesleyan authorities facilitated a more precise definition of this attitude, particularly when the pronounced political views of opponents dispelled all hope of a sympathetic hearing. In the early stages of controversy when there were few clear impressions of an alternative system, the Free Methodists saw themselves as the casualties of an ecclesiastical junto whose ready response to the first signs of trouble was to classify all critics as dangerous political rebels. Irritation soon turned to anger when complaints met the oft-repeated argument that Wesleyanism could not abandon itself to a politically-inspired faction. The Free Methodists maintained that they were not the chief offenders in the first instance, and they referred to the actions of the Conference leadership in order to prove the point.

There were various shades of opinion concerning the position of Conference and the political behaviour of some of its leading figures. The first and least common view focussed attention on the right or duty of Conference to make political pronouncements. While some individuals held that Conference had been far too aloof especially during periods of serious unrest, others opined that there had been a dangerously increasing volume of instructions from the same source. This second type of criticism was voiced by Richard Farrar, the Liverpool leader, who argued that an understandable concern for slavery had encouraged Conference to take an ever-widening and more contentious interest in other matters. A larger body of opinion rarely objected to Conference's right to make political statements but disapproved of pastoral letters that revealed a conservative disposition. The tone and substance of such addresses gave credence to the belief that the connexional hierarchy upheld what was called the passive obedience and non-resistance theory or what was reduced to the simple formula 'vote for the Conservatives: or meddle not with those given to change'.[10]

The question as to whether Conference welcomed any contact with political life or implicitly accepted certain values scarcely occurred to some of its most vociferous critics who were convinced that Conference operated as a 'Tory political union' on the wrong side of the political divide.[11] Upholders of such a view were less inclined to regard themselves as escapees from a religious community based on the chiliasm of despair than as angry spectators of a clerical body which had its roots in an offensive though nevertheless contemporary political order. Detailed charges usually related to individual ministers like Bunting who was commonly represented as a major opponent of liberal aspirations. If Bunting's views were less rigid than was supposed at times and he had reservations about official involvement in political matters,[12] some of his actions nevertheless appeared to offer sufficient proof of determined partisanship, not least when he and one of his colleagues voted for the moderate Tory candidate, Lord Sandon, in the Liverpool election of 1832. Both the *Circular* and the *Christian Advocate* seized on this act to show that, notwithstanding official advice to pay a conscientious and paramount regard to the slave question, the leadership had demonstrated its true political colours by voting for a gradual rather than immediate emancipationist. The opinions and activities of other ministers intensified suspicions of a Tory-dominated ministry. During the early 1830s Samuel Dunn, a staunch Tory, advised one of the Oldham Street leaders 'to have nothing to do with politics, and especially with the Liberal party',[13] and shortly afterwards, in the midst of his difficult superintendency as successor to Warren, Newton found time to campaign for the Tories against Lord John Russell in the Tavistock constituency. There were of course liberal ministers like Galland and Beaumont, yet they were engaged in an uphill struggle during the 'thirties when the conservative *Watchman* reflected the political views of the Buntingites.

While the party loyalties of ministers provoked adverse comment, Free Methodism also constituted a positive attempt to construct a church order that conformed to a certain set of political beliefs. In this respect the connection between liberal opinion and opposition to Wesleyan government persisted throughout the Association and Reform agitations. A *Circular* editorial made the point and posed the question,

This is the age of reform, every institution is feeling its renovating power, even those deemed most sacred and most ancient are giving up their new, extraneous and injurious redundancies. . . . And why shall not the spirit of reform penetrate even to the Wesleyan Methodist Conference?[14]

Almost twenty years later William Martin, the Manchester Reformer, set denominational squabbles in an even wider context when he criticised Wesleyan government against the background of a strife-torn continent,

Christianity does not merely conform to existing political conditions, it does more. It contributes to the due development of all the political elements existing in society, and consequently to that of democracy among the rest. . . . Despotism of every kind is tottering to its fall. The reign of priestcraft is drawing to a close.[15]

A direct link was thus discerned between political developments and ecclesiastical conflict, and even when events fell short of Martin's expectations and the exiled Kossuth visited England in 1851 the *Wesleyan Times* observed 'It seems a natural transition from the cause of liberty in Hungary to the same cause in Methodism'.[16] At the very least all reformers shared the view that Wesleyan government was at variance with their constitutional and legal rights as citizens. They never ceased to point out that, contrary to the Wesleyan system, each order in society had a voice through its representatives in important transactions, that English law did not permit one man to act as prosecutor, jury and judge, and that the humblest individual could petition monarch and parliament while 'the high and mighty Conference is unapproachable either by petition or otherwise'.

Local conditions gave rise to important nuances as each town had a distinctive political culture that left its mark on the protest movement. In Manchester the conservative character of the Association had its roots in a type of immature liberalism that contrasted with the polished Toryism of certain opponents. Unlike some co-agitators elsewhere the Oldham Street rebels seldom claimed that the source or solution of their grievances had much to do with recent political happenings. Certainly lay delegation involved a shift from restoration to reform, but what distinguished the Manchester Association was a large degree of political inexperience and as much concern for a general loss of prestige as an unrestrained desire to extend the principle of newly-won political rights to the denominational arena. Frequent references to the original but now abused Wesleyan constitution bore a closer resemblance to the tone of the Tory radical than the style of the thoroughgoing reformer. Moreover general interest in political activities was limited before 1835, and while there was no sympathy for the Tory cause nor were there any established contacts with the Whig hierarchy. A sharper definition of political views and a closer alignment with certain sections of opinion often occurred in the aftermath of secession, and even then the range of interest was restricted by individual preferences. Three Association leaders served on the town council in the period 1840–60, but none was renowned for attachment to a major political reform. Temperance politics and sabbatarian campaigns generally formed the limits beyond which they lost interest in public debate. Matthew Thackray waged a vigorous war against beerhouses as an active member of the Watch Committee, Miles Craston was a notable campaigner against Sunday trading, and John Kirkham unsuccessfully sought re-election to the council on a purely teetotal platform.

Most of the Manchester Associationists shared the opinions of the middle-class radical Archibald Prentice, the editor of the *Manchester Times*. Besides general support for the Association, Prentice himself had little liking for Wesleyan leaders whom he classified as 'bitter Tories'. In 1832 he had clashed with some of these leaders when he had led the Chorlton Row leypayers in a conflict with the commissioners; on this occasion several Wesleyan Tories, notably James Wood, John Marsden and Joshua Westhead, had acted on behalf of the commissioners and had refused to concede anything to the popular cause of the leypayers. The Associationists met the same fate, for they were quickly stigmatised as the allies and partisans of political agitation and their proposals were transformed into alarming visions of a secular republic replete with violent demagogues, pot-house orators and deluded followers. Part of one of the more polite pieces of Tory scurrility was intended to convey precisely this impression,

And various measures are projected
By rabble leaders thus collected
A constitution free is framed
Hesketh, their secretary named
And Warren President proclaim'd.   Poor Dr. Warren.[17]

Within weeks of Warren's suspension, moreover, the Manchester
preachers concluded that 'The restless and changeful spirit which
has so long been agitating the political world, is now attempting
to establish its domination over our Connexion, and to bring us
into bondage to the policy of this world.'[18] Yet few of the Association leaders bore much likeness to the political imputations
fastened on them by the Wesleyan hierarchy, and a non-political
protest was virtually impossible in this situation because of the
way in which Tories like Wood and Bunting chose to treat the
crisis.

Dissentient opinion in Liverpool encountered the same solid
resistance, only here there was a more politically motivated response amongst some of the young leaders of the Association.
Both the *Circular* and the *Watchman's Lantern* publicised demands that appeared to arise out of political imperatives. In frequent references to the value of reformist tendencies in society,
Rowland argued that Conference laws destroyed the rights of
'free-born Englishmen' at a time when 'Freedom, Freedom, is the
cry of every Christian and of every Briton'. And while Farrar
pointed to the recent and forthcoming benefits of the Reform Act
and the Municipal Corporation Bill in order to justify his conclusion that 'Everything is reformed, save the Methodist Conference', Picton welcomed the occasion of agitation to rid Wesleyanism of anti-democratic spirit and priestcraft so that it might
be 'assimilated to a secular republic'.[19] Although less extreme than
Picton in their political opinions, some of the Reformers were
also aware of the relationship between the general appeal of new
political forces and the particular condition of church polity. The
leader of the Reform party, John Burrows, found that some of his
activities as Vice-President of the local Peace Society and more
especially as a befriender of continental liberals on the run not
only went beyond the conventional behaviour of a mid-nineteenth
century Wesleyan but had a direct bearing on his attitude towards
the character of connexional administration.

Decidedly political interpretations of the Association dispute
in Liverpool soon flowed from Wesleyan sources, and leading
Tories seized on disaffection as a means to extend their influence
over loyal Wesleyans whose political inclinations were different
from their own. The agitators were denounced as political devia-
tionists or as a bad radical faction, and since radicalism was normally equated with irreligion and with diverse ogres like Robert

Owen and Daniel O'Connell the agitators were vulnerable to a
two-pronged attack which was often mounted in a seemingly
non-partisan manner and yet skilfully executed to elicit the desired response. An *Illuminator* editorial vigorously denied any
Wesleyan bias towards a particular party when it commented,

We know of classes of religious persons who are all of one mind on
these questions—who congregate and unite to carry their favourite
views, and if poll-books were examined, would be found as nearly as
possible to have voted all on one side. This may be called a love of,
and the support of freedom; it is bigoted, sectarian, anti-rational, and
slavish subjection of soul and feeling to petty and party views and
interest. To this the agitators of the Wesleyan Society desire to reduce
you, our brethren.[20]

Such ostensible tolerance betrayed a strictly conservative if not
Tory predisposition. Familiar claims concerning a monopoly of
patriotism, of disinterested motives and of well-founded principles may have suggested otherwise, whereas the poll books actually disclosed solid Wesleyan support for the Tory candidates in
the Liverpool parliamentary elections of 1835 and 1837. Any
other outcome was unlikely in view of the enhanced authority
and party loyalties of laymen like Sands, Kaye, Crook and Atherton who were not only prominent critics of the Association but
also served the Tory cause on the town council. In particular,
Sands' sterling opposition to the Association was intensified by his
strong distaste for Whig opponents who, according to his own experience, exhibited the vile purposes of a deceitful and dishonest
party. Similarly Kaye, the proprietor of the Tory *Courier*, used
his press facilities to inveigh against the Association and to impress on his fellow Wesleyans the importance of party differences.

The Rochdale wing of the Free Methodist movement represented the least ambiguous and most determined attempt to carry
over certain political concepts into the organisation of the church.
In particular the local leadership demonstrated what exactly was
meant by references to democratic government both here and elsewhere. Democracy was in effect synonymous with the liberal
ideal of self-government and as such the concept took on a different meaning from that understood by working class radicals of
the 'thirties. Basically, appeals in favour of democratic values implied ecclesistical government by a responsible and educated lay
leadership, as was evident after 1835 when the tight control
exercised by the trustees and leaders reduced the popular Quarterly Meeting to executive impotence. The authority of a conclave
of ministers had been transferred to what could be construed as
an equally close-knit body of laymen. At the connexional level,
moreover, it was no accident that the first delegates' meeting de-

cided to restrict lay delegation to officers. Nor was it only the Wesleyans who claimed that the early organisation of the Association consisted of self-appointed bodies, for even the *Christian Advocate* complained that the Central Committee was a self-chosen lay oligarchy in that it was restricted to leaders who had attended the inaugural meeting.

In conjunction with the influence of political trends the agitation also arose out of an unrelieved sense of alienation from an organisation whose official attitude towards deviant political behaviour ranged from oppressive tolerance to outright opposition. Specific complaints were thus combined with a more general protest against the deadening effects of a Wesleyan upbringing that inhibited the expression of certain opinions. At the height of the first Reform Bill controversy Conference issued familiar advice, 'Let not worldly politics engross too much of your time and attention', yet persistent counselling of this kind often had the effect of directing political energies towards the achievement of changes in Wesleyan government. In 1804 an anonymous writer had argued that radical Methodists like Kilham and his associates had 'imbibed, in some measure, the disorganising spirit of the times' and had turned to reforming Methodism itself, largely because 'their religious economy prevented them from entering into the turbulent and dangerous field of politics'.[21] As a safety valve some forms of political activity might have reduced the intensity of internal controversy in so far as the hostile feeling which flared up in 1834 and 1849 may have burnt itself out in the proper forum. It was also possible that essentially political desires may have continued to find satisfaction within the organisation, had there been less stringent controls over various agencies like the Sunday schools. The Wesleyan establishment entertained no such notions and indeed several of their opponents would not have been retained even had it done so.

For some Free Methodists as for more famous erstwhile Methodists like Richard Oastler and Samuel Bamford, the abandonment of Wesleyanism signified the rejection of an entire system, of which the prevailing and distasteful climate of political opinion was but one aspect. Such individuals cast aside the allegedly unhealthy habit of viewing everything through denominational spectacles in the manner of one Manchester leader who was not content with the simple assertion that the Wesleyans had helped to combat crime and pauperism but proceeded to calculate how far they had thereby reduced the local rates. When set against the subsequent careers of men like James Picton and Charles Rawlins of Liverpool or Edward Taylor of Rochdale, the Association provided an appropriate platform to rebel against the galling experience of a strictly evangelical environment and to proceed on a course that led to a close relationship between radical politics and liberal theology. The fact that Rawlins became a Unitarian, that Taylor emerged as a radical politician of ill-defined theological views, and that Picton was convinced of the value of biblical criticism, was no doubt received by the Wesleyans as proof of their argument that liberal ideas would result in a latitudinarian attitude towards theological standards.

Most Associationists, however, did not follow the same path nor did their subsequent conduct confirm their opponents' suspicion that, as a motley group of politico-religionists, they would 'put away the authority of the Bible'.[22] Instead they exhibited a mood of resentment especially in Manchester and Liverpool where their protests were in part against a mainly non-participant political culture both within and beyond the chapel. Ministerial supervision and centralised control were viewed as a major attack on what Wesleyanism had come to represent in the opinion of some members. For besides its other functions the chapel had served as a political organism which facilitated the acquisition of various social skills and which was often viewed as the only available means for political expression, leadership and organisation. Associationists clearly believed that they were now deprived of such facilities whether in the official meeting where their managerial role was undermined by the minister or in the Sunday school which had always been supervised by laymen, some of whom regarded the institution as 'a secondary academy for the promotion of culture – or rather, perhaps, a sort of gymnasium for exercise in the arts of self-government and mutual improvement'.[23] Furthermore, the conflict in both towns also indicated how far general conditions restricted the expression of political feeling. As a minority movement ignored by political and social superiors, the Association tapped a reservoir of unsatisfied yearnings in these circumstances. Wesleyanism had provided some outlets for quasi-political campaigns in the recent past, yet the popular appeal or relevance of these movements had waned by the mid-1830s Moreover new causes like temperance or disestablishment constituted extra-mural activities that evoked no official sympathy. In its campaigning phase, at least, the Association often appeared as an ersatz political organisation. The introduction of political phraseology into an ecclesiastical setting filled a vacuum in the lives of individuals ordinarily denied political status and meaning. Some of the language and gestures of the political world were particularly evident in the adoption of an impressive though somewhat non-religious title like the Grand Central Association; Wesleyan critics were quick to draw parallels with the Catholic Association. Similarly the delegates proudly and frequently referred to the 'mandates' which, they claimed, had been bestowed upon them by 'numerous constituents', while public meetings often created an atmosphere akin to that of the hustings. The Rochdale Associationists, however, rarely displayed the same symptoms if only because of a different type of environment. They had less need of a national platform on which to voice their opinions, nor did they require a form of political entertainment to make up for the absence of the genuine article.

In the years immediately after the Association division the Wesleyan Tories so tightened their grip on local opinion that there were considerable changes in Wesleyan voting patterns. This development was most evident in Manchester where, seven years after expressing a decided preference for the Whigs, Wesleyan voters swung behind the Tory candidate in the parliamentary election of 1839. General and growing disenchantment with the Whig administration naturally enhanced Tory prospects. More particularly the education issue and a virulent anti-Catholic campaign gave the local Wesleyan Tories solid foundations in religious prejudice; they attacked the government's education proposals as the worst form of Whig treachery, 'a great and threatening evil' according to one petition, and they vied with the most active spokesmen in raising the loudest 'No Popery' cry from the Protestant Association platform. Wesleyan voters were also influenced by the fact that the Whig candidate, Robert Grey, was a Unitarian and that relations between the Wesleyans and the Unitarians had been recently strained by Lady Hewley's case.

But this consideration carried much less weight than internal conditions which worked to the advantage of the Tories. In the aftermath of 1835 loyal members were more susceptible to Tory appeals and clearly fearful of identification with the disreputable liberal opinions of the Associationists. With the exception of one or two Whig manufacturers like George Chappell, whose non-Wesleyan upbringing largely explains his antipathy to the 'church and Tory Wesleyans', the bulk of the membership was subjected to a barrage of propaganda that played on denominational sympathies and business interests. The election campaign itself had more than an ordinary amount of insidious influence and corruption, and some Wesleyans were charged with offences on both counts. Percy Bunting found himself at the centre of controversy when it was alleged that he had forged letters in order to ensure the absence of a number of Whig voters from the polls; evidently he possessed prior knowledge of the letters, although he was innocent of the charge. More orthodox electioneering techniques within the Wesleyan circles took the form of pro-Tory printed circulars as well as canvassing methods which, especially amongst the tradesmen and skilled artisan class, caused one Wesleyan to complain, 'This is the most unpleasant part of this kind of interference, and is evidently intended to put the poor elector into the very annoying position of violating his conscientious opinions, or of displeasing a customer.'[24] For the first time the local press referred to the Wesleyan body as a formidable political interest group which had become aware of its growing influence and was most responsive to the appeals of a particular party. The Tories had been unable to create this impression in 1832, but they benefited by the different circumstances of a post-secession age.

Similar developments occurred elsewhere. The Tory high command in Liverpool had no sooner hammered the Association by disclaiming political motives and denouncing individual reformers in the same breath than it began to ensure that the rank and file supported the Tory cause. Once secured this support was easier to maintain than in Manchester, largely on account of peculiar local conditions which made the town a stronghold of popular Toryism. In 1837 the connection between internal conflict and electoral behaviour caused one newspaper to comment on the extent to which both ministers and local preachers aimed 'to establish it as a principle in their Societies that every Wesleyan, to be comfortable among them, must be a Tory, and believe all the party say and do. . . .'.[25] There is no reason to suppose that such influence was ineffectual, however much the Whig press atempted to convince the Wesleyans of the errors of their political ways by periodic references to selected extracts from the works of John Wesley and Adam Clarke. Whereas a malicious Tory placard purportedly issued by the Unitarians and promising confiscation of all Wesleyan chapels for the Catholics had failed to win Wesleyan votes in 1832, the Tory leadership now turned the religious sympathies of Whig opponents into a party argument that impressed most Wesleyans. For the ordinary member who wished to retain a reputation for theological orthodoxy there were obvious dangers in alignment with a party that consisted of Unitarian leaders, Catholic followers and of course an assortment of Methodist rebels. Anti-Catholic opinion alone was sufficient to prevent any serious consideration of Whig claims, as evidenced in the parliamentary election of 1847 when a meeting of Wesleyans resolved to plump for the Orange candidate.

In Rochdale the Wesleyan rump of 1835 hardly constituted a sizeable section of the electorate, but here also internal conflict had an immediate political effect. Much attention was paid to the Methodist vote in the two parliamentary elections of 1837. The Tories had scored what proved to be a rare triumph in the election of 1835 when the reformers and radicals had been at loggerheads with each other. Only a handful of votes, however, separated the two parties, and the Tories fought hard to win the

Wesleyan vote and dared to hope for some support from the Association. Tory efforts met with a far more favourable response amongst the Wesleyans, some of whom were quite prepared to dissociate themselves from the party loyalties of the Associationists. This reaction was typical of the way in which local party political divisions were influenced less by class and occupation than by other factors such as religious loyalties.[26] Several election addresses were issued by Wesleyan Tories who presented themselves as the defenders of Protestantism; one such address maintained that the Wesleyan voter could not remain neutral in the contest and concluded that neutrality or, worse still, a vote for the Whigs 'would draw down the wrath of God upon our unhappy land'.[27] While some leading members like William Healey, an ex-Radical voter, did adopt a neutral position, most of the former Reform voters like Henry Cartwright, one of the main architects of the post-secession reconstruction period, now turned to the Tories. There was never any doubt about the party sympathies of the Associationists: 'Most of those who go to the Association chapel are Radicals, there are hardly any Tories amongst us' observed one of the first trustees.[28] Some of the Baillie Street leaders in fact countered Tory propaganda by satirical pieces on the political influence of the Wesleyan hierarchy and of Bunting in particular; part of one squib (see page ix) clearly indicated what the dutiful Wesleyan was expected to do,

Bid each of thy servants who values his place
In the eyes of his Master would wish to find grace,
To be and bestir him, and do what he can
To send Tory Royds as a Parliament man.[29]

Wesleyan Tory leaders had scarcely capitalised on a fortunate conjuncture of national and local events in the late 'thirties before massive support began to crumble and they themselves revised their political views. This reversal was most evident in Manchester where the parliamentary election of 1841 indicated that the Tories were unable to repeat the performance of 1839, even though they might have been expected to do so in view of the national trend. Nobody felt inclined to disagree with one correspondent in the *Manchester Guardian* who maintained that his fellow Wesleyans were far more likely to share liberal political views than Tory sympathies. Lord Ashley, indeed, made the same observation in a confidential letter to Jabez Bunting in which he predicted that the Whig candidate, Milner Gibson, 'will be returned to Parliament, I fear, by the votes of Wesleyans . . .'.[30] Certainly Wood, Westhead, Bunting and other Tory leaders made a determined bid for support. Once again the Whigs were attacked on the education issue, and an anonymous writer, who described Gibson as a contemptible person and clamorous deceiver, urged all Wesleyans not only to deny their votes to papists, socinians, and opponents of the Sabbath, Divine Providence and the Bible but to apply the test 'will you to the best of your power save me from being taxed to support Popery and Socinianism?' Moreover members were warned that, whatever might be their views on the Anti-Corn Law League, they would be ill-advised to set free trade before protestantism, as one leader presented the choice shortly afterwards. Such arguments had little impact on most Wesleyan voters, largely because the Tory leadership appeared to overreach itself. The triumph of 1839 had been secured at the expense of exposing supposedly religious motives as an increasingly shabby disguise, and liberal spokesmen were now far less prepared to allow the Tories to exploit 'religious politics' in order to further their partisan aims. Furthermore as the events of 1834–5 became more distant so there was a reversion to the political heterogeneity of the pre-secession period, unwittingly encouraged by certain leading ministers who made no secret of their disregard for the 'no politics rule'. In effect the constant harangues of unrepentant Tories like William Bunting and James Dixon, both of whom were stationed in Manchester in the periods 1838–41 and 1840–3 respectively, all too often proved counterproductive. Some members left their services in disgust and even an influential moderate Tory, Holland Hoole, had occasion to remind Bunting of the dangers involved in political allusions from the pulpit.[31]

Nothing was more ruinous to the cause of Wesleyan Toryism, however, than the performance of the Peel administration between 1841 and 1846. Tory policies roused furious opposition throughout the connexion. In particular, the education clauses of Graham's Factory Bill in 1843, the Dissenters' Chapels Act in 1844 and the proposal to increase the grant to the Maynooth Catholic College in 1845, all fell as hammerblows on Wesleyans of all political persuasions. Only a few stubborn Tories failed to oppose the education clauses and none was prepared to subsidise the Maynooth College. Party loyalties underwent dramatic changes in these circumstances. At the height of the Maynooth conflict William Bunting did not hesitate to declare his own position, 'I, who have taken some pains to lift the present Conservative party to power will, in my own place, as a Minister of religion, do my very best to help them out of power'.[32] Two years later his brother Percy, who was equally disenchanted by Tory measures, voted for John Bright in the Manchester parliamentary election of 1847. Similarly Joshua Westhead, who had once been called the keeper of the conscience of Sir George Murray (Tory candidate in the Manchester parliamentary election of 1839), threw his support behind any parliamentary candidate opposed to the Maynooth grant. Moreover Westhead embarked on his own political career at this time and showed how far the blurring of party lines after 1846 allowed for the development of a new political stance. He won the Knaresborough election in 1847 on the basis of an address in which he claimed that he was unable to describe his political opinions in conventional party terms, and ten years later he was returned as the liberal Member of Parliament for York.

Such changes marked the beginning of a more general trend relating to the disappearance of some of the older generation Tories and the emergence of less combative if not more liberal individuals. The death of James Wood in 1849 removed the linchpin of the traditional brand of Wesleyan Toryism in Manchester in much the same way as Thomas Sands, the comparable standardbearer in Liverpool, had a diminishing influence after his retirement from local politics in the mid-1840s. Their successors on the public platform lacked the features of party activists and instead they were imbued with a strong sense of disinterested civic duty. In the council chamber they avoided party conflict and appeared as fairly colourless characters. Robert Barnes of Manchester typified this new élite. During his period of office on the town council between 1848 and 1858 he was elected to the mayoralty on two successive occasions, largely because his non-party position suited the needs of the time. John Farnworth of Liverpool cut a similar figure as he, too, finally achieved the office of mayor in 1865 after ten years of council activities in which he rarely participated in council debates and in the course of one year intervened on only two occasions, once in defence of his own firm. His preoccupation with religious and charitable affairs and evident disdain for the hurly-burly of political life caused the *Porcupine*, the gadfly of many local worthies, to describe him as a person who was 'somewhat devoted to hobbies, and who regards his own mission as something less profane and mundane than the performance of mere municipal duties'.[33] Some of the Rochdale leaders belonged to the same mould, although few entered local politics and only one, James Booth, earned a reputation. Booth held the same political views as his relatives in the Association but possessed little of the avid political interest and pugnacity of the Baillie Street stock. He shunned controversial issues during his involvement in council affairs and devoted his time to the foundation of the Free Library.

This avoidance of partisanship created a situation in which young mid-century Wesleyans could begin to explore the territory of liberal politics within a less hostile climate of opinion. In the early years of his Manchester life Thomas Champness, the future connexional evangelist, found himself in sympathy with some of the Chartist demands, and he gained far more of his political education from Bright's speeches than from the *Watchman*. Likewise in the more persistently pro-Tory circles of Liverpool Wesleyanism there was still room for one of Champness' contemporaries, William Oulton, to commence a political career which in the first instance made him the acknowledged spokesman of the young radicals in the Junior Reform Club. While these Wesleyans had more in common with nonconformist liberalism than with 'Church and State' Toryism, their ideas were being shaped at a time when the Wesleyan Reform controversy offered the Tories a last chance to take advantage of internal conflict But although Reform leaders spoke the political language of their predecessors and the Tories did lead the current opposition to 'Papal Aggression', only in Manchester was there anything approaching a deliberate attempt to use the opinions of the Reformers in order to frighten Wesleyans into a conservative reaction. The leaders of this campaign were Percy Bunting, who had now overcome recent political doubts, and Peter Wood who inherited his father's political beliefs. Both men actively opposed Bright in the parliamentary election of 1852 to such an extent that the candidate attacked Bunting's 'determined and not very scrupulous opposition to the Whig government and Whig principles'.[34] Local Reformers lodged similar complaints against the way in which Bunting used his influence for party purposes, as in a much-reported case when he prevailed upon one of the leading ministers in the town to set an example by voting for the Tories. There was also evidence of what the Reformers viewed as the double standards of the ministers, particularly when George Osborn dismissed reformist opinion with the familiar argument that Wesleyanism had nothing to do with vote by ballot and universal suffrage. Osborn's emphasis on purely spiritual matters might have been heeded if some of his colleagues and himself had been more circumspect about their own political activities particularly in relation to education. Wesleyan opposition to the Lancashire Public School Association was effectively exploited for party purposes, since Bright was a leading member of the Association.

This minor repetition of past endeavours was yet another example of the effect of denominational troubles on Wesleyan political behaviour. Clearly, the monochrome political character of Free Methodism did prolong the supremacy of conservative elements within the parent body. Tory pressure, however, was never sufficiently strong nor durable to overwhelm all opposition, and consequently Wesleyanism always exhibited a greater variety of political opinion than Free Methodism. In the latter case a sect rather than church-type organisation was associated exclusively with liberal causes. Local conditions determined the nature and extent of any participation in public life, as illustrated by the contrast between Liverpool and Rochdale.

The major social and religious divisions in Liverpool left the Free Methodists in an anonymous position, simply excluded from the familiar and influential political categories. Consistent support for the Whigs failed to yield any contact with the well-defined coterie at the apex or the mass Irish support at the base of the party. It was only after the discovery of new denominational loyalties that some individuals acquired the necessary political qualifications. Hence the admission of Charles Rawlins to the upper echelons of the Whig party followed his move into the Unitarian community, and just as James Picton entered the town council after he had forsaken the Association for Independency so William Byrom did not become a skilled organiser in Tory ward committees until he had joined the Anglicans, after much, possibly instructive, experience of pressure group organisation in the disputes of 1834 and 1849. In these circumstances, therefore, the Association played an instrumental role in the articulation of political views that required new surroundings for full expression.

Even when abandonment of an ailing Association offered more inviting prospects for the furtherance of political careers, however, there could remain a sense of uncertainty or lack of identity with the forces that shaped civic life, as was evident in the twists and turns of Picton's pilgrimage. Denied some of the local recognition that he felt was his due, Picton ascribed to himself at different times the qualities of the municipal socialist, the radical, the moderate liberal and the non-party man. His son characterised his attitudes in later life as those of 'a philanthropic opportunist, anxious for social reform, but doubtful of the human material out of which reformers are made, or in which reformed institutions have to work',[35] and no doubt his early experiences in the Association contributed to the formation of such a judgment. However much he shifted his position or moved in new circles it proved difficult to shake off the description of himself by a social superior as a half-educated Methodist Radical. This was an unfair taunt in view of his cultural pursuits and pioneer work in the development of the Free Library. Moreover Picton did seek to expend political energies in the appropriate quarters, unlike some of his fellow agitators who attempted to do the same with less beneficial effect through their own ecclesiastical foundation. Political rabble-raising found little satisfaction in such close confines, as David Rowland's strife-ridden passage into eventual obscurity showed only too clearly.

By way of contrast the Rochdale Free Methodists figured at the head of the town's big battalions and virtually turned Baillie

Street into the stronghold of local liberalism. Unlike the rest of
the religious denominations, the Association contained a rich
blend of reformist and radical opinion that formed the stuffing of
local politics. Other bodies like the Unitarians may have attracted more working class radicals but none took in a cross-
section of opinion that included Edward Taylor, who could be
bracketed with the more popular radical spokesman Thomas
Livesey, and John Petrie one of the doyens of the manufacturing
class and member of the General Council of the Anti-Corn Law
League. At a general level they were protagonists of the Liberal
Party as it appeared in the 1870s rather than defenders of the
Whig administrations of the 1830s. They cut their political teeth
on the first Reform Bill agitation, fully expressed their political
and social ideals through organisations like the Literary and
Philosophical Society and the Reform Association, and soon afterwards joined and gradually dominated the Board of Commissioners. In the second half of the century they formed an unrivalled army of civic leaders. During the period 1856 to 1893
Free Methodists held mayoral office on sixteen occasions and
monopolised the post between 1878 and 1884. Moreover prominence in the council chamber was matched by considerable
influence in parliamentary politics. In a town where the Tories
won only three parliamentary elections in the sixty years after
1832, none of the Liberal candidates like Edward Miall and
Richard Cobden could afford to ignore the views of many of their
chief backers who had Free Methodist connections.

The eldest son of John Petrie, James (1814–92), was a typical
product of the Baillie Street leadership, exceptional only in so far
as he never served on the town council. His political views and
activities were summarised by his obituarist,

he was a staunch Radical Reformer and a loyal member of the Reform Association. There was no truer Radical in Rochdale than Mr
James Petrie, and his political faith remained firm to the end, for he
followed Mr Gladstone with confidence on the question of Home
Rule. . . .[36]

Radical and reform emphases were not always as easily combined
as was suggested here. The Baillie Street leadership shared a common belief in the union of the industrial classes, and while John
Petrie, as local President of the League, emphasised that the
organisation was designed to harmonise middle class and working
class interests Oliver Ormerod and John Ashworth pressed the
same case as leaders of the local Complete Suffrage Union. It was
particularly difficult to uphold this view in periods of economic
distress and social unrest, yet the tensions between radical and
reformist opinion, which periodically burst into open conflict, did

not destroy the Reform Association, an organisation designed to provide a united opposition to the Tories. Baillie Street reflected some of these differences, particularly in the disputes of the early 1850s. One of the main consequences of the Holland Street division was that some of the leading Associationists lost contact with radicals like Taylor who joined the independent congregation. During the incorporation controversy of 1856, in fact, representatives of the two bodies found themselves on opposite sides. The Holland Street leadership supported the popular cause of an extended franchise, and George Ashworth thus secured a seat on the new council. The Association leaders, however, were classified as liberal Tories because of their refusal to contemplate any such proposal, and accordingly they experienced a rare defeat in the first elections to the new council.

In conclusion the political differences that underlay and in part accounted for Wesleyan troubles signified a conflict between the supporters of a conservative order and the advocates of political change. During the course of this struggle the fragile 'no politics rule' was disregarded by individuals who believed that religion and politics were inseparable whether in relation to the character of ecclesiastical institutions or with reference to the purpose and policy of civil government. Thus the real distinction between James Wood and James Picton, for example, lay in their positions at different ends of the political spectrum; neither individual could resist the temptation to justify his own conduct in political terms. It was understandable that the Tories sometimes mistook party interests for the greater connexional good, if only because they viewed the 'no politics rule' as an expression of their own political opinions. There was therefore no room for party politics in pulpit or vestry, since the Tories believed that by definition Wesleyanism belonged to their own side of the political fence. Once this assumption was challenged they were duty-bound to dismiss the rebels, even if they dropped their most useful guise in the process.

REFERENCES

[1] *Illuminator* 18 November 1835.

[2] *Minutes of the Wesleyan Association Annual Assembly of 1839*, p. 27.

[3] B. Gregory, *op. cit.*, p. 164.

[4] D. O'Connell, *A Second Letter to the Ministers and Office-bearers of the Wesleyan Methodist Societies of Manchester* (Manchester, 1839), p. 8.

[5] *Manchester Guardian* 21 August 1841.

[6] For the electoral behaviour of the Wesleyan and Association leadership, see the appendix and my thesis, 'Methodist secessions and social conflict in South Lancashire, 1830–1857', Manchester Ph.D. thesis, 1966). Voting lists in the thesis are based on the poll books for the following parliamentary elections: Liverpool 1832, 1835, 1837 and 1853, Manchester 1832 and 1839, and Rochdale 1832, 1837, 1841, 1852 and 1857.

[7] C. Welch, *The Wesleyan crisis: or, the coexistence of Wesleyan Methodism, and the 'Central Association', totally incompatible* (London, 1835), p. 57.

[8] *Manchester Times* 10 July 1841.

[9] *Illuminator* 4 March 1835.

[10] *Manchester Times* 5 August 1837.

[11] *Watchman's Lantern* 31 December 1834.

[12] See MSS. J. Bunting to M. Tobias, 23 February 1829; J. Bunting to J. Beecham, 19 February 1833.

[13] J. T. Slugg, *Reminiscences of Manchester fifty years ago* (Manchester and London, 1881), p. 153.

[14] *Circular* 30 June 1831.

[15] *Wesleyan Times* 18 March 1850.

[16] *Ibid.*, 3 November 1851.

[17] MSS. An anticipatory epitaph on Dr Warren.

[18] *Statement of the Preachers of the Manchester District* (Manchester, 1834). p. 13.

[19] *Watchman's Lantern* 21 October 1835; J. A. Picton, *op. cit.*, p. 136.

[20] *Illuminator* 18 November 1835.

[21] A Careful Observer, *Strictures on Methodism* (London, 1804), pp. 77–8, 85.

[22] *Illuminator* 4 November 1835.

[23] J. A. Picton, *op. cit.*, p. 68.

[24] *Manchester Guardian* 4 September 1839.

[25] *Liverpool Mercury* 1 September 1837.

[26] See J. Vincent, *The Formation of the Liberal Party, 1857–1868* (London, 1966), pp. 96–118.

[27] *Rochdale Poll Book* 1837.

[28] *The Methodist Church, Baillie Street, Rochdale. A centenary history, 1837–1937* (Rochdale, 1937), pp. 14–15.

[29] *Rochdale Poll Book* 1837.

[30] *Manchester Guardian* 28 June 1841; MSS. Lord Ashley to Jabez Bunting, 11 July 1841.

[31] A Wesleyan, *Whig-Radicalism v. Wesleyan-Methodism; or sayings and doings of certain liberal divines and statesmen, touching the Wesleyans and Methodism* (London, 1841), p. 32; *Manchester Guardian* 16 April 1845, 22 February 1840.

[32] *Proceedings of the Anti-Maynooth Conference of 1845*, ed. A. S. Thelwall (London, 1845), p. 164.

[33] *Porcupine* 29 September 1866.

[34] *Manchester Guardian* 26 June 1852.

[35] J. A. Picton, *op. cit.*, p. 298.

[36] *Rochdale Observer* 22 June 1892.

CHAPTER 7

CONFLICTING SOCIAL INTERESTS

In conjunction with the worst influences of secular politics Wesleyan spokesmen also detected dangerous tendencies in some of the popular causes of the Free Methodists. Different assessments of the purpose and value of several institutions contributed to the division and subsequently shaped contrasting policies. Three issues assumed particular importance, for opposing views on education, on the Church of England and on teetotalism amounted to a major disagreement over the proper response to matters of public interest.

The connection between the introduction of the Theological Institution and the formation of the Association was only the most obvious aspect of a conflict concerning the use and organisation of educational facilities. Although certain conservative and revivalist elements objected to the academic purpose of the Institution, much of the opposition viewed the enterprise as a means of reinforcing the ministerial hierarchy. Moreover criticism of learned expositions from the pulpits of wealthy chapels usually demonstrated class differences rather than a lack of educational aspirations; the *Circular*, for example, complained of a modest scheme for the instruction of young ministers yet admitted no inconsistency in its accompanying plea for 'educated and studious local preachers'.[1] In any event the question of ministerial training often generated far less friction than the control and status of local agencies responsible for elementary education, and Bunting faced much sterner resistance as the architect of Sunday school policy than as the President of the Institution.

The early nineteenth-century Sunday school popularised Wesleyanism to a far greater extent than any other single institution. By 1840, after fifty years of rapid expansion, the connexion contained 3,019 Sunday schools, 57,181 teachers and 328,056 scholars.[2] Early development raised acute problems of management. The schools could be made to serve a number of religious, social and educational functions. Furthermore their predominantly lay and local character was not only more marked than that of the chapel but also represented both a challenge to ministerial leadership and a possible source of support for any dissident group. During the 1820s connexional policy was mainly influenced by arguments in favour of regulations to counteract the often undenominational, civic and quasi-independent status of the schools. After several pronouncements the Conference of 1827 issued a comprehensive directive that reiterated an earlier ban on instruction in writing, that emphasised the need to vest school premises in chapel trustees, and that insisted on the formation of new school committees consisting of Wesleyan majorities. In South Lancashire, the heartland of the Sunday school movement, opposition to such measures was particularly strong in Manchester and Rochdale.

The Manchester schools had been formed as a result of an undenominational initiative in 1784 when Anglicans, Dissenters and Roman Catholics established a committee and appealed for public subscriptions. This venture fell foul of denominational rivalries, and the Anglicans withdrew in 1800 while the Dissenters organised a Sunday School Union in 1824. In the meantime the schools were largely financed and manned by Wesleyans, and it was customary for scholars to attend a Methodist chapel once monthly. Although the schools remained public institutions beyond Wesleyan jurisdiction, the circuit authorities began to ignore this consideration and in the Peterloo crisis refused admission to any teacher or scholar who sported political badges. This action was the prelude to a more intensive effort to gain control of the schools. Much of the support for reorganisation came from preachers like John Riles who, in 1824, complained of the absence of Wesleyan schools in Salford and claimed that the Sunday school party was 'doing more harm than good' in view of its lack of contact with the chapel and its insufficient respect for the ministers.[3] As superintendent of the Manchester South circuit two years later, Bunting pressed the case for full incorporation of the schools into the Wesleyan system on the grounds that all trace of an undenominational enterprise had vanished and that the present arrangement hoaxed the public and provided inadequate supervision.

At the circuit meeting in which he first raised the subject, Bunting encountered strong opposition on all sides. Members of the schools committee, annually elected by subscribers and friends, maintained that they were bound by the deeds to act as servants and stewards of the public and insisted that the presence of a large number of Wesleyan teachers guaranteed the sound condition of the schools. Some of the teachers themselves were even more strongly critical of the proposal and particularly objected to the view that ministerial intervention was required in order to ensure that the Sunday school leaders – superintendents, conductors and teachers – properly discharged their duties. There was, besides, a considerable body of opposition amongst the chapel trustees. Of the twenty-four Oxford Road and Irwell Street trustees, eighteen rejected the proposal partly because they were alarmed by the prospect of additional financial responsibilities for the schools and partly because they had no sympathy for schools which were susceptible to periodic outbursts of radical opinion. It was also recognised that closer ties between the chapels and the schools meant more frequent attendance by the children at Sunday services and this presented the unwelcome possibility of disorderly scholars apparently uninfluenced by the well-developed system of rewards and punishments; good attendance and conduct were generally rewarded by promotion to one of the select classes or to the post of monitor, by admission to the weeknight writing class and by membership of the school library, while misbehaviour was punishable by various means as at the London Road school, the second largest in the town, where the cane was administered by the school visitor and persistent offenders had their names entered in a black book 'and read from the pulpit and if found entered there three times shall be marched to the door by six of their own classmates and there publicly expelled'.[4]

Despite this opposition it was clear that the already parlous state of school funds could be combined with veiled threats to discontinue Wesleyan contributions in order to promote the required changes. The preachers were so successful in applying this pressure that by 1830 the finances had deteriorated to such an extent that the committee finally accepted its inability to maintain the schools except in the service of exclusively Wesleyan interests. A few of the schools had already been purchased by the Wesleyans at knock-down prices, and the rest were now reorganised as 'The Sunday Schools for children of all denominations in connexion with the Wesleyan Methodist Society'. The management of the schools was transferred to a new committee which was dominated by members of the Society, was presided over by the superintendent minister, and was attended by all preachers.

Public opposition to this change surfaced in 1834, by which time the Wesleyans supervised eighteen schools and 9,066 scholars while only the Anglicans had a slightly larger establishment.[5] Many of the members of the Association were closely identified with the old undenominational schools and like some of the teachers, who had no Wesleyan affiliations, they resented the imposition of denominational control and seized the opportunity to contest the decision of 1830. In the ensuing conflict the Wesleyans kept the property but lost a substantial number of conductors, teachers and scholars. In the Oldham Street circuit the Tib Street school, the first temporary headquarters of the rebel leaders, and the David Street school, the venue of the inaugural meeting of the Association, were eventually re-occupied as empty buildings. In the Irwell Street circuit Grindrod swiftly ousted all Association teachers, many of whom complained that he had never set foot in the schools in the previous two years; the number of scholars consequently declined from 3,142 to 2,182 in the period 1829–37. Much of the general agitation in the Grosvenor Street circuit was associated with the schools, and a large majority of the teachers and scholars, 100 and 800 respectively at London Road and sixty and 800 respectively at Chancery Lane, joined the Association. In both cases there were fierce contests over equipment especially in connection with one of the most prized possessions, the school library, which was entirely financed out of the subscriptions of teachers and scholars. The Wesleyans kept control, largely because they commanded majorities in the circuit Sunday school committee where the subscribers, many of whom were not actively involved in the schools, outvoted a majority of the teachers. Large losses were also reported in some of the outlying schools as at Blackley and Moston where the entire body of teachers and scholars went over to the Association.

The size of Association gains became apparent in 1836–7. In February 1836 there was a major bid to end the Wesleyan occupation of the old undenominational schools, and at the annual meeting of subscribers and officers of these schools the Wesleyan contingent only narrowly defeated an Association amendment to allow non-Wesleyan conductors in the schools. All Association leaders were removed from office and now concentrated on their own school system which included twenty-four schools and 6,500 scholars by 1837, the fourth largest unit in the town. The subsequent decline in the number of scholars to 4,976 by 1854 was less dramatic than the contraction in membership and was in part due to the fact that one of the largest schools, Bank Meadow, eventually fell into Wesleyan hands.

Initially the Association provided schools that were less orientated towards denominational and religious interests than the Wesleyan institutions. After 1835 the officers and teachers of Wesleyan schools were almost entirely members of the Society. Supported by teachers who had never belonged to the Society, however, the Association attracted an assortment of leaders; in 1845 the Grosvenor Street circuit schools were managed by 165 officers and teachers, of whom 114 were members of the Association or of another denomination. There was also a different attitude towards the provision of secular education. Sunday writing lessons had been a short-lived feature of the undenominational schools. The opposition of the preachers to such instruction had long been viewed in some quarters as a blow against the education of the poor, particularly since the schools catered for the children of poor parents and the preachers had shown no interest in campaigning for a shortening of the working day in order to facilitate attendance at weeknight schools. Nor did the wealthy Wesleyans see any reason to subsidise writing lessons in the schools; some maintained their own factory schools and all sent their own children to respectable day schools. The Wesleyan schools served solely religious functions or were gradually obliged to do so where, as at Middleton, it was reported in 1839 that the contributions to school funds from the wealthy members had fallen off because of the refusal to give up Sunday writing. Meanwhile the Association schools pursued more expansive designs, 'in our Sabbath Schools' commented one of the leaders 'we not only taught reading and writing, but in some instances grammar, arithmetic, and the higher branches of the mathematics . . .'.[6] In the short run this emphasis may have given the Association a competitive advantage over its Wesleyan rivals but in the long run it reinforced support for a voluntaryist system whose defects were more quickly and clearly discerned by the Wesleyans.

While the Wesleyans were assimilating the undenominational schools in Manchester, the Sunday school interest in Rochdale steadfastly refused to contemplate any changes that undermined the valued independence of the schools. The first school in Rochdale had been opened by James Hamilton, a tin-plate worker, in 1784. As a result of Wesleyan support the school was soon removed to the Toad Lane chapel and later transferred to Union Street. During the period 1800–20 the Union Street school underwent rapid expansion, attracting seventy teachers and 1,235 scholars by 1806, and also organised and financed sixteen schools in the neighbourhood. There were two main reasons for this success. First there was no major rival. The Anglicans failed to provide any school facilities until 1843 and showed little interest in the Union Street project. During the 1800s, in fact, the parish church authorities were so appalled by the presence of noisy scholars in the morning services that the practice was soon discontinued and instead it was resolved that 'the Children go into the Chapel to receive instruction by way of exhortation from some of the local preachers'.[7] Secondly, the school always maintained a civic character in that it avoided denominational regulations, provided both secular and religious instruction, and recruited teachers on the basis of sound moral character and religious principle. Thus the school officers always insisted that the school existed for the education of children of parents of all denominations and that the children were free to attend any place of worship.

Amongst the teachers there were different views of the instrumental value of the school; the extension of elementary education, the inculcation of moral standards and the propagation of religious beliefs attracted varying degrees of interest. All teachers, however, were determined to ensure that 'no general rule or rules be made for the government of the schools but by the quarterly meeting of the teachers', and consequently the Conference regulations of 1827 were so unacceptable that it was not until December 1835, in the aftermath of the Union Street division, that the new Wesleyan trustees seized the opportunity to implement official policy. A substantial majority of the teachers protested against such interference and claimed that 'the school was built by them and secured to them in equity by the agreement with the trustees . . .'.[8] The teachers had entered into negotiations with the trustees in 1818, when the possibility of a new school building was first raised, and they had concluded an agreement in 1822 whereby they bore the cost of erection while the trustees rented out the land and recognised the independence of the school. But this agreement had never been stamped and was therefore void in law. Once it was clear that the teachers were unwilling to acquiesce in the new regulations the superintendent minister promptly barred their entry to the school, whereupon virtually the whole establishment, 100 teachers and 1,000 scholars, joined the seceders at Hoyle's warehouse. After similar school divisions elsewhere in the locality, the Association eventually accommodated the largest local school system, comprising twelve schools and 5,560 scholars by 1837. Both secular education and the independence of the schools were preserved under this arrangement until the 1840s when the circuit authorities established formal links with the schools.[9]

Whereas child employment in the textile towns facilitated the proliferation of Sunday schools and restricted the growth of day schools, the situation in Liverpool allowed for a different set of priorities. The Conference regulations of 1827 presented no problems here, since the Sunday schools had always been denominational institutions. These schools rarely enjoyed substantial official support, and by 1830 only two of the main chapels, Brunswick and Leeds Street, provided accommodation. There was a much greater degree of interest in the day schools which were established at Leeds Street (1815), Jordan Street (1819) and Brunswick (1826), in addition to which the Society financed the first deaf and dumb school in the town in 1823. Such facilities offered 'a more efficient method of promoting our interest than the Sunday schools', and by 1825 the day schools attracted a larger number of scholars, 1,420, than the Sunday schools, 1,000. All schools were supervised by the day school committee which largely consisted of ministers and chapel trustees. In 1830, however, a Sunday school committee was formed in order to boost the declining membership.

The new committee put on such an effective recruiting drive

that the number of Sunday schools and scholars increased from 7 to 13 and from 709 to 1,859 respectively in the period 1830-5. Although previously denied official representation the teachers elected most of the committee, and by 1834 the Leeds Street teachers, in particular, occupied a dominant position. Wealthy laymen and ministers alike were now strongly criticised for their neglect of the schools; the former had singularly failed to offer any assistance while the ministers, it was noted, all too often occupied the Sunday dinner tables of their influential friends but rarely visited or encouraged the 'low set' of teachers. Such complaints were scarcely consistent with the anti-clerical views of the schools as 'nurseries of independent thought and manly feeling', yet they had a telling effect and forced the Wesleyan leadership to take drastic action in order to unseat the Associationist members of the committee. The committee was dissolved and the pre-1830 controls were restored in January 1835. As elsewhere the Association failed to secure the property but gained a large number of teachers and scholars; it had seven schools and 1,177 scholars by 1837 and later maintained its position as the fourth largest Sunday school organisation in the town, despite ever dwindling congregations.

Besides the Sunday school conflict, day school policy also revealed considerable differences between the Wesleyans and Free Methodists. On the formation of the Wesleyan Education Committee in 1838 there were only nine infant schools and twenty-two day schools throughout the connexion; Manchester had no such schools and Rochdale possessed only one small cause at Bagslate. The immediate concern of the Committee was to oppose government schemes. In 1839 massive petitions were returned against Whig plans for a normal school based on the Irish scheme of 1831 with provision for denominational and undenominational instruction. Four years later there were equally hostile reactions to Graham's Factory Education Bill with its heavy weighting towards the church. The corollary of the rejection of government proposals was the provision of denominational schools on a voluntaryist basis. In 1843 the connexional management made an appeal for £200,000 in order to build 700 schools by the end of the decade, but it was evident that the resources did not exist for such a massive programme; only 200 schools were functioning by 1850. The tardy response to this appeal was largely due to the fact that the Centenary Fund had recently attracted large subscriptions and that the deepening of the commercial depression had dire effects. James Fildes, a Manchester wholesale grocer and long-standing superintendent of the London Road Sunday school, reminded Bunting of the reduced circumstances of many members at this time when he declined to make further contributions to the connexional coffers, 'the cloud is still thick upon us. . . . I really must also be excused giving you the names of friends to apply to. These times one scarcely knows the position of one's nearest and dearest relations and friends'.[10]

Existing day schools, moreover, clearly demonstrated the principal weaknesses of voluntaryism. The Jordan Street school in Liverpool had once numbered its scholars in hundreds and was originally one of the most advanced local institutions of its kind, yet it had fallen on hard times by the mid-1840s when it was reported that costly and inferior education, uncertain financial support, defective discipline, and poor, irregular attendances, all contributed to a most unsatisfactory state of affairs. By 1850 the Manchester Wesleyans had opened six schools comprising 1,277 scholars, but only the prestigious Rusholme Road schools secured a considerable degree of support. Meanwhile some of the leading Whig sympathisers at the Oxford Road chapel were increasingly critical of the voluntaryist principle. George Chappell and John Mayson, for example, argued that opposition to Graham's Bill should be followed by support for any system of education financed from a public rate evenly divided between the religious denominations. It was of course generally understood that no undenominational enterprise and least of all an entirely secular system should be allowed to obscure essentially religious interests. Against this background the Education Committee finally accepted State support in 1847. The decision was welcomed by most local leaders. In Liverpool the day school management committee immediately approved of the prospect of financial relief at a time when its income was falling far short of its annual expenditure of £500. In Manchester there was also considerable support for rate-aided education when a parliamentary bill was promoted for such a purpose in 1851. George Osborn, the Oxford Road superintendent, reflected the change in voluntaryist opinion, for in 1849 he still held the view that there was 'no reason why private charity might not be infinitely extended, so as to meet the necessities of the people' but two years later he came out in support of rate-aided education.[11]

No such major change occurred in Free Methodist policy. In 1847 the Assembly identified itself with the dissenters' protest against the Privy Council minutes, and after 1849 the Reformers expressed their dissatisfaction at the way in which the connexional leadership had opted for State assistance. Government initiatives and supervision were viewed with the same hostility as Conference interference with the management of the Sunday schools. The Association officially supported the British and Foreign School Society, yet shortage of funds and mixed results exposed the limitations of this commitment. Three of the Manchester Sunday schools were utilised as day schools but all had failed by 1850; Gould Street had a short-lived existence as a 'ragged school' rather than a British school, Bank Meadow was supervised by the Wesleyans after 1844, and London Road was always bedevilled by financial problems. Notwithstanding this poor showing, the Manchester leaders continued to oppose State intervention and objected to local proposals for rate-aided education; two of the town councillors, Craston and Thackray, insisted that the parliamentary bill in favour of rate-aid was not necessary and would invade the rights of conscience if passed', while George Swallow, a Lever Street leader, successfully moved a resolution in support of voluntaryism in a major debate on State aid at the Assembly of 1857. The Liverpool leaders shared the same views and had more reason to believe that their own efforts were sufficient, for by 1845 they supervised five schools and educated some 800 scholars. They were hard-pressed, however, to maintain this establishment in the face of declining congregational support and rising costs, but no serious consideration was given to any alternative system. In Rochdale the Baillie Street chapel played a significant role in local education in that it accommodated the first British school in the area and it was later occupied by the first Board school in the town. Unlike the Manchester and Liverpool leadership moreover the Baillie Street officers were willing to consider new schemes and particularly approved of the Lancashire Public School Association, one of the successor organisations of the Anti-Corn Law League, which campaigned for unsectarian and comprehensive education based on local rates and independent of central government. Some of the Reformers also advocated this scheme; William Martin of Manchester considered that it was 'infinitely superior to any other . . .' while Joseph Dickin of Rochdale was a leading local spokesman. Clearly neither unmodified voluntaryism nor State-assisted denominational enterprises commanded unanimous support. In 1847 one member of the Manchester Association concluded that voluntaryism had patently failed to offer sufficient benefits, and three years later a Manchester Wesleyan local preacher claimed that connexional education policy had been formulated by ministers and wealthy laymen without reference to intelligent artisans and operatives who required only a sound system of secular education.[12]

The education issue was related to the second division of opinion concerning policy and attitudes towards the Church of England and, by extension, towards the Dissenting community. In this area of controversy the Wesleyans and the Free Methodists were convinced that their respective positions in the ecclesiastical spectrum represented the logical development of Methodism.

Early nineteenth-century Wesleyanism officially adopted a neutral position between churchmen and dissenters, yet historical influences and a continuing concern for public order perpetuated the idea of a special relationship with the church. During the debate on the Stephens case Bunting provided a classic exposition of the conventional wisdom and concluded that in the event of abandoning Methodism 'I would go to the Church rather than Dissent'.[13] Mixed reactions to such a preference immediately became apparent in the course of the Associationist agitation and formed part of a prolonged crisis of identity concerning the status of the connexion.

Most of the Wesleyan leaders in South Lancashire occupied a fairly similar position in the major battles between militant dissent and the church during the 1830s. They believed, in effect, that the struggle against 'popery, socinianism and infidelity' and the defence of the Protestant constitution involved at the very least a friendly disposition towards the church or else a positive determination to uphold the practices and privileges of the church. Leading dissenters and liberal press alike viewed such leanings with a mixture of incomprehension, dismay and ridicule. Robert Halley, the Manchester Congregational minister, voiced a widespread opinion when he referred to the Wesleyans as only supplemental and auxiliary to the Church, while newspapers such as the *Manchester Times* and the *Liverpool Mercury* despaired of attempts to entice the Wesleyans into the dissenters' lobby and proceeded to liken leaders of the Society to 'fawning sycophants and spaniels'.

In these quarters Wesleyan participation in church rate contests often provided sufficient cause for disparaging comment. During the Manchester church rate controversy of 1831–5 few public figures supported the compulsory rate as keenly as James Wood; his call for a scrutiny in 1833, after a very narrow victory by the anti-rate party, actually saved the rate until 1835 when it was continued on a voluntary basis. The local Tory press acknowledged the value of Wood's public services and the support of the Wesleyans at large; the *Herald* was confident that the Wesleyans would never abandon the church and the *Courier* concluded that they had a rightful place 'in the bosom of our maternal establishment. . .'. Fifteen years later another Wesleyan, the Tory town councillor Charles Ashmore, played an equally prominent role in an unsuccessful attempt to maintain payment of the optional rate by the corporation. In Liverpool a mounting campaign against the rate in 1834 occasioned an impressive demonstration of support for the church. The Brunswick leadership composed a loyal address, for which there was such strong congregational support and general approval that Thomas Kaye, the principal or-

ganiser whose *Courier* newspaper regularly identified the Wesleyans with the church party, was able to report

No circumstance, as far as I am capable of judging, has tended so
much to raise the cause of Methodism in the estimation of respectable
society, as this very event,—the signing at Brunswick having been
talked about freely, and hailed as a full redemption of that pledge
which has for years past been given, that there was no hostility on
the part of the Wesleyan body towards the Church of England.[14]

There was a similar response in Rochdale where the rate controversy reached a climax in two vigorously contested polls in 1840.
On both occasions the church party was supported by the Wesleyans, some of whose leaders played a particularly active part in the
contest and deliberately sought to embarrass some of the anti-
rate Associationists. Thomas Wilkinson, a Union Street trustee
and Churchwarden, unsuccessfully attempted to secure a verdict
against the Baillie Street leader, John Petrie, who had refused to
pay the rate.

Besides the specific issue of church rates Wesleyan susceptibility
to Anglican appeals was evident in the support for the Protestant
platform in the late thirties. For when low church evangelicals
like the Ulsterman Hugh McNeile in Liverpool and the Manx-
man Hugh Stowell in Manchester emerged at the head of a noisy
anti-catholic crusade, they had the backing of influential Wesleyan leaders in both towns. In Manchester James Wood and
Percy Bunting figured as tireless supporters of the Reformation
Society, no less moved by a 'wholesome horror of popery' than
Stowell and always intent on ensuring that their religious politics
did the maximum amount of damage to the whigs. Wood denounced the education scheme of 1839 for playing popery and
protestantism upon the same ground, and when he supported the
Tory parliamentary candidate at the hustings in the same year it
was scarcely necessary for him to declare himself in favour of a
national religious establishment, for he was by now one of the
most active defenders of the church outside its own ranks. Although they never achieved the same prominence in the local
Protestant Association, the Liverpool leaders were equally inclined to uphold the church cause especially in relation to
the question of the two corporation schools which had been
founded on the Irish scheme and which were as strongly supported by the Whig council (1835–41) as they were opposed
by the Tories. At a large Protestant meeting in 1836 James
Dixon, the South circuit minister and renowned protestant
campaigner, was loudly cheered when he seconded the resolution in favour of more church schools and prayed that 'the
Church of England would be preserved in all its glory . . .'. In the

course of the increasingly bitter debate on the corporation schools, moreover, the Protestant Operative Association congratulated the Wesleyans for their refusal to support the dissenters, and in town council discussions on the issue Thomas Sands so emphasised the similarities between Anglican and Wesleyan policies that he caused one of his Whig opponents to comment, 'I cannot as a true churchman allow the Wesleyans to belong to the church (laughter). No sir, I cannot – it is quite impossible'.[15]

When the tide turned against the Wesleyan Tories in the 'forties it was clearly difficult to maintain a fund of goodwill for the church. Any popular notion of a special relationship with the church was continuously strained by the criticism of high churchmen and eventually crumbled as a result of Peelite policies. Both Wilkinson and Sands, for example, hopelessly failed in their defence of Graham's Bill. After the Rochdale poll for churchwardens in 1843 it was reported that this issue had caused all Wesleyans except Wilkinson to desert the church party in favour of neutrality or support for reform candidates. Sands meanwhile exhausted the patience of his Liverpool audience when, as chairman of a Wesleyan meeting, he argued for the Bill but finally vacated the chair 'in manifest ill-humour and with a significant shake of the head.'[16] Opposition to the Bill necessarily aligned the Wesleyans with the dissenters but this did not mean unqualified support for all dissenting causes. In Rochdale there were few contacts between the Wesleyan and dissenting chapels, and although the Union Street leadership no longer sided with the church it showed no corresponding acceptance of the often extreme demands of Miall-type dissenters. There was a more marked change in Liverpool where the ministries of Joseph Beaumont and Francis West in the 1840s and 1850s facilitated cooperation with the dissenters especially in the interdenominational mission agencies and also in the sabbatarian controversy. Yet a fairly strong pro-Anglican element remained in existence and found expression for example in the Stoneycroft Society which erected St Paul's chapel in 1868, adopted Anglican usages, and provided a squire's pew for the leading member, Edwin Green of the toffee firm Sharp and Green. Moreover there was also local evidence of a connexional phenomenon in that some Wesleyans, either pulled by the various social attractions of the church or pushed by the disheartening spectacle of internal conflict, abandoned the chapel for the church. Some of the principal families in the Manchester agitation of 1834 illustrated this leakage, for besides Warren and Read the brothers of two circuit stewards, John Burton and John Marsden, and the son of Jonathan Crowther, all became Anglican clergymen.

Free Methodists were scarcely surprised by the fact that some

Wesleyans finally drifted into the church nor by the knowledge that a larger proportion of the preachers' sons at the Kingswood School entered the church rather than the Wesleyan ministry. Both the Associationists and the Reformers protested against pro-church influences and favoured the adoption of a dissenting position. This development was marked by two recurring themes concerning the independent status of Wesleyanism and the question of Church-State relations. Widespread opposition to Anglican usages and expressions was evident in 1834 when the controversy raged fiercest in chapels which had been either by-passed by the Anglican tradition or superseded by others as the heirs of this tradition. In Manchester the liturgy had been transferred from Oldham Street to the Oxford Road chapel, in Liverpool from Pitt Street to Brunswick, and in Rochdale any resemblance to the set order of worship at the parish church had begun to disappear at the beginning of the century. Unlike some of their main opponents, moreover, Association leaders often had little knowledge of the peculiar origins of Methodism and whenever they appealed for a return to primitive Methodism this was always of a non-Anglican variety. Some leaders were dissenters by birth or by upbringing. Amongst the Manchester officers, for example, John Green had been an Independent Methodist, Edward Hodson had been a member of an Independent congregation, John Kirkham had been converted at a Primitive Methodist camp meeting, William Ward belonged to a New Connexion family, and William Clegg was of Unitarian stock. In Rochdale, too, there were leaders of mixed origins like Oliver Ormerod, who was the son of Quaker parents, and John Pollitt, a former Baptist and long-standing secretary of the local Sunday School Union, who joined the Association largely because of the Sunday school issue.

The objections of these and other leaders to pro-church tendencies were twofold in terms of the internal development of Wesleyanism. Firstly and most commonly they argued that imitation of church practices gave a false impression of popular Wesleyanism and buttressed a particularly offensive view of the ministry. What was especially distasteful was the idea that the chapel was some kind of mission station of the church. In 1820 a Manchester correspondent was particularly critical of the 'fickle, servile disposition manifested by Methodists, in adopting the forms of that Church from which, notwithstanding their professions to the contrary, they have so obviously dissented'. Thirty years later a similar point was made in one of the Reform addresses which emerged from the village of Waterloo in the Liverpool North circuit, 'we deny that the Wesleyan Church is merely a voluntary Society, having since its separation from the Established Church, ever claimed for itself and all its ministrations and proceedings, the authority and dignity of an independent Christian church . . .'.[17] In effect continued use of appellations like 'society', 'connexion', and 'body' suggested a makeshift arrangement which, if not designed to facilitate a speedy return to the Anglican fold, implied closer ties with the church than with dissent.

Secondly, some Associationists not only viewed the Theological Institution as but one detestable example of a conscious effort to introduce a ministerial order reminiscent of an unreformed church but they were also convinced that the plan was part of a deeper plot. Thomas Barlow of Manchester was characteristically blunt in his assessment of the sinister intentions of the connexional management, 'The preachers and the rich men want to divide us into three parts – the poor – yes, the poor Methodists to go to the Primitives, and middle class to the New Connexion, and the rich are to be the Wesleyan Methodists – and then with their fine chapels and college-bred parsons go to the church and tories'. While the more perceptive Associationists disagreed with this crude analysis and recognised that the institutional independence of Wesleyanism precluded organic union in the near future, nevertheless they shared the view that the connexion had inherited the worst features of the church. And this opinion was echoed by Reform leaders like Josias Browne of Manchester, who argued that ministerial pretensions were at variance with proper Wesleyan discipline and that some of the ministers should therefore seek livings rather than circuits.[18]

In their attitudes towards the church as opposed to their view of the influence of the church on Wesleyanism, the Free Methodists showed their dissenting colours in several campaigns, but the degree of involvement and support varied considerably between localities. The Stephens' case drew hostile comment from the three towns; some of the Manchester leaders were dissatisfied with the outcome, the Rochdale leadership was entirely opposed to the verdict, and the Liverpool editor of the *Watchman's Lantern* voiced local opinion when he attacked 'The friendly leaning of Wesleyanism towards the Church of England, so grandiloquently, but gratuitously, trumpeted forth by the Conference of 1834 . . .'. Two of the Manchester Association leaders, William Wood and William Hesketh, were particularly active in the local dissenters' campaign. At a large meeting of dissenters in the town in March 1834 Wood seconded the key resolution in favour of disestablishment, maintained that Wesley himself had demonstrated the evil results arising from the church being united with the State, and secured appointment as one of the honorary secretaries of a standing committee with general oversight of dissenters' grievances. From the same platform Hesketh insisted that his fellow Wesleyans had equipped themselves to join the dissenters' crusade and that even if many of the influential members were unlikely to commit themselves there would be a considerable body of rank and file support. Although Warren and his closest associates held no such extreme views, and Warren jun. claimed that his father was basically a warm friend of the established church, and abhorred the attempts to separate it from the State, the Associationists generally shared the pre-occupations of the dissenting world, and the tory press was predictably scathing in its characterisation of the Oldham Street rebels as double schismatics who formed a latitudinarian and uncharitable set.

The conflict between church and dissent in Liverpool never acquired the same importance and bitterness as struggles in other towns, nor did the Free Methodists ever possess sufficiently distinguished speakers to make any impact in this situation. The anti-rate platform of the 'thirties was dominated by a few colourful personalities usually of Independent or Presbyterian persuasion. Some of the Associationists were by no means inclined to rage against the church; Henry Pooley, for example, publicly applauded 'the tolerant conduct of our venerable Church Establishment'. Yet a large majority shared the dissenting instincts of Rowland and Picton. At the height of the anti-rate campaign in 1834 it was reported that 'Some few also of the Methodists have joined in the outcry, though altogether discountenanced by the leaders of that flourishing sect . . .', and the fact that the Brunswick loyal address was not turned into a circuit document reflected the dissenting views of the Leeds Street leadership. Rowland himself constantly claimed that all parliamentary legislation concerning religious affairs was both unscriptural and unjust, and during his Liverpool ministry James Carveth made frequent appearances on the public platform to argue the case for disestablishment.[19]

While the Manchester and Liverpool Associationists lacked the influence though shared the concerns of larger dissenting congregations, the situation was altogether different in Rochdale where Baillie Street was in the forefront of a continuous battle against the church. In the course of the early contests concerning the church rate the Friends and the Baptists provided the most prominent anti-rate propagandists in John Bright and William Whittle Barton, yet Methodism commanded the largest amount of congregational support and organisational ability. The attitude of the Baillie Street leadership became apparent during the first main clash in 1834 when a call for the refusal of the rate was carried by a majority of ratepayers but the churchwardens nevertheless proceeded to levy a rate. John Petrie was amongst the first to suffer distraint of goods, and the removal of the dining room table by the bailiffs was vividly recalled by his daughter 'For a week or two we picnic'd in the front kitchen – we youngsters glorying in the notion of persecution for truth's sake, but enjoying the whole thing immensely. There was some talk of imprisonment, and I think we were rather disappointed that our father had not to go to prison, like John Bunyan, for conscience sake'.[20] During the contest of 1840 Petrie and other Association leaders took the lead and after a second poll resulted in a victory for the church the anti-rate party called a meeting in Petrie's iron foundry. Under the chairmanship of John Howard, Chief Constable and Association leader, this meeting declared the rate illegal and resolved to refuse payment. The test case occurred in January 1841 when nine defaulters were summoned before the magistrates. The charges were dismissed on a technicality and it was now virtually impossible to maintain the rate. This was no mean achievement for the Association, particularly since four of the nine defaulters, John Petrie, Edward Taylor, Robert Heape and John Whitaker belonged to Baillie Street.

That the church interest in Rochdale and more particularly the vicar, John Molesworth, regarded the Association as the chief source of opposition was evident on the appearance of the *Common Sense or Everybody's Magazine*. Between May 1842 and September 1843 Molesworth used this publication for a general defence of the rate and always took the opportunity to cast the whole Baillie Street leadership in the worst possible light. It was a measure of the extent to which Molesworth was fighting a losing battle that he turned trivial offences into major issues; John Peters, the Association preacher, was strongly and persistently criticised for wearing a hat as he was leaving one of the ratepayers' meetings in the parish church. Baillie Street responded with the *Vicar's Lantern* which was edited by Edward Taylor and managed by four other leaders, Oliver Ormerod, Thomas Booth, Thomas Schofield and Robert Schofield, all of whom served notice on Molesworth that the rate contest was only the start of a concerted effort to strip the church of its privileges in order to advance religious equality. For such a purpose the Association threw its weight behind the local Religious Freedom Society, the inaugural meeting of which was held at Baillie Street in 1840, and subsequently dominated most of the local activities concerning the Anti-State Church Association and its successor organisation the Liberation Society. At the parish level moreover Association leaders continued to oppose some of the public interests of the church, as in the 'fifties when they rejected a proposed compulsory rate for a new burial ground and also campaigned for the use of churchland revenue for educational purposes and for the relief of the poor. There could be no truce between these parties even when a conciliatory gesture was possible; thus, it was reported that the funeral of George Ashworth jun. in 1873, a large civic event, was marred only by the fact that the parish church authorities refused to toll the bell for a lifelong critic of the church.

The third important division of opinion between the Wesleyans and the Free Methodists concerned the early development of the temperance movement and found formal expression in 1841 when Conference and Assembly dealt with the subject. Against the immediate background of teetotal controversy in the Cornish societies and of the preoccupations of certain ministers, Conference issued several declarations that effectively withheld official support for temperance and teetotal organisations; chapels were closed to temperance meetings while superintendents were empowered to restrict the free movement of pro-temperance ministers between circuits and also instructed to avoid use of unfermented wine in the administration of Holy Communion. In its annual address of 1841, however, the Assembly acted in accordance with its assimilation of small groups like the Temperance Methodists of Hayle and the Teetotal Methodists of Cambourne; the address extolled the principles and practical advantages of the temperance movement, encouraged members actively involved in the campaign, and warned only of the need for restraint in the temperance/teetotal conflict. Such pronouncements merely reflected what had become apparent in Lancashire during the 1830s when the new movement had gained its earliest and largest support in the area. In 1829 Liverpool was the first English town to witness temperance publicity. Three years later the Preston Teetotal Society was formed and appointed the first nationwide missionaries. By 1834 Lancashire accounted for almost thirty percent of the membership of the British and Foreign Temperance Society.

At an early stage Wesleyan opinion was divided over the value of an organised temperance movement and was even more seriously split on the teetotal question. In the light of existing rulings against the use of strong spirits and the immoderate consumption of beer and wine, it appeared that no Wesleyan could object to the project. Certainly this was the view of William Pollard, an Oldham Street local preacher and early temperance campaigner, who made a speech at the inaugural meeting of the Preston Society that 'almost electrified the audience for a considerable time', and who subsequently declared that 'if the methodists should array themselves against temperance societies, with the rule of John Wesley upon their books, he for one would run after them exclaiming "Stop thiefs" . . .'.[21] Substantial backing for a purely temperance programme was always decidedly limited in extent, and significantly only two of the chapels largely unaffected by the agitation of 1834–5, Brunswick and Stanhope Street in Liverpool, maintained small, denominational societies which eventually perished on the emergence of teetotalism.

The growth of teetotal societies during the mid-1830s had a telling effect on Wesleyan attitudes as certain initial suspicions were increasingly confirmed by the dubious credentials, means and objectives of the teetotallers. In 1836 a Manchester temperance paper concluded that the statement of one local Wesleyan, in favour of intoxicating liquors for working men, was 'only a solitary verbal expression of what many practically declare . . .'.[22] Wesleyan opposition to teetotalism was based on several considerations. Besides a natural preference for temperance, it was always unlikely that members involved in the drink trade as publicans, innkeepers and brewers would be prepared to jeopardise their business interests. In Manchester the well-known Sandbach family owned a wine and spirit shop that was patronised by members of the Oxford Road chapel, while the Wesleyan landlord of an Oldham Street hotel, J. Youil, was so convinced that teetotalism was opposed to reason, to providence, and to Scripture that he tried to disrupt the outdoor meetings of the Association teetotallers. There were similar interests in Liverpool where the Pitt Street trustees leased the chapel basement to a wine and spirit dealer, Daniel Leather, who was a leading member of the Stanhope Street chapel. The early temperance movement in Liverpool exhibited most of the general features that the Wesleyan leadership considered so repugnant. Formed in 1830 the first society was supervised by Presbyterians and Independents who, although comparable in social standing to the Brunswick and Stanhope Street officers, were associated with political dissent that immediately prejudiced their efforts in Wesleyan quarters. There was even less sympathy for the Liverpool Total Abstinence Society which was formed in 1836, manned by the socially inferior members of minor religious bodies like the Primitive Methodists and the Christian Society, and counted amongst its chief publicists the Unitarian John Finch, exponent of millenarianism and friend of Robert Owen. This type of management, soon beset by sectarian conflict, easily convinced the respectable Wesleyan that teetotalism was a disreputable cause that incorporated the worst forms of radical politics and religious fanaticism. What seemed to justify such impressions and no doubt hardened the opposition was the fact that the Associationists were identified with the movement and, as the *Illuminator* put it, that they had turned teetotalism into a household god.

The Manchester Association included some of the most active pioneers. Before 1835 the few temperance meetings on Wesleyan premises were held in the Oldham Street circuit where Warren was an early supporter and Ralph Grindrod was the principal spokesman. Grindrod was a natural innovator and publicist. Besides his authorship of a major teetotal textbook *Bacchus* and his lengthy lecture tours in the forties when he claimed some 200,000 converts, he presented himself as the first medical practitioner to sign the teetotal pledge, as the founder of the earliest exclusively teetotal society at Miles Platting in 1834, and as the originator of the Band of Hope idea. Some of these claims were disputed, but he was certainly responsible for the first demonstration of Associationist support for teetotalism after his delivery of three lectures in the Stevenson Square tabernacle in August 1835. A year later one of the Manchester Association preachers commented on the proliferation of total abstinence societies, 'Abstinence is bearing down all opposition and spreading like the light of heaven, evidently God's hand is at it, and it is surely vain to contend with Jehovah . . .'.[23] In Liverpool some leaders like Rowland and Picton gave little indication of public support for teetotalism and others like Anthony Barnes, proprietor of a once famous coaching inn, were disinclined to do so. There was nevertheless some criticism of the Wesleyan attitude towards drink, and while the main Pleasant Street chapel did not form a teetotal society until later the largely working class congregations of Bispham Street and Heath Street formed adult and Sunday school societies at the outset.

Attitudes towards teetotalism were shaped by different social conditions and denominational concerns. Members of the Manchester Association, for example, invariably lived in areas which gave reality to contemporary surveys of poverty and squalor associated with intemperance. As inhabitants of the Oldham Road district they had an immediate contact with the seamier side of urban life often beyond the daily experience of Chorlton Row Wesleyans. In a period of bitter anti-Catholic feeling no Wesleyan would have suggested, as did one of the Lever Street leaders, that it was preferable 'to witness the multiplication even of Roman Catholic chapels, than of beershops and spirit vaults . . .',[24] nor would any self-respecting Wesleyan have chosen a cause that involved loose alliances with diverse parties. The Associationists had no qualms about co-operation with various teetotal organisations, and this feature was as much a consequence of social class as of dissenting inclinations. In Liverpool there was support for non-sectarian concerns like the Total Abstinence Home Mission Society, and in Manchester all of the Association chapels appeared on a town plan of temperance (as yet interchangable with teetotal) speakers that served a number of denominational and non-denominational bodies.

The teetotal movement was also a means whereby Methodist reformers demonstrated their moral superiority to the Wesleyan leadership. It was frequently maintained that Wesleyanism had lost its pristine moral earnestness in unevangelical respectability and that new social habits were undermining hitherto categorical imperatives concerning drink, theatres, dances and gaming rooms. One contributor to the *Watchman's Lantern* observed, 'That the preachers, generally speaking, are in the habit of indulging in a cheerful glass of punch is as notorious as the sun at noon-day',[25] and proceeded to relate how several members of the Liverpool South Quarterly Meeting had been silenced by the preacher when they had suggested enforcement of Wesley's rule on the subject of spirit drinking.

Teetotal societies also provided more scope for leadership of an independent enterprise. None of the Manchester Associationists, for example, played a major part in the anti-slavery campaign during the early 1830s, for this kind of venture was largely managed by the influential Grosvenor Street and Oxford Road officers. The teetotal movement, however, offered a form of organisation that was unrestricted by denominational controls and was open to all and sundry. Furthermore, it was beyond the influence of the minister and the wealthy layman, and it lent itself to the employment of evangelical imagery and conversion techniques. This last feature was particularly marked in Manchester where teetotal experience meetings were frequent occurrences and where each of the Association chapels organised quarterly services, communions and rallies on behalf of the cause. It was reported of one such chapel which actually collapsed during the course of a teetotal meeting, 'The Tabernacle, Oldham Road is one of the best attended of any in town, it is situated in a densely populated and very drunken neighbourhood. . . . The spirit of the cause is more lively here than in many other places, owing to the excitation kept up by the officers . . .'. In this setting the horror tales of reclaimed drunkards had the same effect as personal testimonies of spiritual destitution in the period before religious conversion. And long after it became apparent that the Association was unlikely to benefit by a providential outbreak of revivalism, the teetotal societies continued to flourish as agencies that reproduced the atmosphere of the band room meeting and often betrayed signs of what has been called 'the secularisation of the conversion experience'.[26]

Rochdale Methodism was associated with the temperance movement at an early stage. The first local organisation, the Auxiliary Temperance Society, held its inaugural meeting in the Union Street Sunday school in July 1832. Under the chairmanship of John Petrie this meeting elected eighteen committee members including eleven Wesleyans, nine of whom joined the Association. The Society commenced as a civic enterprise but was soon affected by social and denominational divisions. Official Wesleyan support was withdrawn in 1839 when the superintendent, Richard Felvus, refused to accommodate Society meetings at Union Street. This move coincided with a period in which Chartist and Primitive Methodist leaders began to dominate Society proceedings. The Associationists shared the teetotal emphasis of such working class elements and arranged for regular teetotal meetings and lovefeasts at Baillie Street. Such support, however, tended to wane in the early 1840s when the teetotal Chartists came to the fore and when only one of the Baillie Street leaders, Oliver Ormerod, remained on the committee. As the author of the Society's fourth annual report in 1836 Ormerod had noted that many reformed drunkards 'instead of being in the Synagogues of Satan are found in the Temples of the Lord', but it soon became clear that the Primitive Methodists and Baptists, in particular, were gaining more recruits by such means than the Association. Moreover some of the violent language of working class spokesmen not only caused John Bright, a founder member of the Society, to absent himself from public meetings but also induced several Associationists to form their own ventures. In 1847 the teachers at the Belfield Association Sunday school complained of improper statements made by Society speakers at a school meeting,[27] and in the same year two of the Baillie Street leaders, John Petrie and Thomas Schofield, formed a small teetotal society which, as one newspaper reported, consisted of a respectable band of assistants and offered an alternative to the working class societies. Yet the Association never severed its links with the Society and throughout this period it helped to finance some of the main public enterprises, notably the first local temperance hotel and coffee room as well as the Rochdale Public House Coffee Company in which the Baillie Street leaders had a controlling interest.

In spite of official rulings Wesleyan support for teetotalism remained in existence throughout the 'forties, but it was usually a mark of reformist inclinations. In Manchester a Wesleyan Union of Total Abstainers was founded in the late 'forties and sought refuge in dissenting chapels. Its management was largely confined to Reform leaders like Richard Hardman and Joseph Simpson whose attempts to establish branches in all chapels met with resistance from several ministers who regarded the movement as a dangerous compound of the political effusions of the teetotal Chartists and the fervour of an experience meeting. At the Cheetham Hill chapel in 1850 the minister, Samuel Simpson, was informed by one teetotaller that some Sunday school scholars had taken to gambling, smoking and drinking in a nearby beershop, yet he saw no reason to introduce a teetotal organisation and, in fact, 'in no very measured terms expressed his dislike of total abstinence, and his opinion, that, as religion was higher, it was also independent of any other moral reform'.[28] A similar organisation was formed in Liverpool where one of the ministers, Joseph Beaumont, did provide a rare example of keen and intelligent support for temperance principles. A founder member of the first English temperance society (Bradford), Beaumont was medically qualified to argue the physiological case against alcohol and in the period when he was explaining the precise effects of drink to large Liverpool audiences he was also leading the opposition to the platform party in the Conference of 1841. As on other matters his independent stand influenced local Wesleyans who subsequently formed the nucleus of the Reform party. John Burrows, in particular, was convinced by Beaumont's arguments and he became one of the earliest advocates of teetotalism in the local medical profession. In 1847 Burrows formed a Wesleyan Temperance Union. The exclusively denominational character of this organisation was designed 'to remove the objections made against uniting with such persons as generally compose temperance societies', and as such it was criticised by a number of dissenters and by the historians of the local temperance movement.[29] Prospective Reformers immediately joined the Union, while the attitudes of Liverpool Wesleyans at large soon began to change in the 1860s and even more so in later years as the pendulum swung to the other extreme and as the popular Charles Garrett, for example, emphasised teetotalism at the expense of other social issues. In some respects the formation of exclusively Wesleyan teetotal societies was characteristic of a general response to public issues. In their handling of the Church-State, education and temperance questions the Wesleyan leadership frequently demonstrated how far political opinion, social interests and denominational concerns told against any formal and enduring alliance with militant dissenters or secular reformers. In the meantime Free Methodism presented the altogether different spectacle of an advanced form of Methodist nonconformity towards which Wesleyanism gravitated in a later period.

REFERENCES

[1] *Circular* 27 February 1830.

[2] *Wesleyan Education Report*, 1840; For the early development of the Sunday schools see W. R. Ward *op. cit.*

[3] *Report of the Minutes of Evidence, taken before the Select Committee on the State of Children employed in the Manufactories of the United Kingdom* PP. 25 April–18 June 1816; MS. Minutes of Manchester Sunday School Committee, 24 September 1819; MSS. J. Riles to J. Bunting, 21 January 1824.

[4] MS. Minute Book of London Road Sunday School, 7 March 1813.

[5] *Report of a committee of the Manchester Statistical Society on the state of education in the borough of Manchester in 1834* (Manchester, 1834).

[6] *Circular* 29 June 1833; *Manchester Guardian* 26 April 1843.

[7] MS. Minutes of Rochdale Sunday School Teachers' Meeting, 1806.

[8] H. Howarth, *op. cit.*, p. 22.

[9] See Chapter 3.

[10] MSS. J. Fildes to J. Bunting, 14 July 1843.

[11] MS. Minutes of the Committee of the Wesleyan Schools, Liverpool South Circuit, 5 November 1847; *Manchester Guardian* 31 March 1849.

[12] *Manchester Guardian* 21 February 1852; 29 April 1847; 1 May 1850.

[13] B. Gregory, *op. cit.*, p. 162.

[14] MSS. T. Kaye to J. Bunting, 9 July 1834.

[15] *Manchester Guardian* 8 February 1840: 7 September 1839; J. Murphy, *The religious problem in English education: the crucial experiment* (Liverpool, 1959); *Liverpool Mercury* 15 July 1836, 3 December 1841.

[16] *Liverpool Mercury* 14 April 1843.

[17] *Manchester Gazette and Weekly Advertiser* 17 June 1820; *Wesleyan Times* 4 March 1850.

[18] *Manchester Times and Gazette* 15 November 1834; *Wesleyan Times* 22 August 1850.

[19] *Liverpool Mercury* 19 September 1834; J. Carveth, *Nonconformists defended: or, an attack resisted* (London (1848).

[20] I. Mills, *op. cit.*, pp. 14–15.

[21] *Moral Reformer* 1 April 1832; *Manchester Guardian* 3 December 1832.

[22] *Manchester and Salford Temperance Journal* 26 November 1836.

[23] MS. Diary of Rev. John Peters, 26 February 1836.

[24] *Wesleyan Methodist Association Magazine* January 1851.

[25] *Watchman's Lantern* 20 May 1835.

[26] *Manchester and Salford Temperance Journal* 12 November 1836; B. Harrison, *Drink and the Victorians: the temperance question in England 1815–1872* (London 1971).

[27] MS. Minutes of the Rochdale Auxiliary Temperance Society, 12 July 1832: 7 November 1836: 8 December 1847.

[28] *Manchester Temperance Reporter and Journal of Progress* 19 January 1850.

[29] P. Winskill and J. Thomas, *History of the Temperance Movement in Liverpool and District from its introduction in 1829 down to the year 1887* (Liverpool, 1887).

CONCLUSION

Methodist secessions in the three towns originated in serious internal pressures and disruptive external forces, some of which had more extensive significance than others. The mixture of similarity and diversity between the dissentient parties in these towns was indicative of the common set of conditions and the peculiar local circumstances which affected the process and outcome of a particular conflict. The evolution of early nineteenth-century Wesleyan organisation generated similar tensions throughout the connexion. Strained relations between ministry and laity, conflicting attitudes towards central authority and local controls, and the disputed powers and functions of institutions and individuals, were all recurrent and widespread features of a body which was shedding the identity of a movement for that of a denomination. Yet the precise character of acute unrest often reflected contrasting motives, interests and perceptions. The dissentient leaders were the products of a specific social milieu. They also possessed varying degrees of experience, and they were so given to an assortment of opinions that Dr. J. S. Simon, a late nineteenth-century Wesleyan writer, once described their medley in terms of the ' "wild and wandering cries" which rang through the Methodist societies in 1834–5'.[1]

The transition from a societary to a church-type organisation constituted a major though varied form of discord in each town. Two different views of ecclesiastical government produced upheavals in the face of this development. In defence of a professedly deeply-rooted conception of the functions, duties and prerogatives of the ministerial office, Wesleyan apologists maintained that the ministry exercised powers and responsibilities which could not be shared with nor surrendered to the laity. It was a change of title, one of the most obvious aspects of the transition, as opposed to a change of function that distinguished the late eighteenth-century itinerant preacher from the mid-nineteenth-century regular minister. The supreme authority of Conference, the jurisdiction of the District meeting, and the judicial power of the superintendent, all originated in what Wesley had bequeathed to the preachers. The *Illuminator* was thus able to refute the arguments of its opponents,

Did you, gentlemen of the Association, raise up this ministry, as you require the surrender of its power into your hands. No. Instrumentally, it is the ministry trained and raised up by John Wesley . . .[2]

And since post-1791 developments had preserved 'the sacred deposit inviolate', it followed that the opposition completely misunderstood both the nature of the Pastoral Office and the exact meaning of connexional polity. This polity could be neither illuminated nor modified by misleading analogies with civil government, for it was shaped by a concept of pastoral authority which had no foundations in popular notions of representative government.

The Free Methodists argued that exponents of this view were not simply elaborating an established if undefined tradition but were fashioning an altogether unscriptural and unconstitutional order which was heavily biased towards a certain understanding of authority and subordination in society. In their view Methodism had emerged from the crises of the 1790s with a constitutional government which had been founded on a contract between preachers and people. The preachers had subsequently broken this contract by acting in defiance of the lay-dominated local courts and by assuming unprecedented powers on the basis of a wholly mistaken view of their office. It then became a question as to whether the preachers would admit to their sins of commission and omission or, failing this, how far the dissentients would proceed to construct a new model of government.

This study has sought to explain the factors responsible for the rifts in the Wesleyan communities in the three towns and to account for the distinctive features of the seceders in each case. While a more comprehensive and less regional analysis would be required to test claims concerning the disputed ancestry of the Pastoral Office, the struggles in the three towns demonstrate in an early and far-reaching manner that no defence of the theoretical soundness and historical validity of the official position could overcome formidable practical obstacles to the implementation of an authoritarian concept of the ministry. At the grass roots level the relationship between minister and layman was subjected to considerable strains. The increasingly sharp differentiation of ministerial and lay roles meant a heightening of the contrast between the primarily connexional and professional interests of the minister and the essentially local preoccupations of the layman. From the point of view of the laymen the chapel was a principal and enduring form of association which, at least for those who had not yet begun to discover other forms of communal activity, served numerous social as well as manifestly religious functions. For the minster, however, the chapel was a temporary sphere of labour in which he could not hope to exercise the same influence as the lay officer and in which, more importantly, he could so easily fail to acquire in fact the position he was said to hold in theory.

Besides other barriers between the two parties, the ministers were too thin on the ground to cultivate close contacts with a rapidly growing membership and thus to secure full recognition of their undivided pastoral authority. Between 1800 and 1830 the connexional ratio of ministers (including supernumeraries) to members increased from 1 : 268 to 1 : 295, but this latter figure was appreciably higher in some circuits like Rochdale (1 : 683). Moreover even where the ratio was much lower as in the Liverpool North circuit (1 : 177), the ties between laymen could be far stronger than the bonds between ministers and people, or as one member observed on the expulsion of a class leader in this circuit,

My leader is an Israelite, indeed, in whom there is no guile. His God shall be my God, and his people my people. He is always here at the appointed hour of class meeting, and gives us good advice; and when sick or in trouble, he visits and comforts us, and prays with us. As long as I have been a Methodist, never a preacher came to see me at my house.[3]

No determined upholding of the Pastoral Office could change this situation, for it was virtually impossible to persuade such members to regard class leaders as anything less than their faithful pastors and fathers in the Gospel. Even if there had been fewer signs of social discrimination on the part of the ministry and more evidence of an unambiguous, well-developed polity, the scope for ministerial management would still have been restricted so long as such primary relationships remained in existence.

The scale of lay involvement in the organisation and expansion of the societies presented a constant challenge to any central authority based on an elevated view of the ministry. Dissentient opinion always rejected official statements on the indispensability of the ministry as so many inflated claims. In its address to the societies in 1835 Conference asserted that 'The ministry amongst you, against which so much malignity is manifested, is that very ministry by which the Connexion has been brought to its present state of efficiency . . .'.[4] Such declarations had substance yet they might have carried more weight if the ministry had been primarily responsible for pioneering a range of agencies like the Sunday schools, the village societies and the town preaching rooms. It was in such circumstances that it proved particularly difficult to reconcile a ministerial system of government at the highest level with lay leadership and popular culture in the societies. This was particularly the case as a burgeoning connexional administration not only denied an increasingly trained, organised and educated laity any representation in the rule-making body but also blocked the institutional means for the expression of grievances, thereby intensifying the opposition and drawing an impassable dividing line between active participation in decision-making and total exclusion from the centres of influence.

The reformers firmly believed that the connexional system operated only for the benefit of the ministers and their chief supporters. It was in the light of this experience that the case for a reformed, yet powerful connexional authority had limited appeal in comparison with the determined bid to eradicate all trace of a ministerial oligarchy and to demolish much of the apparatus of central authority. In the three towns, moreover, some seceders were so intent on escaping from the clutches of an unamenable bureaucracy that they continued to harbour doubts about minimal connexional ties and eventually opted for independency. In particular, the Liverpool and Rochdale divisions of the early 'fifties showed that no recognisably Methodist pattern of organisation could contain disparate elements. Furthermore, these divisions signified that the Association itself had turned full circle in dealing with two issues, the disciplining of a preacher and the organisation of the Sunday schools, which had figured so prominently in the original protest movement.

Opposition to an authoritarian system of government was everywhere accompanied by a set of political opinions, social attitudes and cultural values at variance with the predominant influences and interests that governed connexional policy. This area of conflict encompassed divisions of opinion on questions such as political reform, Church-State relations, temperance, and education. More generally, controversy turned on the marked contrast between the conservative inclinations of the ministerial and lay hierarchy and the liberal political attitudes and nonconformist leanings of the dissentients. Political and social divisions were most evident in the differences between Wesleyan Toryism in Manchester and Free Methodist Liberalism in Rochdale and in the distinctions between rising and depressed social groups in Liverpool and Manchester. Wesleyan leaders frequently depicted themselves as the guardians of a connexion which resisted any alliance with a political party or with an ecclesiastical grouping; Wesleyanism held a position that was as much removed from high church and low dissent attachments as it was from ultra Toryism and ultra Liberalism. But even if these extremes were avoided, the reformers never failed to point out that such a view merely obscured the partisan character of the leadership. There was, in effect, no mistaking the meaning of official policy and attitudes especially at times of political and social turmoil when unqualified support for the existing order was combined with punitive action against radicals or dissenters in the societies.

In view of the lack of consensus over polity and policy it was always unlikely that a major conflict could be concluded without a division. Any moderating influence proved ineffectual as the emotive language, extravagant gestures and intransigent attitudes of the hard men on both sides served only to poison relations and allowed for no accommodation short of unconditional surrender. The Wesleyan hierarchy was never disposed to enter into formal discussions if only because it occupied a doctrinaire position, it commanded majority support, and its strategic interest in ordered growth and consolidation was advanced by the removal of a fractious minority. Uncompromising opposition to dissentient demands was tersely expressed by Bunting in 1835, 'It is no sin for a man to think that our discipline is wrong, providing that he quits us', and at the same time Conference did not hesitate to classify rebellious proceedings as acts of hostility against the kingdom of Christ. The dissentients for their own part frequently observed that they could be good Christians but bad Methodists under this regime. Yet their excesses and distortions provided little room for manoeuvre, and they were equally inclined to adopt inflexible positions and to make uncharitable judgments whether by resorting to extreme measures or by turning Bunting-ism into a branch of demonology.

Besides these general features, the conflicts in the three towns reflected the heterogeneous character of a dissentient movement that served as a vehicle for a number of causes. The Association embodied several types of protest which ranged from conservative to radical emphases and which expressed varying degrees of re-vivalist interest, anti-clerical opinion, political influence, and social antagonism. The Liverpool and Manchester divisions had much in common as early examples of an urban membership in-creasingly affected by geographical and social class separation. In both cases specific disputes over internal controls and external alignments signified both the general influence of social class status on relationships within the societies and the particular effects of a growing distinction between the wealth, authority and customs of a middle class element and the aspirations, frustra-tions and practices of a predominantly artisan class. In this situa-tion Wesleyan polity and fellowship, hitherto designed to protect a wide social spread, conformed to the demands and interests of the dominant group which primarily consisted of the ministry and the better off laity.

There were substantial differences, however, between the characteristic features of dissentient opinion in both towns. The Warren case, the Theological Institution question and the Sun-day school issue had a far greater bearing on the controversy in Manchester than in Liverpool. More importantly the pro-nounced theme of the Manchester leadership was essentially con-servative in perspective and in programme; it amounted to a reaction against the displacement of early Methodist attributes and agencies by a highly institutionalised order and, in particular, against the transformation of preacher into minister, against the diminishing appeal and value of the traditional means of grace, and against the social pretensions and declining fervour of the hierarchy. Such emphases fell far short of revolutionary designs and soon provided an unpromising foundation for independence. Ironically though not unexpectedly the new organisation was itself the victim of the waning enthusiasm that had appeared so offensive in the parent body. Yet the Manchester Association retained an identifiable albeit shrinking constituency and it played a part in the dissenting life of a town which was less hostile to such a body of opinion than Liverpool.

The initial popularity and subsequent decline of the Liverpool Association exposed a mixture of elements and crippling internal tensions. No collective view of Wesleyan ills emerged from this situation and thus there was no uniform vision of the purpose of a separate body. Some leaders were less disturbed and disturbing personalities than others, and some were wholly inspired by political imperatives while others wished only to protect their existing rights. The lack of a common will was a disastrous defect in a town where Methodist sects attracted little public interest and commitment, and where the new Association chapels were soon left stranded by rapid movements of population. Furthermore the Liverpool cause was an extreme example of a strong anti-authoritarianism that turned in upon an increasingly sour, introverted organisation and left a ruinous pattern of dissident dissent.

The far more robust Rochdale Association originated in and drew strength from an altogether different set of conditions. Its leadership belonged to a powerful social group which was identified with a rising tide of militant dissent and which had a clear perception of its radical interests within and beyond the chapel. The important Sunday school revolt here rested on a defence of the undenominational enterprise, yet on the broader question of the management of the societies the Baillie Street leaders were far less concerned to preserve the societary character of early Methodism than to institute a form of denominational government in accordance with their political concepts and aspirations. There was no point at which the Wesleyan hierarchy could tolerate either the general programme or aggressive campaigning tactics of such a party. It was equally plain, however, that the Baillie Street leaders shared the same attitudes towards worship, fellowship and recruitment as the middle class, suburban Wesleyan.

Finally, the fact that none of these towns yielded substantial support for the Wesleyan Reformers was a reflection of changes in the denominational and social environment. Despite previous purges it was commonly assumed that the large South Lancashire circuits would figure in the vanguard of a new reform movement; as late as 1852 a Leeds Reformer expressed the hope that 'Manchester, the great Free Trade emporium, . . . would yet furnish a powerful opposition to the monopoly of Conference, to take its proper place in the advent of Reform'.[5] But the Reformers failed to build up a head of steam in the absence of the same degree of political and social conflict that had characterised the earlier period. It was most evident in Liverpool and Manchester that Wesleyanism had consolidated its position in the paying suburbs and had undergone further contraction in formerly troubled districts. The contrast between the serious disorders of the 'thirties and the mild outbreaks of the 'fifties was a measure of how far the three towns had exhibited advanced support for and resistance to the authority and instruments of social control most clearly defined in the person of Bunting. Each town presented unfavourable conditions for the preservation of social diversity within one religious community. And the process of fragmentation in each case was a demonstration of the conflicting interests of particular social groups within Wesleyanism.

REFERENCES

[1] *London Quarterly Review* 1893 J. S. Simon, 'The Theological Institution Controversy in Methodism'.
[2] *Illuminator* 27 May 1835.
[3] *Watchman's Lantern* 25 February 1835.
[4] *Minutes of the Wesleyan Conference*, vii, p. 596.
[5] *Wesleyan Times* 17 August 1852.

WESLEYAN AND ASSOCIATION LAY LEADERSHIP (1835)

This Table consists of leaders who either signed the pro-Wesleyan declaration of the Sheffield meeting (24 July 1835) or attended the two delegates' meetings held in Manchester (20–3 April 1835) and Sheffield (30 July–7 August 1835). Office refers only to trustees (t) and local preachers (lp). Besides circuit and society records, the following extant circuit plans have been used to identify local preachers: Liverpool (1825), Liverpool North (1830), Manchester North (1825), Manchester Oldham Street (1836), Manchester Grosvenor Street (1834), Manchester Great Bridgewater Street (1829), and Rochdale (1833). Neither town directories nor other sources provide clear evidence of the occupations of certain leaders. Evidence of voting behaviour is derived from the Liverpool (1837), Manchester (1839) and Rochdale (1837) parliamentary election poll books; w and t denote whig and tory voters respectively.

WESLEYAN

	Office	Occupation	Voting
LIVERPOOL			
David Appleton	t, lp	blockmaker	t
Michael Ashton	t, lp	ironfounder	
William Atherton	lp	collector	t
Thomas Crook	t	accountant	t
Josiah Churchill		smallware dealer	
John Davies			
John Deane	t	druggist	t
Matthias Hall		leather merchant	
George Heald	t	builder	
Samuel Hunt		ironmonger	
Thomas Kaye	t	newspaper publisher	t
George Leigh	t	book publisher	t
William Lewis	lp	accountant	
John Mathison			
George Millard	lp	book-keeper	
Joseph Russell	t, lp	shipbuilder	t
Thomas Sands	t	merchant	t
John Townley	lp	watch manufacturer	t
Thomas Vernon	t, lp	shipbuilder	t
John Walthew			
MANCHESTER			
William Allan		manufacturer	
Percy Bunting	t	attorney	t
George Chappell	t	manufacturer	w
Thomas Davies	t	grocer	

	Office	Occupation	Voting
MANCHESTER *continued*			
James Fernley	t	manufacturer	t
John Fernley	t	manufacturer	
James Fildes	t	wholesale grocer	t
John Harrison	t	merchant	
Robert Henson	t	merchant	t
Holland Hoole	t, lp	manufacturer	
Thomas Jackson	t	calico printer	t
William Johnson	t	glass manufacturer	t
John Lomas	t	merchant	
John Marsden	t	cotton merchant	
Joshua Rea	t	calico printer	t
Thomas Read			
William Read	lp	tobacco manufacturer	t
William Robinson	lp	machinist	
Robert Townend	t	manufacturer	
Joshua Westhead	t	manufacturer	t
James Wood	t, lp	manufacturer	t
Peter Wood		physician	t

ASSOCIATION

	Office	Occupation	Voting
LIVERPOOL			
Anthony Barnes		innkeeper	w
John Beynon	t, lp	grocer	
John Bridson		ironmonger	w
Charles Cole		draper	
William Coulthurst	lp	warehouseman	
Richard Farrar		coffee dealer	w
John Gleave		bookseller	
Joseph Hiles		confectioner	w
William Johnson		silk dyer	w
Wilson Ledger		gentleman	w
James Martin			
William Morgan		shoemaker	w
John Norris			
James Pearson			
David Rowland	lp	secretary	w
John Stephenson			
John Stoward		painter	
Richard Widdows		tax collector	
John Wood			
MANCHESTER			
Thomas Barlow	lp	army captain rtd.	
Joseph Brooke		chapel-keeper	
Adam Cottam		mechanic	
John Greenhalgh	lp	schoolmaster	
Ralph Grindrod		surgeon	
John Hart			
John Haywood			
William Hesketh	lp	corn merchant	w

	Office	Occupation	Voting
MANCHESTER *continued*			
George Hughes		painter	
William Jones			
Robert Lowe		manufacturer	
Thomas Lucas			
William Matthews	lp	locksmith	
Joseph Peak		coal dealer	
William Procter			
Jabez Sanderson		dyer	
Thomas Taylor	t, lp	watchmaker	w
Matthew Thrackray		bookseller	w
William Wood		woollen manufacturer	w
ROCHDALE			
George Ashworth	t	woollen manufacturer	w
Thomas Booth	t	chemist	w
Stephen Broad		wool-stapler	w
Samuel Heape	t, lp	merchant	w
John Howard	t	wool-stapler	w
James Hoyle	t	corn merchant	
John Petrie	t	engineer	w

SELECT BIBLIOGRAPHY

Notes: (1) This bibliography is confined to nineteenth-century manuscript and printed sources of a selected and mainly local type. (2) Only pamphlets which are not contained in the collections of the John Rylands Library are listed below.

I MSS. AND PAMPHLET COLLECTIONS

Champness Hall, Rochdale:
Minutes of Rochdale Wesleyan Leaders Meeting 1828–60; Minutes of Union Street Chapel Trustees Meeting 1835–60; Cash Book of Union Street Chapel 1792–1826; Seat Rents Account Book of Union Street Chapel 1824–44; Marriage Register of Union Street Chapel 1850–63.

Chetham's Library, Manchester:
Minutes of Manchester Sunday School Committee 1784–1839.

Liverpool Methodist Central Hall:
Minutes of Liverpool Wesleyan Quarterly Meeting 1802–26; Minutes of Liverpool South Quarterly Meeting 1826–55; Minutes of Liverpool South Schools' Committee 1841–56; Minutes of Mount Pleasant Chapel Trustees Meeting 1814–51; Pew Lists of Mount Pleasant Chapel 1831–50; Minutes of Stanhope Street Chapel Trustees Meeting 1826–60; Minutes of Stanhope Street Chapel Leaders' Meeting 1829–50; List of Stanhope Street Chapel Class Leaders 1828–59.

Liverpool Central Library:
Minutes of Liverpool North Local Preachers Meeting 1839–57.

Manchester Methodist Central Hall:
Minutes of Irwell Street Chapel Trustees Meeting 1826–46; Minutes of London Road Sunday School 1811–50; Marriage Register of Oldham Street Chapel 1851–60; Minutes of Manchester District Meeting 1825–38; Grosvenor Street Wesleyan Sunday School Visitors' Book 1829–58.

Manchester Central Library:
Minutes of Broughton Road Wesleyan Day School Trustees 1839–60; Minutes of Broughton Road Wesleyan Sunday School Committee 1846–60; Minutes of Bury Street Association Chapel Trustees Meeting 1850–2; Account Book of Gravel Lane Chapel Leaders Meeting 1829–42; Baptismal Register of Gravel Lane Chapel 1841–75; Minutes of Lever Street Leaders' Meeting 1836–42; Minutes of St. Stephens Association Chapel Trustees Meeting 1852–5; Class Book of Thomas P. Bunting 1825–8.

Manchester Register Office:
Marriage Registers – Lever Street Association Chapel (1842–50), Grosvenor Street Association Chapel (1845–50), Grosvenor Street Wesleyan Chapel (1845–50).

Methodist Archives and Research Centre, London:
Minutes of Liverpool District Meeting 1830–7; A list of the names of the

Societies in the Manchester Circuit beginning May 1759; Correspondence of
Jabez Bunting; Diary of James Everett, 12 vols.; Scrapbook of James
Everett; Diary of George Marsden, 7 vols.; Share certificates of Baillie
Street Chapel, Rochdale.

Plymouth Grove Methodist Chapel, Manchester:
Minutes of Chancery Lane Schools Teachers Meeting 1843–58; Minutes of
Grosvenor Street Wesleyan Quarterly Meeting 1824–65.

Private Collection:
Diary of Rev. John Peters 1836–41.

Public Record Office:
Home Office Papers: Religious Census of 1851 – Manchester Returns
(129/20), Liverpool Returns (129/20), Rochdale Returns (129/21), Salford
Returns (129/22). Non-parochial Baptismal Registers (R.G.4): Manchester
– Great Bridgewater Street Chapel (1801–37), Chorlton Chapel (1806–35),
Oldham Road Chapel (1811–37), Oldham Street Chapel (1814–37), Gros-
venor Street Chapel (1824–37), Oxford Road Chapel (1827–37); Corres-
pondence: Francis Marris to Lord Sidmouth H.O.42/198.

Rochdale Central Library:
Minutes of Baillie Street Chapel Trustees Meeting 1836–56; Minutes of
Baillie Street Chapel Leaders Meeting 1845–60; Minutes of Baillie Street
Chapel Foreign and Home Missions Committee 1836–54; Baptismal Register of Baillie Street Chapel 1855–60; Cash Book of Baillie Street Chapel
1836–50; Cash Book of Baillie Street Chapel Town Steward 1843–62; Minutes
of Rochdale Association Quarterly Meeting 1836–52; Journal of the trans-
actions in the Rochdale Circuit 1813–34; Statistical account of the numbers,
attendance and contributions of the members in connection with the Wesleyan Methodist Association Rochdale Circuit, for the quarter ending
September 1848; Rochdale Sunday School Entry Book 1817–19; Minutes of
Rochdale Sunday School Teachers Meeting 1802–19; Minutes of Rochdale
Auxiliary Temperance Society 1832–53; Correspondence relating to the
Ashworth dispute of 1851; Diary of John Ashworth 1859–73; John Bright
Papers.

Wesley Church, Hulme, Manchester:
Register of teachers and officers of Great Bridgewater Street Wesleyan Sunday School 1829–52.

Pamphlet collections, John Rylands Library, Manchester:
Methodism Warren Controversy 4 vols.; *Methodism Reform Agitation* 10
vols.

II NEWSPAPERS AND PERIODICALS

a) *General*
The Beacon (Rochdale).
The Christian Reformer.
The Christian Witness and Church Members' Magazine.
Common Sense or Everybody's Magazine (Rochdale).
Cowdroy's Manchester Gazette and Weekly Advertiser.
The Liverpool Chronicle.
The Liverpool Courier.
The Liverpool Journal.

The Liverpool Mercury.
The Liverpool Review.
The Liverpool Times and Billinge's Advertiser.
The Looking Glass : or Rochdale Reflector.
The Manchester Courier.
Manchester Guardian.
Manchester Herald.
Manchester Observer.
The Manchester and Salford Temperance Journal.
The Manchester Temperance Reporter and Journal of Progress.
Manchester Times and Lancashire and Cheshire Examiner.
The Pilot and Rochdale Reporter.
The Porcupine (Liverpool).
The Poor Man's Advocate and People's Library.
The Rochdale Observer.
The Rochdale Recorder.
The Rochdale Sentinel.
The Rochdale Spectator.
The Rochdale Standard.
The Rochdale Weekly Banner.
Transactions of the Rochdale Literary and Scientific Society.
The Vicar's Lantern (Rochdale).
b)   *Methodist*
The Christian Advocate.
Circular to Wesleyan Methodists (Liverpool).
The Free Methodist.
Illuminator (Liverpool).
London Quarterly Review.
The Proceedings of the Wesley Historical Society.
The United Methodist.
The United Methodist Free Churches Magazine.
The Watchman.
Watchman's Lantern (Liverpool).
The Wesley Banner and Revival Record.
The Wesleyan and Christian Record.
The Wesleyan Methodist Magazine (the *Methodist Magazine* to 1821).
Wesleyan Methodist Association Magazine.
Wesleyan Methodist Penny Magazine.
Wesleyan Times.
Wesleyan Vindicator and Constitutional Methodist.

III   REPORTS

a)   *General*
Laws, Regulations, and General Polity of the Christian Society, in connexion with the Rev. Robert Aitken . . . *Liverpool, 1836.*
Manchester Statistical Society, *Report of a committee on the state of education in the borough of Manchester in 1834.* London and Manchester, 1835. *Report of a committee on the state of education in the borough of Salford in 1835.* London and Manchester, 1836.

Report of a committee on the state of education in the borough of Liverpool in 1835–6. London and Manchester, 1836.

Minutes of the Fourth Annual Convocation of the Christian Society in connexion with the Rev. Robert Aitken. Liverpool, 1839.

Parliamentary Papers, *Select Committee on the State of the Children in the Manufactories of the United Kingdom* 1816 (397) iii. *First Report of the Commissioners appointed to collect information in the manufacturing districts relative to the Employment of Children in Factories . . .* 1833 (450) xx. *Report of Religious Census of 1851 for England and Wales,* 1852–3, lxxxix.

b) *Methodist*

Minutes of the Wesleyan Conference.

Minutes of the Annual Assembly of the Wesleyan Methodist Association.

Proposals for the erection of a Methodist Chapel and Schoolroom in Baillie Street, Rochdale in shares of one pound each. Rochdale, 1836.

Proposals for the formation of a literary and theological institution, with a design to promote the improvement of the junior preachers in the Methodist Connexion. London, 1834.

Report of the Liverpool Methodist Tract Society, 1830–1. Liverpool, 1831

Reports of the Wesleyan Education Committee.

Rules of the Oldham Street Methodist Chapel Friendly Society. Manchester, 1794.

Rules of the Wesleyan Methodist Local Preachers' Friendly Society. Manchester, 1833.

c) *Poll-books:*

Liverpool, 1832, 1835, 1837, 1853, 1857 Elections.

Manchester, 1832 and 1839 Elections.

Rochdale, 1832, 1837, 1841, 1852, 1857 Elections.

IV   PAMPHLETS

Anon. *A Letter to the Rev. John Stephens occasioned by some recent transactions and occurrences in the Methodist Society in Manchester.* Manchester, 1820.

Anon. *A catechism for Wesleyan Methodists in three parts : particularly for class leaders and local preachers : wherein the various points at issue between the conference and the people are taken up and discussed in familiar dialogue.* Liverpool, 1834.

Anon. *Observations on the resolutions adopted at David Street Sunday School Room, and privately circulated for signature among the members of the Wesleyan Methodist Societies in Manchester and elsewhere.* Manchester, 1834.

Anon. *A word to the Wesleyan Methodists of Liverpool and Manchester, and the Society in general.* Liverpool, 1834.

Anon. *Memoir of the Rev. Samuel Warren, L.L.D.* (extract from the *Imperial Magazine,* August 1826).

Anon. *More Light on the Radcliffe Affair; or the gratitude of 1829 and*

1831 contrasted with the ingratitude of 1834, in Letters from Samuel Warren, Esq. Manchester, 1834.

Anon. *Memoir of the Rev. Samuel Warren, L.L.D., with a brief review of the recent proceedings of the Manchester Special District Meeting.* Leeds, 1836.

Anon. *Wesleyan Methodism and Religious Education defended from attacks of John Stores Smith, in his reply to the Revs. H. Stowell and G. Osborn.* Manchester, 1849.

Anon. *The Fly Sheets.* London, 1844–9.

Ashworth, John. *An Account of the rise and progress of the unitarian doctrine : in the societies of Rochdale, Newchurch in Rossendale, and other places formerly in connexion with the late Rev. J. Cooke.* Rochdale, 1817.

Barlow, Thomas. *A narrative of the blessed battle fought . . .* Manchester, 1834.

Carter, William. *The Case tested : being an inquiry into the character and labours of the Rev. James Caughey . . .* London, 1847.

Carveth, James. *A new and practical scheme of reform developed; or the way to political equality and equitable taxation made plain.* Manchester, 1849.

Carveth, James. *Nonconformists defended : or an Attack resisted . . .* London, 1848.

Carveth, James. *Recantation demanded and refused : or a rejoinder to an "Appeal to facts" . . .* London, 1850.

Crowther, John. *Observations and arguments, showing a Wesleyan Theological Institution to be unnecessary.* Manchester, 1834.

Crowther, John. *A reply to sundry misrepresentations contained in pamphlets of Dr. Warren and J. Hull.* London, 1835.

Eckett, Robert. *An exposition of the laws of Conference Methodism . . .* London, 1846.

Eckett, Robert. *The "Fly Sheets" and the Conference condemned . . .* London, 1847.

Eckett, Robert. *Question by penalty examined . . .* London, 1853.

Garrett, Philip. *The Rev. Philip Garrett's Protest against the vote of thanks passed to him by the anti-Methodistical meeting of leaders held in Manchester.* Manchester, 1834.

Greenhalgh, John. *An authentic report of the trial and expulsion of Mr. John Greenhalgh . . .* Manchester, 1834.

Greenhalgh, John. *An account of the antichristian and reckless conduct of the Rev. John Anderson . . .* Manchester, 1835.

Hoole, Holland. *A letter to the Right Honourable Lord Viscount Althorp M.P., Chancellor of the Exchequer : in defence of the cotton factories of Lancashire.* Manchester, 1832.

Hull, John. *A short and plain answer to the statements in Mr. William Read's "Candid Address" . . .* Manchester, 1834.

Hull, John. *A final answer to Mr. William Read's "Address" and "Appeal".* Manchester, 1835.

Martin, William. *Unscriptural Assumptions of the priesthood.* London, 1851.

Martin, William. *Words of explanation and warning to the Wesleyan Reformers.* London, 1855.

Oastler, Richard. *A letter to Mr Holland Hoole in reply to his letter to the Right Honourable Lord Viscount Althorp M.P.* . . . Manchester, 1832.

O'Connell, Daniel. *A letter to the Ministers and Office-bearers of the Wesleyan Methodist Societies of Manchester.* Manchester, 1839.

Pyer, John. *Six letters to a trustee of Canal Street Chapel, Manchester in answer to a pamphlet lately published by Samuel Stocks, jun.* Manchester, 1830.

Read, William. *An appeal to facts in answer to the charges of J. Hull.* Manchester, 1834.

Read, William. *A candid address to the members of the Wesleyan Societies* . . . Manchester, 1835.

Rowland, David. *An appeal to the members of the Wesleyan Methodist Association* . . . London, 1851.

Scott, John. *A letter to Mr. Webster Morgan in reply to a circular entitled "Liverpool North Circuit".* Liverpool, 1829.

Stephens, John. *The mutual relations, claims and duties of the rich and poor.* Manchester, 1819.

Stocks, Samuel, jun. *A reply to the Rev. John Pyer's "Few plain and indisputable testimonies" explanatory of the affairs of Canal Street Chapel.* Manchester, 1830.

Taylor, Thomas. *An Account of the Complete Failure of an ordained priest of the "Latter Day Saints"* . . . Manchester, 1840.

Vevers, William. *An appeal to the Wesleyan Societies* . . . London, 1835.

Warren, Samuel, jun. *My first circuit : Law and facts from the North.* London, 1838.

Watmough, Abraham. *Observations on teaching the art of writing in Sunday Schools.* Rochdale, 1832.

Watson, Richard. *An Affectionate Address to the Trustees of the London South Circuit.* London, 1829.

Westhead, Joshua. *Remarks on the occurrences of the last few days in the township of Chorlton Row.* Manchester, 1832.

V. GENERAL STUDIES

Barrett. Alfred. *The Ministry and Polity of the Christian Church.* London, 1854.

Baxter, Matthew. *Memorials of the United Methodist Free Churches.* London, 1865.

Beecham, John. *An essay on the constitution of Wesleyan Methodism.* 2nd ed. London, 1850.

Boyden, W. and Askew, E. *Hand-book of the United Methodist Free Churches.* London, 1877.

Everett, James. *The Disputants.* London, 1835.

Gregory, Benjamin. *Sidelights on the conflicts of Methodism, 1827–1852.* London, 1899.

Kirsop, J. *Historic sketches of Free Methodism.* London, 1885.

Myles, W. *A chronological history of the people called Methodists.* London, 1813.

Smith, George. *History of Wesleyan Methodism.* London, 1864.

Swallow, Thomas. *Disruptions and secessions in Methodism : their causes, consequences and lessons.* London, 1880.

Warren, Samuel. *A digest of the laws and regulations of the Wesleyan Methodists.* London, 1835.

VI.   LOCAL STUDIES AND HISTORIES

Anon. *The Methodist Free Church in Openshaw.* Manchester, 1891.

Anon. *Sketches of Methodism in Manchester.* Manchester and London, 1872.

Allen, W. S. *The present position of Wesleyan Methodism in Manchester.* Manchester, 1873.

Aspinall, James. *Liverpool a few years since.* Liverpool, 1885.

Axon, W. E. A. (ed.). *The annals of Manchester.* Manchester, 1886.

Davies, T. *Memorials of Irwell Street Wesleyan Chapel and Schools.* Manchester, 1876.

Davies, T. *London Road Wesleyan Sunday School Centenary Memorial.* Manchester, 1885.

Everett, James. *Wesleyan Methodism in Manchester and its vicinity.* Manchester, 1827.

Faucher, L. *Manchester in 1844.* London, 1844.

Fishwick, H. *History of the Parish of Rochdale.* Rochdale, 1889.

Gill, R. *Gravel Lane Chapel, Salford.* Manchester, 1890.

Holyoake, George Jacob. *History of the Rochdale Pioneers.* Rochdale, 1893.

Howorth, H. *A brief account of Baillie Street Sunday School, Rochdale.* Rochdale, 1883.

Hume, A. *Condition of Liverpool, religious and social.* Liverpool, 1853.

Love, Benjamin. *Manchester as it is.* Manchester, 1839.

Orchard, B. G. *Liverpool Exchange Portrait Gallery.* Liverpool, 1884.

Picton, James. *Memorials of Liverpool.* London, 1873.

Prentice, Archibald. *Historical Sketches and personal recollections of Manchester.* Manchester, 1851.

Robertson, W. *Rochdale past and present.* Rochdale, 1875.

Robertson, W. *The social and political history of Rochdale.* Rochdale, 1889.

Shimmin, Hugh. *Liverpool life: its pleasures, practices and pastimes.* Liverpool, 1856.

Shimmin, Hugh. *Pen-and-ink sketches of Liverpool town councillors.* Liverpool, 1886.

Standring, Robert. *Sunday schools among the mountains as they were fifty years ago.* Rochdale, 1874.

Thom, D. *Liverpool churches and chapels: their destruction and removal or alteration.* Liverpool, 1854.

Walkden, A. *The Sunday School at Sudden Brow and Brimrod.* Rochdale, 1888.

VII. BIOGRAPHIES AND AUTOBIOGRAPHIES

Atmore, Charles. *Methodist memorial*. Bristol, 1801.

Barrett, Alfred. *Consolator: or recollections of a departed friend, the Rev. John Pearson*. London, 1856.

Beaumont, J. *The Life of the Rev. Joseph Beaumont, M.D.* London, 1856.

Beech, John. *Outer Life of a Methodist preacher*. London, 1884.

Boaden, E. *Memoir of the Rev. Richard Chew*. London, 1896.

Breeden, Henry. *Striking incidents of saving grace*. London, 1878.

Bunting, Thomas Percival. *The Life of Jabez Bunting, D.D.* London, 1859, 1887.

Calman, A. L. *Life and labours of John Ashworth*. London and Manchester, 1873.

Chew, Richard. *William Griffiths: Memorials and Letters*. London, 1885.

Chew, Richard. *James Everett*. London, 1873.

Dinnick, J. D. (ed.). *Samuel Dunn: Memoirs and Sermons*. London, 1890.

Dixon, R W. *Life of James Dixon*. London, 1874.

Entwisle, J. *Memoir of the Rev. Joseph Entwisle*. London, 1843.

Everett, James. *Adam Clarke portrayed*. London, 1843, 1844, 1849.

Felvus, Richard. *The Methodist preacher: or recollections of the late Rev. Philip Garrett*. London, 1864.

Grose, J. *Memorials of the Rev. Daniel Chapman*. London, 1852.

Guttridge, John. *Life among the masses*. Manchester, 1884.

Harrison, R. *The Life of Henry Bowers Harrison*. London, 1895.

Holyoake, George Jacob. *Life of Joseph Rayner Stephens*. London and Edinburgh, 1881.

Hulbert, C. *Memoirs of seventy years of an eventful life*. Shrewsbury, 1852.

Hussey, W. *The Christian believer justified, sanctified and glorified: shown in the religious experience of Mrs. Ann Gibson of Cheetham Hill*. Manchester, 1848.

Jackson, Thomas. *Memoirs of the life and writings of the Rev. Richard Watson*. London, 1834.

Jackson, Thomas. *The Life of the Rev. Robert Newton, D.D.* London, 1855.

Jackson, Thomas. (ed.). *The Lives of early Methodist preachers*. London, 1871–2.

Jackson, Thomas. *Recollections of my own life and times*. London, 1874.

Johnson, S. *Edward Sunners: the Liverpool cabmen's missionary*. Liverpool, 1886.

Lomas, T. *Memorials*. London, undated.

McOwan, J. *A man of God: or providence and grace exemplified in a memoir of the Rev. Peter McOwan*. London, 1873.

Miller, M. *Biographical sketch of the Rev. John Guttridge*. London, 1886.

Mills, I. *Threads from the life of John Mills, banker.* Manchester, 1899.

Milner, J. T. *Memoirs of the Rev. Joseph Hollingworth.* Sheffield, 1836.

Picton, J. A. *Sir James A. Picton: a biography.* London, 1891.

Pope, W. B. *A memorial of Richard Haworth J.P. of Manchester.* Manchester, 1885.

Rowe, G. S. (ed.). *Memorials of the late Rev. William Bunting: being selections from his sermons, letters and poems.* London, 1870.

Sanderson, William. *Life and labours of William Sanderson of Liverpool.* Wigan, 1899.

Smith, R. *The Life of the Rev. Mr. Henry Moore.* London, 1844.

Stoddart, A. M. *Life and letters of Hannah E. Pipe.* London and Edinburgh, 1908.

Warren, Samuel. *Memoirs and select letters of Mrs. A. Warren, with biographical sketches of her family.* London, 1827.

West, F. H. *Memorials of F. A. West.* London, 1873.

West, R. A. *Sketches of Wesleyan preachers.* New York, 1848.

VIII. FICTION

Anon. *The autobiography of a Methodist preacher's daughter,* London, 1850.

Love, Benjamin. *Records of Wesleyan life.* London and Manchester, 1843.

GLOSSARY

Wesleyan Methodist organisation

Circuit: a circuit consisted of a number of societies within a particular area. Conference appointed ministers to a circuit.

Class: the class was the smallest organised, unit within the connexion. Each class consisted of members of the society and met weekly under a class leader.

Conference: the Conference was the governing body of the connexion. It was composed of ministers and met annually.

Connexion: the connexion was the whole organisation of Wesleyan Methodism. The term originated in the societies which met "in connexion with the Rev. Mr. John Wesley".

District: the District consisted of a group of circuits within a particular area. The District Meeting, ministerial in composition, was supervised by the District Chairman and was responsible to Conference for the execution of the laws.

Itinerant preacher: the itinerant preacher was a full-time regular preacher assigned to a circuit by Conference. The term was used in the eighteenth and early nineteenth-century but was thereafter replaced by "Minister".

Leaders meeting: the Leaders meeting originated in regular meetings of the class leaders to review the spiritual condition of the society. It had a particular responsibility for the admission and disciplining of members.

Local preacher: the local preacher was a layman qualified to preach and appointed to do so within a circuit.

Quarterly Meeting: the Quarterly Meeting exercised general oversight of the societies forming a circuit. It had an undefined composition until the mid-nineteenth century but always consisted of the ministers and stewards in the circuit and sometimes included class leaders, local preachers and trustees.

Society: the society consisted of a number of classes supervised by one Leaders meeting. Membership of the society was recognised by use of the class ticket.

Stewards: Society and Circuit stewards were laymen appointed by the Leaders Meeting and Quarterly Meeting respectively with particular administrative duties concerning society and circuit finances.

Superintendent: the Superintendent was the senior minister in a circuit. He had considerable powers and presided at the Quarterly Meeting, the Leaders' Meeting and the Trustees' Meetings.

Trustees: the trustees were responsible for the maintenance of the chapels, for the servicing of their debts, and for ensuring that the chapels were used for purposes in accordance with the Conference Deed.

INDEX